TESTIMONY OF A CONFUCIAN WOMAN

TESTIMONY OF A CONFUCIAN WOMAN

THE AUTOBIOGRAPHY OF MRS. NIE ZENG JIFEN, 1852–1942

TRANSLATED AND ANNOTATED BY
THOMAS L. KENNEDY

EDITED BY
THOMAS L. KENNEDY
AND
MICKI KENNEDY

THE UNIVERSITY OF GEORGIA PRESS
ATHENS AND LONDON

Set in Palatino with Lithos Display by
Tseng Information Systems, Inc.
Printed and bound by Thomson-Shore
The paper in this book meets the
guidelines for permanence and durability
of the Committee on Production
Guidelines for Book Longevity of the
Council on Library Resources.

Printed in the United States
of America

97 96 95 94 93 C 5 4 3 2 1

Library of Congress Cataloging in
Publication Data

Tseng, Chi-fen, 1852–1942.
Testimony of a Confucian
woman : the autobiography of
Mrs. Nie Zeng Jifen, 1852–1942 /
translated and annotated by
Thomas L. Kennedy ; edited by
Thomas L. Kennedy and Micki
Kennedy.
p. cm.
Includes bibliographical references
and index.
ISBN 0-8203-1509-5 (alk. paper)
1. Tseng, Chi-fen, d1852–1942.
2. Women—China—Biography.
I. Kennedy, Thomas L., 1930–
II. Kennedy, Micki. III. Title.
CT1828.T688A3 1993
951.04'092—dc20
[B] 92-22989
CIP

British Library Cataloging in Publication
Data available

FOR OUR GRANDCHILDREN,
PAMELA MEJIA
AND PENG PENG XIAO

CONTENTS

Foreword by Hsin-i Fei ix

Preface xiii

Acknowledgments xix

Introduction: Cultural and Historical Setting xxi

Part One: In the House of My Father (1852–1872) 1

1. A Soldier's Daughter 5

2. Zeng Guofan's Final Years 22

Part Two: In the House of My Husband (1872–1911) 31

3. My Marriage and Life in Hunan 36

4. Life in Nanjing and War with France 49

5. Life in Shanghai and Financial Ruin 57

6. End of a Dynasty: Rebirth of a Family 70

Part Three: In the House of My Son (1911–1942) 83

7. Widowhood 87

Epilogue by Qu Duizhi 101

Translator's Afterword 104

Notes 111

Works Cited 177

Glossary 191

Index 195

FOREWORD

Hsin-i Fei

My grandmother, Madame Nie Zeng Jifen, was born in 1852 and lived until she was ninety-one. She was the youngest daughter of Marquis Zeng Guofan, and she married into the Nie family when she was twenty-four. She was thrifty and diligent, following closely the teachings of her father and passing them down to her children and grandchildren. She had thirteen children, seventy-two grandchildren (sixty-two of whom grew up into adulthood), and thirty-eight great-grandchildren (during her lifetime). My grandfather died in 1911 when Grandmother was sixty years old. During the next thirty years the Nie family was centered on her. The children and grandchildren respected and loved her, not with awe but with affection, because she was kind and fair, gentle and amiable. To this day, long after she has passed away, the mere mention of Grandmother brings pleasant memories to her grandchildren, who are now scattered all over the world, drawing them closer and dearer to one another.

When I came into this world she was more than sixty years old. Every Sunday, all her children and grandchildren went to her house. I remember her wearing a long black silk skirt and a dark blue silk jacket. Her silver hair was tied into a knot with a jade hairpin and protected by a black silk turban decorated in the front with a jade piece surrounded with pearls. She carried herself straight, wearing an unforgettable smile on her face.

She lived a well-regulated life. She rose at six o'clock every morning and had breakfast at seven. Then she would read the Bible, say her prayers, read the newspapers, and practice calligraphy. Unless interrupted by visitors, that was her daily routine. When the grandchildren came to pay their respects, she would smile and nod, still doing her daily work. Although she did not pay any special attention to me, I still loved to linger in her

Mrs. Nie Zeng Jifen

room. From her serene and peaceful attitude I gained a sense of strength and security that I could not get elsewhere.

After I grew up, I began to understand her better. During her ninety-one years, she lived through many important world events: the Taiping Rebellion, the Boxer Rebellion, the fall of the Qing dynasty, the First and Second World Wars. She herself had also changed from the daughter of a marquis to the wife of a governor and then the mother of a business tycoon. She was brought up in the Confucian tradition. After she was sixty, she became a devout Christian. She set aside one-tenth of her property as a charity fund—she was thrifty in her own expenses but generous in giving to and helping others. Social prestige, thousands of acres of family land, and two cotton mills had had no effect on her sense of values.

During the Sino-Japanese War (1937–45), we all had to evacuate our homes. I was fortunate enough to share the same house with her, thus having many opportunities to be with her. I had breakfast with her every morning, and she was fond of me. At the breakfast table she talked about her friends and relatives, family traditions, and her philosophy of life.

The longer I knew her the closer I felt to her. I remember her sitting at her sewing machine sewing winter clothing for our soldiers. I remember her concocting Chinese herbs to make medicine. I remember her talking over financial matters and the distribution of her charity funds with my sixth uncle. I remember her accepting respect and greetings from her grandchildren. I remember her mingling with the Chinese and American guests at Dr. Stuart's* tea during her visit to Beijing. I remember her smile, her serenity, her generosity, and her modesty.

She was unforgettable—a great lady, a grand personality, and a fine example of a Chinese lady.

*Dr. John Leighton Stuart, president of Yanjing University, Beijing, and later United States ambassador to China (1947–49).

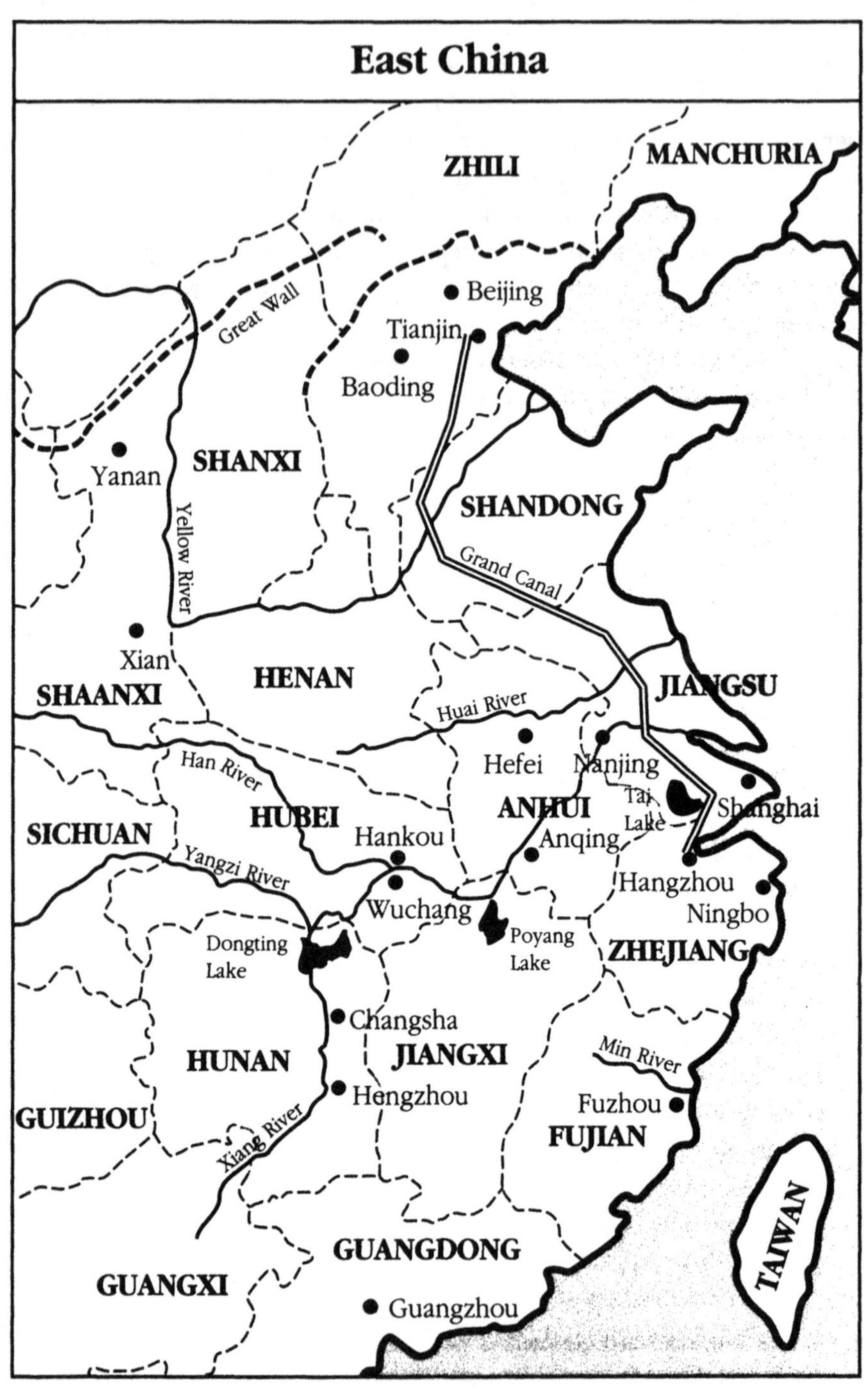
East China
ZHILI
MANCHURIA
Beijing
Tianjin
Great Wall
Baoding
Yanan
SHANXI
SHANDONG
Yellow River
Grand Canal
Xian
HENAN
JIANGSU
SHAANXI
Huai River
Hefei
Nanjing
Han River
Taj Lake
Shanghai
HUBEI
ANHUI
SICHUAN
Hankou
Anqing
Yangzi River
Hangzhou
Wuchang
Ningbo
Dongting Lake
Poyang Lake
ZHEJIANG
Changsha
HUNAN
JIANGXI
Min River
Hengzhou
Fuzhou
GUIZHOU
Xiang River
FUJIAN
TAIWAN
GUANGDONG
GUANGXI
Guangzhou

PREFACE

Mrs. Nie tells her readers the story of her life, disclosing something of herself and something of the world around her. As a document of social history, her autobiography is a rich source of information concerning the customs and social practices of her day: the role of women and girls in a wealthy traditional family, clothing, hairstyles, cuisine, concubinage, nepotism, official corruption, and more. As a memoir, it recounts the effects of major political, social, and economic events of the late nineteenth and early twentieth centuries on her life and the lives of family members and friends.

Moreover, Mrs. Nie's recollections deal also with human experiences which evoke from the reader an empathy that reaches across time and cultural barriers: the death throes of her father and the family's bereavement, the effect of war on a soldier's family, and her undisguised admiration for her father's character. As the years passed, the intensity of Mrs. Nie's experiences remained undiminished. The reader feels her anxiety as she nudges her husband up the ladder of bureaucratic success, and her maternal pride as her son establishes himself in the business world in Shanghai. Scandalized by the new freedom enjoyed by Chinese women in the 1920s and 1930s, Mrs. Nie looks back longingly on the elite society in which filial piety and Confucian mores governed the lives of women. The student of the humanities will find familiar themes here, developed in the context of Chinese family life and expressed with the subtlety and reserve that were the literary hallmark of China's Confucian elite.

It is the dual character of this work—social history and autobiography—that poses a problem for the translator. Its value as a document of social history could be realized by selection, translation, and explanation of passages representing the evolution of Chinese society. I have decided not to limit my treatment of the text in this way, principally because it is the autobiography of a remarkable person. I believe that students of modern China and students of human nature—and who among us is not the latter—will find the story of Mrs. Nie's life, as I have, a rich source of humanistic knowledge and wisdom. For this reason I decided to translate the text in its entirety.

With the goal of capturing the meaning of Mrs. Nie's life as she recalled it, it has been necessary to introduce some changes in order to find an idiom suited for the Western reader. The most fundamental change was the rearrangement of materials. Mrs. Nie prepared her autobiography for publication about the time of her eightieth birthday in 1931.[1] I have been unable to ascertain how long she had been collecting the materials. She arranged her work in the format of the *nianpu,* or chronological biography (a more informative translation would be "year-by-year biography").[2] The *nianpu* includes a separate section for each year of her life. Precise dates are given for many, but not all, of the events she entered for each year. She departed from the strict chronological format in some years to reflect on earlier background events or recount how the events of the year related to subsequent developments. In most cases, however, she dealt only with events that occurred in a given year. When an event is one in a sequence that took place over several years (such as the arrangement, preparation, postponement, and celebration of her marriage), or if events in different years are otherwise related, it was necessary for us to integrate the entries that she recorded under several years to achieve thematic coherence for the reader. We have done this whenever it seemed to further understanding. The Epilogue, which covers the final decade of Mrs. Nie's life, is based on an addendum to the autobiography written by her son-in-law, Qu Duizhi, following her death in 1942. It is adulatory in tone, departing from the neutral and self-effacing rhetoric of the autobiography.

A second type of change made throughout the text is my integration of additional related materials. I had two aims in mind when doing this. First, I have employed published biographical materials concerning Mrs. Nie and her relatives and associates to clarify and elaborate personalities and personal relationships. In some cases it was necessary to include such information simply for identification. In each instance where

I have employed additional materials to supply information other than basic identification, I have noted the sources. For those figures for whom biographical data are available, I have included a brief sketch in an endnote at the first occurrence of their names in Mrs. Nie's autobiography. I have also included their life dates in the text to provide the reader some sense of age relationship. Second, I have included historical, geographical, and cultural information necessary for a Western reader to comprehend the context of Mrs. Nie's life and her environment. These additions may be apparent to some readers and may create the impression that she is belaboring the obvious. The alternative would be to ask the reader who is not familiar with China's history and geography to consult annotations endlessly to make sense of the narrative.

A brief cultural and historical introduction with bibliographical citations is included to provide an overview of Chinese society in the years during which Mrs. Nie lived and to supply a frame of reference for understanding the historical events mentioned in the text. In the text itself I have endeavored through annotations to explicate the cultural and historical context of her life. The result is two types of notes: the bibliographical citations in the Introduction, where the interested reader may find further information in English-language literature regarding the interpretations I have presented; and the exegetical notes accompanying the text based on Chinese- as well as English-language literature. I have annotated the text wherever I felt a reader unfamiliar with modern Chinese history might require more cultural or historical information than could be incorporated gracefully into the text or presented concisely in the Introduction.

Other changes are less fundamental. All dates have been converted to the Western calendar except in one or two instances where it was essential to the meaning to preserve the lunar calendar dates. This will be apparent to the reader. Date conversions of anniversaries create some confusion. Birthdays celebrated on the same date as the original birth on the lunar calendar usually come on a different day on the Western calendar. This sometimes creates the impression that a person's birthday falls on a different date in different years.

I have translated the Chinese references to individuals' ages directly into English. This results in some slight inaccuracies because of the difference in the way years of age were referred to in traditional China and the way they are referred to in the contemporary West. For example, Zeng Jifen was born on the thirtieth day of the third lunar month of the second year of the Xianfeng reign (May 18, 1852). She referred to herself for the remainder of that lunar year as being one year old (i.e., *yi sui*). After the beginning of the next lunar year she referred to herself as two years old, and so on. This system of reference thus designates individuals as one year older than in the Western system. In 1862, when Zeng Jifen returned to her natal home after a period with an uncle, she referred to herself as eleven. By Western terms of reference she would have turned ten that year. Similarly, in 1931 when she celebrated her eightieth birthday, by Western calculations she had turned seventy-nine. I have elected not to change these ages to Western equivalents throughout the text since, for example, it would spoil the effect of her becoming an octogenarian if the reader were reminded that Mrs. Nie, by Western calculation, was only seventy-nine.

With respect to personal names, the reader should know that Mrs. Nie when referring to her male relatives and other prominent men usually employed the posthumous honorary titles conferred on them by the court. For example, she referred to her father as the revered Mr. Wenzheng (cultivated and upright one). Males without such honorary titles she called by their rank or title, if they held one, or the formal term translated as the revered Mr. So-and-so. She referred to her sons and daughters by their given names. Older women such as her mother, mother-in-law, and the wives of officials she referred to by the term equivalent to Madam. She even called her husband's concubines by their imperially designated rank, if they had one. I have departed entirely from this elaborate nomenclature of persons, though I have no doubt sacrificed some of the formal flavor of the text in so doing. Instead I have used the name by which each person appearing in the text is usually referred to in Western historical writing about China. I have dropped the Zeng family name of Mrs. Nie's siblings after the initial mention of each. To spare Western readers the rhetorical irritant of Mrs. Nie repeatedly referring to her father and husband in the third person as the revered Mr. Wenzheng and Governor Nie, I have introduced expressions such as "my father" and "my husband."

Apart from formality in the use of names, Mrs. Nie employed other rhetorical devices that reflect the cultural assumptions underlying her writing. One is the language used to record births. In most instances of childbirth she mentioned that the *father* had a baby and did not mention the mother at all. I have broken with her practice in this respect for the sake of sparing readers such awkward sentences as "My son Qiwei gave birth to a girl on the seventh of June" and to give credit where credit is due. While she painstakingly recorded the births of her sons' offspring, she mentioned the children of her daughters only in passing, reflecting the tradition that after marriage, daughters and their children were regarded as members of their husband's family.

Other conventions reflect her acceptance of the anonymity of women. She rarely referred to her sisters by name, but usually indicated their position in the Zeng family and the family into which they married. For example, "My third sister who married So-and-so." I have not followed this practice, again sacrificing a cultural nuance for the sake of clarity. Mrs. Nie included little biographical background on her own mother, though her mother-in-law is the subject of extensive comment. She was careful to employ precise terminology to show the relationship of individuals in her family: their generational status, whether related through the mother's or the father's family, and her uncles' ages in relation to her father as well as other more detailed considerations. She did not always make a clear distinction between her cousins, the children of her father's brothers, and her siblings if they were of the same generation as she. The reader will note that the Zeng family and Mrs. Nie's descendants followed the popular custom of using disyllabic given names with one character the same in all given names in one generation (e.g., Mrs. Nie's sons were Qibin, Qichang, Qijie, etc.). It would appear from the names given in the text, however, that the Nie family had not always followed that custom. Neither character in the given names of Nie and his brothers was the same. His grandfather and great-uncles, however, did have the same second character in their given names (Samin, Zhenmin, etc.).

In referring to distances and sizes I have converted traditional Chinese units to approximate equivalents in the British measurement units employed in the United States. Exact rendering of monetary terms is made difficult by the regional variation in China's currencies employed during Mrs. Nie's lifetime and by the change of the basic unit from the tael to the yuan.

The standard monetary unit was the *tael*, with a par value of one ounce of silver. Actually, the tael varied greatly from locality to locality in China depending on the weight (i.e., the grains) and the fineness (i.e., purity) of the ounce of silver in the given locality. The tael for each locality bore the locality name and was exchanged with taels of other localities according to a rate based on weight and fineness. The standard was the *haiguan*, or *customs tael*. This was not a real currency but a unit of account in which import duties were levied. Duties were actually paid in *local taels*, which might vary in value by 10 percent or more from the customs tael. From 1880 to 1900, the value of the customs tael fluctuated downward from U.S. $1.41 to U.S. $0.75. From 1901 to 1914 it continued to drop, more slowly, from U.S. $0.75 to U.S. $0.67.

The *cash* was a round copper coin with a square hole in the middle; its par value was one-thousandth of a tael. Actually the value of the cash fluctuated in relation to the tael. The *string of cash* originally consisted of one thousand copper cash strung together through their center holes to equal one tael. A string of cash could contain as few as 160 cash coins, depending on local convention.

Originally, *yuan* referred to foreign silver dollars circulating in China; the most common of these in the nineteenth century was the Mexican silver dollar. Around the turn of the century, yuan, or silver dollars minted in China, began circulating. Chinese yuan carried the inscription that they were 0.72 of a tael, but the exchange rate between taels and yuan varied according to local supply and demand. During the first decade and a half of the twentieth century, the value of the Chinese yuan fluctuated around U.S. $0.50.[3]

I have used the pinyin system for romanizing Chinese words with the exception of a few well-known conventional spellings such as Chiang Kai-shek. The glossary supplies Chinese characters for selected romanized words in the text and notes, excluding personal and place names easily accessed in standard reference works.

ACKNOWLEDGMENTS

At the risk of overlooking someone, I would like to acknowledge the help I received from various individuals at various stages in the preparation of this manuscript. Professor Li Yuning (Bernadette Li) of St. John's University and Professor Samuel Chu of Ohio State University read the manuscript in part or entirely on several occasions and offered valuable criticism. Professor Richard J. Smith of Rice University offered extensive helpful suggestions on the penultimate draft. Professor Thomas Ganschow of the University of Georgia also provided constructive critical comments. Professor Shen Chuanjing of Sichuan University, Professor Yang Tianhong of Sichuan Normal University, and Ms. Qiu Liying of Chengdu University of Science and Technology gave me important help with understanding and with annotation, as did Professor Chao Chung-fu (now deceased) and Professor Chang Peng-yuan of the Institute of Modern History, Academia Sinica, Taipei. Ms. Tang Yuan-hua of National Taiwan Normal University provided critical language assistance in the initial stages of translation. Ms. Sun Yi of Washington State University assisted with the glossary and bibliography. Mr. Thomas Creamer produced the characters for the glossary. The maps are the work of Fred and Aleta Sonnenberg of the Biomedical Communications Unit, and the Washington State University Press. Photographs of Mrs. Nie, Nie Qigui and Zeng Guofan are from a privately published edition of Mrs. Nie's *nianpu* supplied to me by Mrs. Nie's granddaughter, Professor Hsin-i Fei. The photograph of Nie Qijie is from the second edition of *Who's Who in China*, published in 1920 by Millards Review, Shanghai.

I am indebted to the following institutions. Over the years, the Institute of Modern History, Academia Sinica, Taipei, has made its facilities, materials, and personnel available to me without cost, as have Sichuan

University and Sichuan Normal University. Mr. Ye Guangliang of the Sichuan Provincial Commission on Education provided support when it was urgently needed. The Pacific Cultural Foundation of Taipei, the National Endowment for the Humanities, the Graduate School of Washington State University, and the Department of History of Washington State University have awarded me direct financial grants without which my continued effort on this project could not have been sustained.

Professor Hsin-i Fei, granddaughter of Mrs. Nie, and Professor Fei's daughter, Ms. Sylvia Ting of Taiwan, the Republic of China, read the manuscript. Professor Fei graciously agreed to share her remembrance of Mrs. Nie with the readers of this volume. The Foreword was written by Professor Fei for a collection of articles about Mrs. Nie that she is preparing for publication.

The responsibility for the errors and omissions that remain in this text, the introductory material, the afterword, and the annotations are the sole responsibility of the translator and coeditor, Thomas L. Kennedy. The organization, rearrangement of materials, and choice of an English-language idiom are the joint responsibility of the coeditors, Thomas L. and Micki Kennedy.

T.L.K.

INTRODUCTION

Cultural and Historical Setting

Mrs. Nie Zeng Jifen's autobiography is an account of the changes in elite family life in China during the transition from a bureaucratic to a bourgeois society, told from the viewpoint of a daughter, wife, mother, and grandmother. Zeng Jifen was the daughter of Zeng Guofan (1811–72), the victorious leader of the struggle against the Taiping Revolutionary movement (1851–64), the founder of China's first steam-powered machine industry, the governor general of three of China's richest provinces, and a paragon of traditional Confucian virtues. She married Nie Qigui (1855–1911), who became the director of the huge government-owned industrial complex founded by his father-in-law and later a prominent provincial official in east China. After the turn of the century, Nie capitalized on his official connections to launch two of his sons, Nie Qijie (1880–1953) and Nie Qiwei (1883–?), in the textile industry in Shanghai. Nie Qijie eventually became a leader in the Shanghai business community, and his mother, Nie Zeng Jifen, widowed in 1911, assumed the role of matriarch of one of the prominent bourgeois families of twentieth-century China.

Mrs. Nie lived her life in the confines of the traditional elite family; still, she found ways to extend her influence beyond those confines to shape the fortunes and careers of family members at high levels of government and society. Her account of her life provides an insider's view of traditional Chinese society under the stress of modernization, of a proud family steeped in tradition but disposed by the pressure of the times to change essential features of its intellectual and material heritage. The meticulous attention with which she recorded the life cycles, marital unions, and social alliances of her family members reveals the nature of women's involvement in family life in the rapidly changing society in which she lived. She tells her readers of the concerns and commitments not of the social revolutionary vanguard or the hard-pressed working classes but of women in the mainstream of upper-class Chinese society. Her autobiography supplements the portrayals of Chinese women found elsewhere in the literature of this period.[1] Moreover, Mrs. Nie's portrayal of her family reminds her readers that throughout this century of momentous change there flowed a broad stream of social and cultural continuity.

As a daughter, wife, and mother in this elite family, Mrs. Nie's life was molded by the social and cultural environment in which she lived. For her readers to appreciate the forces that shaped her personality, it is essential to have in mind the imperatives that guided the thought and behavior of upper-class Chinese families in the late nineteenth and early twentieth centuries. For readers unfamiliar with the sociocultural landscape of those times there follows a brief introduction to Chinese society, especially those aspects which bore directly on Mrs. Nie's life.

Society and culture were closely interrelated in traditional China. The vastness of China's territory, the diversity of its terrain and climate, and the huge size and dispersed distribution of its population made it imperative for the imperial government to foster cultural integration to achieve a measure of social cohesion. The alternative was territorial and cultural fragmentation and the gradual evolution of separate national states, the historical pattern of early modern Europe. Unlike their European counterparts, China's rulers placed the highest premium on unity. Indeed, the Chinese term for empire, *tianxia* (all under heaven), signified the ideal of a unified state and society.

The cultural strategies employed by the state to unify Chinese society included the recognition of class differences, a system of education designed to promote upper-class solidarity and loyalty to the imperial court, and ritual conformity in all important functions of the life cycle. These cultural forces were at work in nineteenth- and early twentieth-century China; each had some influence in shaping Mrs. Nie's values and beliefs.

The Gentry Class

The ideal stratification of classes expounded in the literature describing traditional Chinese society recognized the educated elite as the ruling class, followed by the agricultural working class on whom the economy rested, the artisans, the makers of tools and weapons, and finally the merchants, whose substantive contributions to society were regarded as small or nil. Though this alignment was sometimes honored more in the breach, in the nineteenth century China's Manchu rulers (ethnically distinct from their Chinese subjects) looked to the educated Chinese upper class, the gentry, as the mainstay of their rule. The gentry presumably had an unshakable commitment to the unity of the empire and an unquestioning loyalty to the imperial institution that symbolized that unity.

Who were the gentry and how was their commitment to the empire and their loyalty to the ruler assured? There has been considerable scholarly debate over the definition of gentry as a class in imperial China. Generally, however, in the literature dealing with the late nineteenth century, the term *gentry*, or *shenshi*, signifies the "social class which from the ownership of land derived the leisure to become educated and thus eligible for public office."[2] According to one scholarly estimate the holders of such educational credentials numbered less than 1 million in a population of more than 400 million during the latter half of the nineteenth century.[3] This figure was augmented, however, by those who acquired educational credentials and gentry status from the state through contributions, or purchase, as it came to be called.

The gentry was the social stratum into which Mrs. Nie was born. She married into a gentry family and lived her life principally among members of this class until the early twentieth century. Then, as the imperial edifice crumbled, the educational system that had molded most of the gentry was replaced, and their numbers began to decline. Slowly, economic change produced a bourgeois class, and gradually the bourgeoisie assumed positions of social prominence and economic leadership and formed a new, fused social group, the *shen-shang* (merchant gentry).[4] The Nies moved easily into this new hybrid social entity but continued to exhibit many of the cultural traits that were the distinguishing marks of the traditional gentry.

The commitment of the gentry to the centralized empire and their loyalty to the ruler were the result of the cultural system fostered by China's imperial rulers. The two most prominent features of this system, and those that most directly influenced the lives of Mrs. Nie and her family, were education and ritual. So strong were these cultural forces that they survived in Chinese society even after the demise, in 1912, of the empire that nourished them.

The educational system was a principal determinant of the gentry class and a source of cultural integration in late nineteenth- and early twentieth-century Chinese society.[5] As early as the eighth century A.D., China had a carefully structured system of competitive civil service examinations. Based on the Confucian notion that government should be staffed by those best qualified through education, the civil service examinations tested the aspirant's knowledge of the Confucian classics and their approved interpretations. The ideal state and civilization derived from these works was the centralized bureaucratic empire presided over by the emperor, the Son of Heaven, and staffed by officials of proven moral and intellectual worth—proven by their achievement on the civil service examinations.[6]

In the late nineteenth century, the civil service examinations were the chief avenue through which male subjects could qualify for an appointment in the bureaucracy. Success in the examinations was also the most sought-after badge of moral and intellectual attainment and lofty social status. As such, preparation for these examinations was the chief determinant of the educational system. Years of classical study produced an intellectually homogeneous class of officials and aspirant officials steeped in the history and moral justifications of China's centralized imperial state and firmly committed to its perpetuation.[7]

The examinations were structured in three tiers. The first tier was administered at the district or prefectural level twice every three years. Success in these examinations resulted in the award of the degree of *sheng-yuan* (government student). As many as thirty thousand degrees could be granted at one time; still, competition was intense and one usually could not attain the *shengyuan* until he had reached his mid-twenties. The second-tier examinations were administered triennially at the provincial level to candidates who had succeeded in passing the entry level. Those who passed the provincial examinations received the *juren* (recommended man) degree and a chance to compete in the metropolitan examinations held triennially in the imperial capital of Beijing. Fifteen hundred *juren* degrees could result from one round of provincial examinations, but only about three hundred passed the third tier, the metropolitan examinations, and received the coveted *jinshi* degree that signified an advanced scholar. One could not customarily expect to achieve the *juren* before age thirty or the *jinshi* before age thirty-five.

The hierarchy of examinations was topped by the palace examinations held in the Forbidden City and presided over by the emperor. The highest of those who passed the metropolitan examinations were eligible to take the palace examinations. Passing the palace examinations meant appointment to the Hanlin Academy, an imperial "think-tank" whose members performed literary, academic, and ritual services for the emperor.

Attainment of the *jinshi* assured placement in the middle range of the nine ranks of the official hierarchy and appointment to an office of significance in the imperial government or a branch of local government. *Juren* were appointed to lower ranks and to minor posts, and *shengyuan* rarely received appointments. Holders of the *juren* and the *jinshi,* as well as officeholders, constituted the upper gentry. *Shengyuan,* for the most part, constituted the lower gentry, pursuing careers as teachers, administrative specialists, and, in some cases, tradesmen. Nevertheless, they enjoyed the legal immunities and elevated social standing that went with gentry status.[8]

In Mrs. Nie's youth, and until the turn of the century, the examination system still commanded the intellectual efforts of those who aspired to elite status, but serious problems developed in the system. The Taiping Revolutionary movement disrupted the administration of the examinations in vast areas of the Yangzi Valley. Though there was a determined effort to restore the traditional system in the 1860s and 1870s, critics of the examinations in the late nineteenth century pointed out, as they had in earlier times, that the examinations placed too great an emphasis on literary style, memorization, and calligraphy and not enough on independent thinking, analysis, and practical application of classical principles to administrative problem solving.[9]

The conferral of degrees in return for financial contributions to the imperial government, a practice followed by earlier dynasties, increased during the financial exigencies brought on by the nineteenth-century rebellions. Purchased degrees qualified the holders for appointment to rank and office and admission to examination for higher degrees just as did degrees earned through examination. Such appointments, however, were usually made initially at relatively low rank and office.[10] In 1905 the imperial government, belatedly committed to educational modernization, discontinued the civil service examinations and replaced them with a national school system based on foreign models.

Gentry status, or the prestige and access to high office that set the gentry apart, could also be achieved through alternative means, the most common of which might be termed "patronage." Because the broad humanistic education that brought success on the civil service examinations did not prepare newly appointed officials to deal with the technical aspects of administration, it became customary for appointed officials to employ a staff of specialists, or private secretaries, to handle the technical aspects of administration at the various levels of government. These specialists included tax experts, legal specialists, corresponding secretaries, bookkeepers, accountants, and others as the situation might require. They were hired by the official who employed them, but they were not government employees. Many were drawn from the pool of lower degree holders who were not eligible for appointment to office. Some had failed the examinations; others had not taken them. Depending on their degree status, specialists were considered the equals of the officials who employed them and relied on them for the performance of essential duties. Because administrative specialists filled such important slots, officials usually chose them with an eye toward securing persons of assured ability. Nevertheless, recommendation by high officials, family connections, and the like could play an important part in getting a qualified person's name before a potential employer.[11]

Although employment as an administrative specialist was not a regularized route to an official appointment, an eighteenth-century imperial edict opened the way for officials to recommend administrative specialists for promotion to official ranks.[12] Furthermore, such appointments were always open to specialists who held degrees, either earned or purchased. In the late nineteenth century, as Chinese local officials began to institute economic and military reforms suggested by Western models, the need for technical specialists increased. Studies of the technical and administrative staffs employed by prominent reformers such as Zeng Guofan (Mrs. Nie's father) and Li Hongzhang, a family friend, show that in the late nineteenth century new avenues of upward mobility were open to their staff members, especially in the new governmental, technological, and economic institutions that appeared at this time.[13] Mrs. Nie's family was intimately involved in the evolution of this new trend toward professionalism in Chinese officialdom. Her husband, Nie Qigui, was clearly a person of considerable ability, industry, and ambition, but he held no educational credentials for appointment to office. Still, as he advanced from tax collector to provincial governor, his career benefited at every stage from the prestige, influence, and connections (*guanxi*) of the Zeng family into which he had married.

Ritual in Chinese Life

The educational system and the officialdom it spawned were the cultural milieu in which the male members of Mrs. Nie's family and their associates pursued their official careers. Ritual, however, was an equally important cultural force guiding not only official conduct but family life and individual behavior as well. A functional definition of ritual may help to illuminate its significance in nineteenth-century China: in Chinese civilization, *ritual* refers to those shared beliefs and practices through which the Chinese have defined their culture and identified themselves as a people. Though ritual beliefs and practices varied from age to age and locality to locality, on the whole ritual exhibited remarkable continuity and geographic uniformity.[14] It constituted a powerful unifying influence, drawing the Chinese people together in support of shared values in the face of divisive forces created by geography and communications.

The rituals that had the most direct influence in Mrs. Nie's life were what we might term the rituals of the life cycle—the beliefs and practices that most upper-class Chinese held to as they passed from one phase of life to the next, from birth to death.[15] Since these beliefs and practices reflected and reinforced the individual's position in the family, an understanding of the nature of the family and its role in Chinese society is essential to understanding ritual.

The Chinese family was organized hierarchically, based on an authoritarian system of subordination of the individual to the group, youth to age, and female to male; it was self-perpetuating through patrilineal succession. In the absence of a strong tradition of civil rights or contract law, an individual's surest protection came from family ties, which sometimes extended far beyond the nuclear family. The importance of kinship was signified by the elaborate terminology for family members; they were designated not simply by gender and general relationship but agnatically, enatically, and by seniority within the generation, as well as by other specifics.[16]

The position of women in the traditional Chinese family was determined largely by the ritual view of how the family should be ordered and by ritual practices that served to reinforce the subordination of women within that order.[17] Though such practices were perhaps honored more in the breach in poverty-stricken families, where the labor of women was important, or in families influenced by foreign values introduced by Western missionaries, Mrs. Nie's family was of the upper gentry and firmly resistant to the intrusion of foreign notions with respect to women. She lived her life largely within the limits that ritual proscribed for the activities of women. In her autobiography she refers frequently to such practices as the training of girls in the tasks of homemaking in contrast to the education of boys in literature and calligraphy, the confinement of pubescent girls and mature young ladies to special quarters, the limitation of female social contacts outside the family, and the impropriety of coeducation.

The best-known ritual practice signifying the subordination of women in the family unit and in the larger society was foot-binding. Foot-binding probably originated in the ninth or tenth century among the nouveau riche of the urban centers of east China. It stemmed from an erotic fascination with the feet of female dancers in certain Buddhist ceremonies, and this fetish gave rise to efforts to replicate the shape of their feet. Foot-binding was not only extremely painful to the little girls (no more than five years old) whose feet were tightly bound with wet bandages that shrank and broke the bones, forcing them to mend in the desired shape; it also crippled these girls for life. It thereby signified the economic power of the male head of the household who maintained such women in a totally dependent capacity. Foot-binding greatly restricted the range of a woman's physical activities and, in one sense, reduced her to a plaything for the man who held her in "foot-bondage." As the erotic qualities of the tiny foot became widely accepted, the practice spread from the wealthy to those in the lower economic strata, and it became necessary for a girl to have small (i.e., bound) feet in order to marry well.[18]

We may assume that Mrs. Nie's feet were bound, though the reader, at first, might wonder why she never refers to the widespread practice of foot-binding. On further reflection, however, it seems likely that Mrs. Nie accepted the inevitability of bound feet as she did the other ritual practices that guided her behavior. But the distasteful nature of foot-binding probably meant that, in honesty, there was nothing she could have said that was positive or even neutral about it; so she said nothing at all. We know that the Natural Foot movement, a harbinger of women's emancipation in China, came into prominence in the late nineteenth and early twentieth centuries. Not surprisingly, Mrs. Nie never mentions it; it was an integral part of a larger movement that sought to relax the ritual restraints on women, restraints of which Mrs. Nie thoroughly approved.[19]

Though Mrs. Nie's account of her early life includes references to ritual practices, it is the death of her father, Zeng Guofan, in 1872 and her subsequent marriage to Nie Qigui in 1875 that disclose the full extent to which ritual guided the passage of important milestones in her life. Zeng Guofan had held strictly to the mourning ritual stipulated in the *Liji* (Book of rites) for relatives according to their degree of relationship, so Mrs. Nie did the same.[20] Not only did she and her family members refrain from proscribed behavior during mourning periods, they resorted to geomancy (a pseudo-scientific analysis of topography) to ensure that their deceased loved ones were buried in sites where their spirits could rest in peace and harmony with the natural surroundings.[21] As the spirit of the deceased joined those of other ancestors the passage was marked by engraving the deceased's name on an ancestral tablet placed on the family altar. Though some, no doubt, believed the spirits of ancestors had direct influence on the lives of the living, among the upper gentry ritual mourning and ancestor veneration in themselves seemed to outweigh any spiritual significance. Popular beliefs became entangled with ritual at times.[22] For example, for a child to cut a piece of his or her flesh for a dying parent to eat was regarded not only as a means of revivifying the parent, it was also a ritual act of filial respect on the part of the child.[23] Many instances of popular belief were expressed as ritual behavior.

After the death of her father, the next major event in Mrs. Nie's life was her marriage. Delayed several times by the ritual proscriptions for mourning following the deaths of her parents, Mrs. Nie's marriage eventually took place in 1875. It conformed to the elaborate ritual that celebrated the union of two families for the purpose of perpetuating the male line of the husband's family and producing future generations to honor their ancestors. These purposes of the marriage rites were set forth clearly in the *Liji;* their realization was ensured by ritual practices that prepared the way for the union and prescribed the conduct of both husband and wife.

The most common form of marriage was that in which the bride left the home of her family to become a wife and daughter-in-law in the family of her husband. Such marriages, agreed upon in advance by senior representatives of both families, were sometimes arranged through an intermediary—a third party known to both families or a professional matchmaker. In some cases the family or matchmaker might resort to divination to predict the compatibility of the couple, analyzing astrological information and seeking the counsel of ancestors. Betrothal gifts that sealed the contract were sent by the groom's family to the bride's; the bride's family reciprocated, supplying a dowry and trousseau. All was negotiated carefully to reflect the relative status of the families and the propriety of the marriage. The couple customarily did not meet until the ceremony when the bride was physically transferred from her family home to the home of her husband. The ceremonies performed at that time were designed to welcome her into her new family. The new bride, for her part, was expected to formally acknowledge her subordinate role in that family. From that time on she owed respect and obedience principally to her mother-in-law; she visited her natal family only as a guest.

There were departures from this pattern: a little girl was sometimes transferred to her prospective husband's family, where she was raised until puberty and the marriage was formalized. In other cases, for reasons agreed on by both families (e.g., the lack of a male heir in the bride's family), the marriage might be matrilocal, with the groom joining the bride's family.

The strict order of the Chinese family, which required subordination and obedience from younger members and females, placed a bride in the arbitrary power of her mother-in-law. Since the groom also owed respect and obedience to his mother, the happiness of the new couple—especially the bride—depended to a great extent on the attitude of her mother-in-law.

A wife's life might be further complicated and her status undermined by her husband's concubines. Since one of the principal purposes of marriage was to beget future generations, concubinage was originally rationalized as a means to beget a son if the wife failed to do so. In practice, concubinage went far beyond this. Males often purchased concubines when their wives had already produced sons, reflecting a general ethos that celebrated male sexual activity but strictly circumscribed that of the female. In theory, concubines were ritually subordinate to the principal wife. Concubines of officials, however, bore imperial titles which designated their status, derived from the head of the household in which they served. Moreover, if a concubine enjoyed the special favor of the head of the household or his mother, she could seriously undermine the status of the principal wife.[24]

The practice of adopting a male heir if none was born also reflected the principal purpose of marriage: perpetuation of the male line. Nephews were often adopted for this purpose. Adoption was sometimes posthumous, reflecting the ritual importance of descendants, which clearly outweighed the consideration of direct biological descent.[25]

Apart from the formal ritual that guided a person's progression through life, numerous inherited beliefs and practices influenced the pattern of day-to-day living. Some of these, such as fortune-telling, were derived from ritual practices of divination originating in the *Yijing* (Book of changes).[26] Others were no more than dietary taboos or sexual superstitions handed down through the generations, possibly originating from popular religious beliefs.[27] The progression of the lunar year was marked by a number of festivals, most of them celebrated according to ritual—such as feasting, ancestor worship, and so on. Festivals such as the lunar New Year derived their importance from the lunar calendar which recorded the continuing relationship of heaven and earth, a relationship that Chinese thought deemed a fundamental force influencing human society. The ritual observances associated with the festivals of the lunar year marked the importance of that relationship and celebrated the family as the cornerstone of human society.[28]

Even leisure activities, though not conducted according to any formal ritual, reflected China's distinctive cultural inheritance. Chinese chess mirrored a strategic tradition in which the ebb and flow of power was more important than victory or defeat; calligraphy bridged ideographically the aesthetic space between painting and poetry; and poetry celebrated man's universal attachment to nature expressed with imagery, musicality, and concision peculiar to the language.[29]

Chinese Medicine

Apart from the educational system and the practice of ritual, Chinese medicine was another aspect of the traditional culture of Mrs. Nie's time that greatly influenced her life. Among the several medical theories and schools of practice employed in China from the earliest times, Mrs. Nie seems to have been influenced principally by the therapeutic school known as pragmatic drug medicine. This school had its origin in third- or second-century B.C. Daoism, an indigenous Chinese religion. Daoism considered life a continuum of corporeal and noncorporeal existence rather than one side of a dichotomy of life and death. The Daoist aim of sustaining corporeal existence into the indefinite future gave rise to various hygiene cults and the employment of natural and man-made substances for the maintenance of wellness and treatment of illness. Over the centuries this school of therapy produced an extraordinarily rich Chinese pharmacopoeia which included herbs, animal parts, and distilled liquids inter alia.[30] The boundary between foods and drugs was also an amorphous one in traditional China, and diet was a respected therapy for the maintenance of wellness or treatment of illness.[31]

Imperial Chinese governments made little effort to regulate the practice of medicine. The first government-supported medical schools, apart from those directly associated with the imperial court, were established at the turn of the twentieth century. In the nineteenth and early twentieth centuries, Chinese medicine and remedies were dispensed by independent practitioners or by pharmacists. The first attempt by the government to codify the Chinese pharmacopoeia and to standardize and regulate the preparation of drugs did not take place until 1930. Western medical practice was reintroduced into China in this laissez-faire environment during the nineteenth century by Western medical missionaries who continued the work begun by Jesuit missionaries in the seventeenth and eighteenth centuries. From the middle of the nineteenth to the middle of the twentieth centuries, the period approximately corresponding to Mrs. Nie's lifetime, Western medicine and Chinese medicine competed for patients and government support, with Western medicine finally gaining the upper hand in the first half of the twentieth century.[32] In this environment Mrs. Nie, following an established tradition in her husband's family, independently and nonprofessionally practiced pragmatic drug therapy among her relatives and friends, thus exemplifying the eclectic and pragmatic Chinese turn of mind that also accounts for the ready acceptance of Western medicine in China during these years.

Historical Background, 1850–1950

Mrs. Nie's life was touched by many of the national and international events that shaped the destiny of modern China. For her readers to appreciate her involvement in these events and the experience she took from them while clinging tenaciously to traditional values, her life must be seen in the setting of recent Chinese history. In the years immediately following World War II, Teng Ssu-yu and John K. Fairbank employed the phrase "China's response to the West" to interpret the evolution of Chinese civilization during the late nineteenth and early twentieth centuries, the period of Mrs. Nie's lifetime.[33] The paradigm of "response" widely employed in Western scholarship on China in the postwar years received limited attention from non-Marxist Chinese scholars.[34] Even the Marxists saw this period more as a futile confrontation with the inexorable force of imperialism than as a response to Western ideas.[35]

As the postwar decades slipped by, the notion that the principal activity of Chinese civilization in the late nineteenth and early twentieth centuries was response gradually lost validity. One study after another, relying on Chinese-language source materials, suggested that China, while responding to international pressures, was equally driven by an internal dynamic entirely Chinese in origin.[36] This revisionist scholarship of the 1960s and 1970s is epitomized in *The Cambridge History of China, The Late Ch'ing, 1800–1911*, published in two parts in 1978 and 1980. This volume includes a penetrating study of Imperial Restoration in the 1860s and 1870s by K. C. Liu which infers that the impulse for change in Chinese civilization came principally, or at least equally, from within and not chiefly in response to external stimuli.[37] Similar views were summarized and evaluated in 1984 by Paul Cohen, who argued cogently that a more accurate interpretation of this century would look at the evolution of China from the inside out rather than the other way around.[38]

At the risk of oversimplification, I suggest that forty years of Western scholarship—culminating in Cohen's work in the 1980s—has changed our view of the century when Nie Zeng Jifen worked out her personal destiny and the fortunes of her family. We saw it originally as a time when China responded to the West. Now it seems that China responded also to itself. The achievements and vicissitudes of Mrs. Nie's life seem to affirm this interpretation. She and her family were part of an internal dynamism that moved Chinese civilization forward during these years. The historical summary that follows represents the setting of national and international events within which Mrs. Nie's life unfolded. Her autobiography itself represents the inner substance of Chinese civilization during these years—what Cohen would call the China-centered view of China's history. Furthermore, Mrs. Nie's portrayal of the emerging bourgeois society in which her family made its fortune raises the question of continuity between China's recent past and its future. Will the socialist revolution of the mid-twentieth century, the evolving capitalism of Mrs. Nie's time, or some blend of the two point the way for Chinese civilization in the twenty-first century?

Before examining Mrs. Nie's recollections, let us look briefly at the principal trends and major events that formed the historical landscape through which she traveled. Two great historical forces influenced nineteenth-century Chinese civilization: population growth and foreign aggression. The growth of China's population, from approximately 150 million in 1700 to 430 million in 1850, brought with it a plethora of economic, social, and administrative problems for the ruling Manchus of the Qing dynasty (1644–1912).[39] In the nineteenth century the Manchu imperial government was highly sinicized (assimilated into Chinese society), yet it seemed paralyzed by complacency and weakened with corruption—a reaction, perhaps, to the astonishing military and economic achievements of the eighteenth century.[40] Beginning in the early nineteenth century, Manchu officials increasingly yielded their authority, especially in the provinces, to ethnic Chinese, some of whom showed remarkable talent for administration.[41] The inertia of a self-satisfied and sometimes self-serving government in the face of mounting socioeconomic and administrative problems induced by overpopulation spawned a series of uprisings in the late eighteenth and nineteenth centuries, culminating in the Taiping Revolutionary movement at mid-century.[42]

The Taipings were a peasant-based socioeconomic movement guided by an ideology that combined Christian egalitarianism and the Confucian vision of a hierarchically ordered family-state. They sought to rescue the empire from the grip of decadent Manchu leaders who, in the 1840s and 1850s, capitulated abjectly to the force of Western arms. The Taipings' aim was to replace Manchu rule with a new theocratic state—the Heavenly Kingdom of Great Peace—presided over by their charismatic leader, Hong Xiuquan (1814–64), the self-proclaimed younger brother of Jesus Christ. The Taipings originated in poverty-stricken regions of south-central China but quickly moved north, establishing their capital at Nanjing in the lower Yangzi Valley in 1853. After an unsuccessful thrust northward (1853–55) that was turned back at the gates of Tianjin, they controlled much of the lower Yangzi, China's richest agricultural region, from the mid-1850s until the early 1860s (see map). In 1864, newly formed provincial militia forces under the overall direction of Zeng Guofan, Nie Zeng Jifen's father, overran the Taipings' capital and effectively put an end to the movement. Other commanders who helped give the ruling dynasty victory over this prolonged rebellion included Zuo Zongtang (1812–85), Li Hongzhang (1823–1901), and Nie Zeng Jifen's uncle Zeng Guoquan (1824–90). All represented the emergent generation of Chinese leaders in the provinces, and all figured prominently in the fortunes of Nie Zeng Jifen and her family.[43]

Second in importance only to the Taiping Rebellion was the Nian Rebellion (1853–68). The Nian were Mafia-like bandit groups who dominated the economically depressed villages of the north China plain between the Yellow and Huai rivers in the early nineteenth century. Driven by severe economic conditions created by the vagaries of the Yellow River in the early 1850s and encouraged by the northern campaign of the Taipings in 1853, the Nian gradually organized their village bands into a regional force. By the late 1850s they had taken over defense of the villages they controlled, usurping the functions of government from corrupt and powerless local bureaucracies. Unlike the Taipings, however, the Nian did not manifest imperial pretensions. Raiding and plundering adjacent areas during the late 1850s and early 1860s, the highly mobile Nian bands became a serious problem for the beleaguered Manchu court, easily resisting the inept efforts of the imperial forces to exterminate them.

In 1865 the court, shaken by the Nian victories and the death of the imperial commander, Prince Senggelinqin (d. 1865), turned to Zeng Guofan, architect of the imperial victory over the Taipings, to lead the Anhui Provincial Army against the Nian. Zeng pursued a policy designed to "strangle the Nian in their nests" for a year and a half but met with limited success. Then, in late 1866, on Zeng's recommendation, Li Hongzhang was named commander of the forces battling the Nian. Li, the founder of the Anhui Army, reinforced his troops with Mongolian cavalry and equipped them with modern weapons from the newly established Jiangnan Arsenal in Shanghai. Other provincial officials emulated Li's efforts. They mobilized provincial armies and, by the summer of 1868, were successful in encircling and exterminating the last of the Nian.[44]

While the dynasty seemed about to buckle under the internal stress of overpopulation and the rebellions it spawned, a virulent imperialism emanating from metropolitan centers of Europe and North America challenged China's long-held assumption of centrality and superiority among civilized societies. In the eighteenth century British traders seeking new markets for mass-produced textiles, the early fruits of the industrial revolution, forced their commercial attentions on a self-sufficient and generally disinterested China. The isolationist Manchu court yielded to the persistent British overtures but permitted trade only at the south China port of Guangzhou (Canton). In the late eighteenth century, contrary to British expectations, the trade developed lopsidedly in favor of China. British textiles found no ready market at Guangzhou. Instead, British traders purchased tea, ceramics, and luxury goods to supply a burgeoning European demand for things Chinese, paying with British silver. To redress this imbalance British merchants from India introduced Bengali opium to the China trade. The result was a dramatic reversal in the balance of trade. Depressed economic conditions in China worsened with the flight of silver from opium purchases as the use of the pernicious drug spread through a disaffected populace.[45]

British importation of opium was not only in violation of Chinese law, it also complicated other contentious issues between the two nations: legal jurisdiction over British subjects in China, international communications, Chinese import tariffs, the opening of additional ports to British trade, and state-to-state relations. A stalemate in the resolution of these issues and the intensifying economic and social ills resulting from opium imports produced armed conflict: first between China and Britain (1839–42),[46] then between China and France and Britain (1856–60). In both of these so-called Opium Wars, China was defeated decisively by superior Western military forces and was obliged to sign treaties known collectively as the unequal treaties. These agreements accorded privileged status in China to Great Britain and to other nations, among them France and the United

States, that had either joined the British side in the Opium Wars or opportunistically exploited China's defeat to demand privileged status. There were no corresponding gains for the Chinese side.

The unequal treaties resulted in the establishment of the treaty port system under which nearly every Chinese coastal or river port was opened to foreign trade and residency. China also conceded administrative and legal control of areas in these ports to the various treaty nations. Shanghai epitomized the "treaty port." There the several foreign concessions—excluding the French—were consolidated into an International Concession extending inland from the west bank of the Huangpu slightly north of the Old Chinese City. The French Concession was sandwiched between the northern limits of the Old Chinese City and the southern fringes of the International Concession. These concessions existed as semicolonial enclaves in the midst of a thriving Chinese metropolis.[47]

The unequal treaties also opened China to Christian missionaries and tacitly permitted the continuation and expansion of opium imports. The mission movement precipitated decades of conflict between the pious, but sometimes arrogant, "soldiers of the cross" and those they called the "heathen Chinese."[48] The use of opium, its import, and the eventual domestic cultivation of the poppies from which it was produced proved to be an unrelieved blight on China's economy and social development well into the twentieth century.[49]

The autumn of 1860 not only marked the conclusion of the Second Opium War and the establishment of the unequal treaty system that guided China's relations with the West for most of the following century, it also witnessed the revival of Taiping vigor after a period of internal dissension and military decline in the late 1850s. The renewed Taiping advance on Shanghai, the new center of Western commerce under the unequal treaties, prompted the intervention of British and French forces in support of the ruling Qing dynasty, with whom they had concluded the treaties. As British merchants in Shanghai sought to bolster the defenses of that city against the onslaught of the Taipings, British and French forces occupying Beijing dictated to China the unequal treaties that concluded the Second Opium War. The sharply contrasting actions taken by the British in the north and in the Yangzi Valley epitomize the inherently contradictory role of the Western powers in China: they attacked or defended the ruling dynasty as their self-interest dictated.

The urgency of the situation prompted some Chinese statesmen to reassess strategies and advocate policies designed to strengthen state power, pacify domestic rebellion, and eventually to turn back the advance of Western imperialism. Prominent among the leaders of this incipient reform movement were the Chinese provincial officials who had led provincial militia in the final pacification of the Taipings: Zeng Guofan, Zuo Zongtang, and Li Hongzhang among others. They rationalized their determination to employ Western military and industrial technology to bolster China's state power through the neo-Confucian precept of "using barbarian techniques to resist the barbarians." This "Self-strengthening movement" was conceived and nurtured during the last years of the struggle against the Taipings in the often close relationship between provincial militia forces fighting in the Yangzi Delta and newly established anti-Taiping Sino-British and Sino-French forces equipped with foreign ordnance and led by foreign officers.[50]

Reform, initiated in 1860, developed slowly over the next sixty-odd years. It was well into the twentieth century before the commitment to rationalize and strengthen traditional civilization spread beyond a handful of enlightened officials into other sectors of society. The commitment to technological modernization of military and industrial aspects of the state broadened at the turn of the century to include a drive to reform the institutions at the basis of society: education, government, the economy, and the armed forces. During the second decade of the twentieth century, Chinese youth and intellectuals went further: they called for a change in the values that lay at the heart of Chinese civilization, principally Confucianism with its emphasis on family, social hierarchy, and classical learning. Science and democracy were the new values that this New Culture movement advocated as it took hold in Chinese cities during and after World War I.

The first phase of reform (1860–95) showcased huge national defense industries such as the Jiangnan Arsenal and Dockyard in Shanghai, the Fuzhou Dockyard, and a score of provincial arsenals all owned and operated by the government. Jiangnan used the most advanced machinery and methods to produce ordnance, ammunition, and steamships comparable to contemporary Western models.[51] It included a translation center and an institute for technical education.[52] In the 1880s and 1890s, the determination to compete with Western imports protected by low treaty tariffs and to counter growing Western influence in China's economy led to the establishment of government-supervised merchant enterprises and jointly operated government-merchant industries: the China Merchant's Steam Navigation Company, the Kaiping Coal Mines, the Shanghai Cotton Mill, and others. The New Huaxin Cotton Mill, a joint government-merchant enterprise, was established in Shanghai in 1890 with the backing of Li Hongzhang. Nie Zeng Jifen's husband, Nie Qigui, served as a director of Jiangnan and was a major stockholder in the New Huaxin Cotton Mill.[53]

In the dog-eat-dog world of nineteenth-century imperialism, China's drive for national survival through military-industrial modernization proved too little and too late. The commitment to military-industrial strengthening spread slowly through a relatively small component of China's leaders. Infrastructural changes in education and the economy needed to sustain and enhance the impetus for modernization were even slower in coming. Important decisions were too often blocked by the indifference or outright opposition of tradition-bound officials.[54] Equally damaging were the virulent thrusts of imperialism that distracted and monopolized the energy of the relatively few leaders who saw the urgent need for reform.[55]

The Christian missions that proliferated under the treaty system spawned cultural misunderstandings and precipitated frequent internal conflicts. Most damaging was the Tianjin Massacre of 1870, which came about when Chinese residents of Tianjin protested what they perceived as child abuse by French nuns who operated an orphanage in that city. Shots fired by an impatient French consul touched off a violent reaction by the protesters, resulting in the loss of French lives and property. The incident was investigated by an ailing and aging Zeng Guofan who exculpated the French nuns. Though the Qing government executed the protest leaders, made a humiliating public apology, and paid a huge indemnity, it was only the German advance on Paris in 1870 that saved China from French retaliation.[56]

More important, the Tianjin Massacre seemed to open the way for a renewed assault on China's dependencies by the imperialist powers. In the 1870s, Japan, itself in the throes of what proved to be a highly successful modernization movement, cast a greedy eye in the direction of Taiwan and China's traditional dependencies in the Ryukyu Islands and Korea.[57] Muslim uprisings in the remote northwest regions of the Manchu Empire provided a pretext for czarist Russia's occupation of the fertile Ili River valley, a pathway for trade in the Sino-Russian borderlands. It was not until Zuo Zongtang led provincial military forces into the northwest in 1878 that these uprisings were ended. In 1881, following several years of tortuous negotiations with czarist Russia, China regained control of the Ili Valley. These talks were successfully concluded by Nie Zeng Jifen's brother, Marquis Zeng Jize (1839–90), as he was known in the West.[58] Only three years later, in 1884, Chinese forces clashed with the French in a struggle for control of Indochina, another of China's traditional dependencies. After French forces destroyed China's southern fleet in the Min River and leveled its largest shipbuilding facility, the Fuzhou Naval Dockyard, in 1885, China conceded control of Indochina to the French colonial empire.[59]

A decade of frantic attempts at naval reorganization and reform following the defeat by France were undermined by inertia, indifference, and ignorance in the imperial government, now dominated by the aging Empress Dowager.[60] Japan's efforts to wrest control of Korea, begun in the 1870s, intensified as czarist Russia's expansion into the Pacific conferred new strategic importance on the year-round, ice-free ports of south Korea.[61] Finally, in August 1894, fighting broke out between Chinese and Japanese forces in Korea seeking control of the peninsula. In a war that tested the military modernization movements in both nations, Japan was the decisive victor. China was obliged to pay a large indemnity, to cede Taiwan and the strategic Liaodong peninsula in southern Manchuria to Japan, and to recognize the independence of its former dependency Korea (which in 1910 became a Japanese colony). The Treaty of Shimonoseki, which concluded the war in 1895, and the Sino-Japanese Commercial Treaty of the following year marked Japan's admission to the ranks of the imperialist powers competing for control in China.[62]

China's defeat in 1895 also opened the door to a new round of imperialist aggression. Japan, pressured by Russia, France, and Germany, relinquished control of the Liaodong peninsula. Within three years the Russians had wrested from China the right-of-way for the Trans-Siberian Railroad to traverse northern Manchuria to Vladivostok with a branch south to the ice-free ports of the Liaodong, the same area that Russia had forced Japan to retrocede to China. By 1898, the other European powers, realizing China's powerlessness to resist foreign demands, had carved out spheres of economic influence comparable to Russia's in Manchuria. Each imperialist nation exercised a quasi-colonial control over China's economy in a given region. Britain's sphere was in the Yangzi Valley; France's was in the southern border provinces; and Germany controlled the Shandong peninsula. Japan's victory in the Russo-Japanese War (1904–5), fought largely on Chinese soil in Manchuria, enabled it to regain imperialist control of the economy, transportation, and administration of the Liaodong peninsula in southern Manchuria.[63]

The renewed pressure of imperialism hastened China's drive for reform in the period 1895–1914. Proposals for reform that had been building in the Neo-Confucian School of Statecraft during the nineteenth century[64] were rationalized and codified by the Confucian scholar and imperial confidant Kang Youwei (1858–1927) and promulgated by young Emperor Guangxu (r. 1875–1908) during the One Hundred Days of Reform in the summer of 1898. The changes envisioned would have transformed China into a constitutional monarchy and effected sweeping reforms in education and the economy.[65] But the changes also posed a serious threat to the entrenched power of the Empress Dowager, a former imperial concubine who had dominated Guangxu for decades and still manipulated the reins of government from retirement, and other high imperial officials. As the reforms gained momentum, the Empress Dowager emerged from retirement and, with the help of the loyal military forces of the Beiyang Army under the command of Yuan Shikai (1859–1916), led a stunning countercoup, executing some of the reformers while others fled to Japan. She placed the young emperor under house arrest and abolished most of the reform measures.[66]

Foreign sympathy for the captive emperor gave rise to a mood of virulent xenophobia in the imperial government in the years following the countercoup. In 1899 and 1900 a grass-roots antiforeign movement emerged in the unstable environment of northwestern Shandong, led by a secret society known in the West as the Boxers (from its Chinese name, Righteous Fists of Harmony). The Boxers rapidly mobilized popular resistance to the growth of foreign economic power and the spread of Christianity, principally in Shandong and the adjacent metropolitan province of Zhili (present-day Hebei). Boxer gangs ravaged Christian institutions, terrorizing and slaughtering foreign and Chinese Christians alike. Their militant anti-imperialism eventually won the support of frustrated Chinese and Manchu officials, including the Empress Dowager, who saw no better way to combat the growing foreign domination of Chinese society.[67]

In 1900, however, the governors of the southeastern provinces, including Nie Zeng Jifen's husband, Nie Qigui, moved to check the spread of Boxer violence in south China. In a gesture that defied the imperial government's support of the Boxers, they guaranteed the lives and property of foreigners in the southeastern provinces in return for a pledge of nonintervention from the foreign consuls stationed in Shanghai. Foreign intervention did come in the north, however, in the summer of 1900, when an eight-nation allied military force penetrated to Beijing where the Boxers, fighting side by side with imperial troops, had placed the foreign legations under siege. The Empress Dowager and her court fled Beijing to the ancient imperial capital at Xi'an. After the allied armies crushed the Boxers, there followed a year of painful negotiations between the allied powers and the imperial government, negotiations based on the fiction that the Boxers were a rebellious movement and the imperial government had welcomed foreign intervention to restore order. The Boxer Protocol signed in 1901, however, left no doubt as to who was the loser. Not only was the protocol punitive and humiliating to the Chinese side, it exacted an indemnity which required the government to pledge its last secure sources of revenue for decades in the future.[68]

Institutional reform resumed in 1901, this time with the halfhearted backing of the impoverished imperial government. Governmental reorganization begun that year was followed in 1906 by the promise of a constitution patterned on the Japanese model. Provincial assemblies elected by wealthy, educated, property-holding groups were convened in 1909; the court also promised a national assembly to be chosen by a similarly restricted franchise.[69] To the dismay of the court, the provincial assemblies proved to be rallying points for those provincial leaders who increasingly opposed the decadence and ineptitude of the imperial government.[70]

Gradually, in the years following the Sino-Japanese War, the provincial elites, comprised chiefly of officials and scholar-gentry, showed an incipient interest in business undertakings. Positions in foreign firms and government-supervised merchant enterprises provided opportunities for individuals to amass wealth, which they invested in business and industry in port cities. Eventually, railroad companies capitalized by provincial elites sought to regain control of China's rail transport from foreign interests operating under the protection of imperialist agreements.[71] As this infant bourgeoisie made its appearance, the time-honored social status that came from passing the imperial civil service examinations began to fade. The diminished relevance of classical learning to the changing socioeconomic climate of the reform years gave rise to a movement for educational reform. A farsighted provincial leader, Governor General Zhang Zhidong (1837–1909) of Hunan and Hubei, produced a plan that in 1905 resulted in the elimination of the centuries-old civil service examinations and the establishment of a new educational system, based on Japanese models, from kindergarten through university.[72]

The adoption of these educational reforms in 1905 sent Chinese students flocking to Japan, a nation that enjoyed new prestige and respect throughout Asia after its stunning victory in the Russo-Japanese War. In Japan, and in Western universities as well, Chinese students sought the scientific and social-scientific training needed to staff the new educational system. But many Chinese students who went to Japan became caught up in a seething reform movement fired by the gospel of nationalism, preached and published by the exiled leader of the One Hundred Days of Reform, Liang Qichao (1873–1929).[73] Even more militant were the followers of the revolutionary leader Sun Yatsen (1866–1925), who, since his escape from China in 1895, had tried vainly to ignite a revolution to replace the moribund Manchu court with a republican government.[74]

On October 10, 1911, after fifteen years of unsuccessful attempts at revolution by Sun and his followers, underground groups in the military garrison at the central Yangzi city of Wuchang that were loosely linked to Sun's foreign-based revolutionary society rose up in defiance of the Manchu regime. Surprisingly, the foreign powers with interests in China remained neutral. Not so surprisingly, the provinces of south and west China, under the leadership of their provincial assemblies and with the support of local military units, one after another declared independence from the Manchu court and support for the revolutionary cause. Sun Yat-sen hurried back to China from a fund-raising tour in the United States to assume the provisional presidency of a new republican government headquartered in Nanjing.[75]

Among the diverse groups represented by this new government were the revolutionaries, the soldiers and other plebeian groups who initiated the uprising, and the Constitutionalists, who included in their number the emerging bourgeoisie. The economic interests of the latter (such as investments in provincial railroad companies) had been damaged by the imperial government's recent railroad nationalization scheme. But before the revolutionary uprising could establish a new government to channel the energies of such disparate provincial groups, it first had to secure a military victory and unseat the infant Manchu emperor. The decisive military power lay in the hands of Yuan Shikai, commander of the Beiyang Army. Although the Beiyang Army was nominally controlled by the imperial government, it responded principally to the commands of Yuan, and Yuan had no personal stake in preserving the defunct Manchu court. Since he controlled the military balance, in the winter of 1911–12 he negotiated to get what he wanted from both sides. The Manchus, powerless without Yuan's protection, agreed to abdicate under favorable terms. In return for Yuan's securing the abdication, the republican government agreed to install Yuan as the provisional president of the Republic. As a result of this deal, the rule of the Qing dynasty officially ended and the Republic of China took up the reins of government on February 12, 1912.[76]

The dream of an independent, democratic, and prosperous China, which had animated revolutionary ideology and rhetoric, was not realized under the presidency of Yuan Shikai. Until his death in 1916 Yuan ruled as a military dictator, snuffed out attempts at parliamentary government by Sun Yatsen's infant Guomindang party, accepted foreign loans with increased imperialist controls, and made a futile bid to restore the monarchy and install himself as emperor.[77]

After the outbreak of World War I in 1914, the imperialist powers' preoccupation with the military situation in Europe provided an opening for Japan to improve its position on the Asian continent. Japan entered the war on the side of its ally Great Britain, seized the German holdings in Shandong Province, and presented Yuan Shikai's government with the notorious Twenty-one Demands. If accepted in toto, the Twenty-one Demands would have greatly increased Japanese economic and administrative control on the mainland and transformed China into a virtual protectorate. The treaty that China finally signed with Japan in 1915, though it did not concede all the privileges Japan sought, was nevertheless extremely damaging to China's sovereignty.[78]

Chinese officials and merchants also took advantage of the relaxation of imperialist controls resulting from the war to establish businesses and industries in the major port cities. The bourgeoisie that had come into being in the first decade of the century developed and prospered during the war years. A tiny proletariat, workers in the new Chinese industries, also appeared.[79] More important were the new intellectuals—students returning from Japan, the United States, and Europe filled with new ideas: anarchism, Marxism, liberalism, and pragmatism. Increasingly, they were determined to rid China of the outmoded Confucian system, which they saw as the cause of China's weakness and economic backwardness among the nations of the world. Thus a third wave of reform moved through the traditional society in the years between 1915 and 1923.[80]

After President Yuan's death in 1916, his military dictatorship fragmented into a plethora of local satrapies headed by military leaders known as warlords. Warlord regimes varied greatly in size and character. Some warlords, such as the British-backed Wu Peifu (1874–1939), aspired to national leadership during the 1920s. Others were little more than local tyrants.[81]

In 1917 the central government—the flimsiest of fictions throughout the decade from 1916 to 1927—led China into World War I on the Allies' side. Its aims seemed to be to secure loans from its east Asian ally Japan, which it did, and to regain control of the Japanese-occupied former German holdings in Shandong Province, which it did not.[82] When the Allies met in Paris in 1919 to sign peace treaties with their defeated adversaries and plan a lasting peace through the League of Nations, China's interests were dealt with arbitrarily. Most humiliating was the Allies' decision, incorporated into the Treaty of Versailles, to award the former German holdings in Shandong Province to Japan rather than return them to China. The Allies' attitude seemed to epitomize the disdain with which the imperialist nations viewed China, underscoring China's powerlessness and the total failure of all prior reform measures, including the republican revolution, to strengthen China against imperialism. The news of the Allies' decision at Paris reached China on May 4, 1919, and touched off a nationwide protest movement. Led by students at Beijing National University, the May Fourth movement called for Chinese youth to break the chains that Confucian values had placed on society and to embrace the new values of science and democracy that had made the Western nations so powerful.[83]

The May Fourth movement ignited the flames of Chinese nationalism and spread from the intellectuals to the bourgeoisie and the proletariat.[84] By the early 1920s the principal aims of Chinese nationalism were clear: end the warlord rule that fragmented and weakened Chinese society from within and the imperialism that controlled it from without. These aims found expression in the program of the Chinese Communist party founded in Shanghai in the summer of 1921, directed by the Communist International (the Comintern) and domestically anchored by Marxist intellectuals from the May Fourth generation.[85]

Sun Yatsen's Guomindang shared these aims with the Communists, but the two held very different visions of China's future as a nation. The Guomindang's moderate reformist program appealed to various sectors of Chinese society to build national unity. Gradually it won the backing of the emerging bourgeoisie, who looked forward to a unified and independent China in which Western-style economic development and prosperity could flourish.[86] The Communists saw socialism as China's future: a classless society led by the party, the means of production owned by the government. The Communists and the Guomindang, or the Nationalists, as they came to be known, joined briefly from 1923 to 1927 under the leadership of Guomindang party chief Sun Yatsen in a United Front against their common foes—the warlords and the imperialists.[87]

This United Front of Communists and Nationalists culminated in early 1926 in the Northern Expedition, a military and political campaign launched from United Front headquarters in south China near Guangzhou to rid China of warlords and imperialism. Following the death of Sun Yatsen in 1925, however, the leadership of the Guomindang passed into the hands of "right-wing" leaders. Foremost among these was General Chiang Kai-shek (1887–1975), who suspected the motives of the Chinese Communists and their Comintern backers. In the spring and summer of 1927, while the Northern Expedition was stalled in the Yangzi Valley, Chiang turned on the Communists, driving them from the United Front into an illegal underground status. Chiang formed alliances with several of the major warlords and gained foreign support with pledges to uphold international treaties. Though he compromised the goals of antiwarlordism and anti-imperialism, by the spring of 1928 he had brought most of China under the rule of the Guomindang, or its warlord allies, and gained international recognition for his government.[88]

Guomindang policies sparked a decade of impressive economic growth in the commercial and industrial centers of east China and the Yangzi Valley[89] but did little to improve the lot of China's huge peasant population and the vast agrarian sector of the economy. Meanwhile, the Communists, at the direction of the Comintern, staged a series of unsuccessful strikes, uprisings, and military takeovers in central and southern Chinese cities, including the seizure in 1930 of Changsha—the provincial capital of Hunan and a city that figured prominently in Mrs. Nie's life. But the Communists' strength was not in the urban areas; these were clearly Guomindang territory. However, the Communists' ability to mobilize tenant farmers and poor peasants in remote rural areas, where they were opposed by a landlord class who enjoyed Guomindang favor, proved a crucial advantage.

In 1931, under the leadership of Mao Zedong (1893–1976), an independent wing of the Communist party sponsored land reform and organized the rural poor of Jiangxi Province into the Chinese-Soviet Republic.

For the next three years the Soviets employed guerrilla warfare tactics to fend off the encirclement campaigns of Chiang Kai-shek's Guomindang armies. Finally, in the fall of 1934, Moscow-recognized party leaders having wrested political control and strategic command from Mao, the Soviets' defenses crumbled as Guomindang forces closed in on all sides. In October, 100,000 Communist troops and party members broke out of the Guomindang's encirclement and fled westward. They fought their way across south China and then north into the remote hill country of Shaanxi Province in an epic struggle that came to be known as the Long March. The leadership dispute was resolved en route in early 1935 when Mao took the top military and political posts back from the group favored by Moscow. The Communists arrived in Shaanxi in the fall of 1935 with their ranks depleted to less than 10,000 and established their new headquarters at Yan'an the following year.[90]

Meanwhile, Japan, sensing the new spirit of nationalism afoot in China after 1928, tried vainly to manipulate warlord puppets in Manchuria to block the extension of Guomindang political authority in that region. Moreover, the Guomindang government's undisguised sympathy for the popular movement to recover Chinese economic rights in Manchuria raised the anxiety of the Japanese military who had guarded and developed the Japanese railroad, ports, and associated enterprises in south Manchuria since 1905. The Japanese military in Manchuria lacked confidence in the determination of the civilian government in Tokyo (which in the 1920s had returned the German holdings in Shandong to China and agreed to sweeping naval disarmament) to defend Japan's interests on the Asian mainland. As a result, young Japanese army officers in Manchuria took matters into their own hands. On September 18, 1931, they blew up a section of track on the Japanese South Manchurian Railroad outside the city of Shenyang (Mukden) and blamed Chinese Nationalists.[91] The incident provided a pretext for the Japanese army to overrun Manchuria, which, the following year, they transformed into the Japanese puppet state of Manchukuo, headed by the hapless Manchu emperor of the Qing dynasty who had abdicated in 1912.[92]

The Japanese continued their pressure on north China, incorporating part of eastern Inner Mongolia into Manchukuo in early 1933 and pressing southward toward Beijing. Chiang Kai-shek's Guomindang government did not resist. Chiang placed first priority on the campaign against the Communists in the south and, after 1935, in the northwest. He seemed willing to yield territory to the Japanese in the northeast to gain time to crush the Communists' insurrection.[93]

As Japanese aggression pushed deeper into north China in 1935 and 1936, popular sentiment increasingly favored suspension of the anti-Communist campaign and the establishment of another United Front of all patriotic Chinese parties to resist Japan. But it was not until December 1936, when Chiang Kai-shek was kidnapped at his northwest headquarters at Xi'an by his own generals, who favored united resistance to Japan, that Chiang agreed to deal directly with Communist leaders regarding a second Guomindang-Communist United Front. Chiang was released on Christmas Day 1936, and during 1937 Communist party leaders and Guomindang officials worked out the terms for the two parties to cooperate against Japan.[94]

The implications of such a united front were, of course, not lost on the Japanese, who seized the initiative on July 7, 1937, by attacking Chinese forces at the Marco Polo Bridge outside Beijing. Japanese forces poured into China, quickly occupying the major cities and lines of communications in the northeast. The Japanese opened a second front in Shanghai on August 13, but there they encountered determined resistance from Chiang Kai-shek's best German-trained Chinese troops. A bitter struggle for control of the city lasted for three months but ended in withdrawal of the Chinese forces, opening the way for the Japanese to advance westward up the Yangzi to Nanjing, which they seized in December 1937. The civilian population of Nanjing was brutalized and tens of thousands were slaughtered by the Japanese. World opinion sympathized with Chiang's government as it withdrew to Chongqing in the remote western province of Sichuan, insulated from the Japanese-controlled east by the precipitous Yangzi Gorges. Meanwhile, in 1938, Japanese forces extended their control over the cities and communication lines of east China by occupying Guangzhou in October and Wuhan in the central Yangzi Valley in December.[95]

The fall of Wuhan marked the end of the first phase of the war. The lines stabilized during the next three years. Hundreds of millions of Chinese lived under Japanese occupation in east China, while the refugee government in Chongqing tried—with scant success—to marshal the resources of west China and collect what foreign aid it could to resist further Japanese advance.[96] During these years, Mrs. Nie lived with her family amid the chaos of wartime Shanghai.

After the Japanese bombed Pearl Harbor and the United States declared war against Japan in December 1941, World War II in the Pacific entered a new phase. The crucial theater of operations shifted gradually from China to the Pacific islands that guarded the maritime approaches to Japan.[97] In those fateful moments in China's modern history in late 1942, Mrs. Nie's life slipped quietly away in Japanese-occupied Shanghai.

PART ONE IN THE HOUSE OF MY FATHER (1852–1872)

Zeng Jifen probably never thought of herself as a very important person, especially during the years she was growing up in the household of her famous father, Zeng Guofan. What she recalled and reconstructed from the years 1852 to 1872 when dictating her autobiography in the 1930s tells of a little girl and young woman who saw herself always in a web of family relationships; rarely did she feel her own sentiments or opinions worthy of record. She dwelt endlessly on the complex network of the extended family that nourished her. Births, deaths, illnesses, betrothals, marriages, and movements, regulated by ritual observances of mourning, celebration, feasting, etiquette, and reverence for tradition, formed the pattern of her family life.

Moreover, Zeng Jifen recalled with pride the military and official careers of her father and her uncle, Zeng Guoquan. Her father's and uncle's protracted campaigns against the Taiping Revolutionary movement, their capture of the Taiping capital of Nanjing, the frustrating and fruitless expedition against the Nian rebels, and their administrative responsibilities, literary accomplishments, and leadership in times of crisis all epitomized for Zeng Jifen, as they do for her readers, a way of life dedicated to service to the Confucian empire.

The institutions that enveloped this young life were the family and the empire. A smaller talent or a duller wit would have been suffocated by the conventions, traditions, and rituals imposed by these powerful societal influences. But Zeng Jifen embraced the Confucian values of her family and the empire and advocated eloquently the homely virtues championed by her father while she wondered about the future in a China where Western learning was persistently insinuating itself. In a sense, Zeng Jifen's intellect, which alternately reached for Western learning and clung to the

Governor General Zeng Guofan

rigid moral principles of her father, mirrored the two-sided intellectual life of Zeng Guofan, the paragon of Confucian values who pioneered the introduction of machine production and steamship construction in China in the 1860s.

Traditionally, in the first stage of a woman's life in Confucian China, she served her father. Subsequent stages were to be devoted to service to her husband and ultimately to her oldest son. In this first stage of Confucian womanhood, Zeng Jifen was indeed the servant of an exceptional master. The individuality and originality that marked her later life were nourished in these years, as was her unbending adherence to the paternally instilled Confucian virtues.

ONE A SOLDIER'S DAUGHTER (1852–1868)

I was born on the eighteenth of May 1852, the year that the Taiping Rebellion swept across China. I grew to young womanhood in the 1850s and early 1860s while the flames of that great rebellion consumed the provinces of central China from which my family had sprung. But I came into the world in north China, in the imperial city, Beijing. My father, Zeng Guofan (1811–72),[1] was a powerful official of the imperial government, vice president of one of its principal ministries, the Board of Rites. His official career and his personality, about which I will say much more, influenced every aspect of my life until his death in 1872, and even thereafter.

The house on Gujia Street where I was born in the small hours of the morning was large. It accommodated our family, which—in addition to my father and my mother, Madam Ouyang (1815–74),[2]—included two brothers, four sisters, and several servants. My firstborn brother died of smallpox when he was only three, and a fifth sister, afflicted with a weakness of the spleen, had succumbed to dysentery. Still sorrowing for her untimely death, my family especially welcomed me and lavished on me their love and attention.

At the time of my birth, my paternal grandparents—Zeng Linshu (1790–1857)[3] and his wife, Madam Jiang (1785–1852)[4]—were living at their family home in the Xiangxiang District of the central Chinese province of Hunan, just west of the provincial capital, Changsha. My mother's ancestral home was in the Hengyang District of Hunan. Her parents, Ouyang Cangming (1787–1869)[5] and Madam Qiu (1787–?),[6] were in their early sixties, having married in 1807, the year my grandfather began his studies in preparation for the imperial civil service examinations.

No sooner had I come into the world than Father's career began to influence the course my life would follow. On July 28, 1852, orders from the court directed Father to proceed to Jiangxi Province in the southeast to preside over the conduct of the imperial civil service examinations. He set out on August 9, leaving us in the capital, and arrived at Xiaochi in northern Anhui Province, more than four hundred miles south of Beijing, on September 8. There, news that his mother had died reached him. He immediately entered mourning and altered his course westward for his parents' home in the Xiangxiang District of Hunan. The situation in Hunan was perilous; the Taipings had placed Changsha under siege.

When the news of my paternal grandmother's death reached our family in Beijing, my mother also entered mourning—together with the children—and began preparations for our return to Hunan. Father's Hunanese friends and colleagues, who had received their civil service degrees the same year as he, went to great pains to assist us, even dispatching a special messenger to determine a route secure from the threat of rebel military activity. My father, however, made arrangements for my mother's brother, Ouyang Muyun, to join us in Beijing and escort us to Xiangxiang. My mother and we children set out from Beijing in the care of Uncle Muyun on what proved to be a long and arduous journey. I would not set foot in the imperial capital again for more than eighty years.

I was nourished on the journey to Xiangxiang by a wet nurse Mother engaged on the eve of our departure. This woman had been employed by a neighbor named Li, but she was a southerner and eager to return to her home in the south. Because of the inadequacy of her own milk, Mother had previously engaged a northern wet nurse; however, Mother never cared for the northern woman's personal traits, and she was pleased to have this newcomer join our caravan.

We traveled overland for more than six hundred miles to Xiangyang in northern Hubei, then by boat for several hundred miles down the Han River to Hankou. From there we sailed west on the Yangzi through Dongting Lake and south on the Xiang River to Changsha, a journey of

CHART 1
Paternal Ancestors of Zeng Jifen

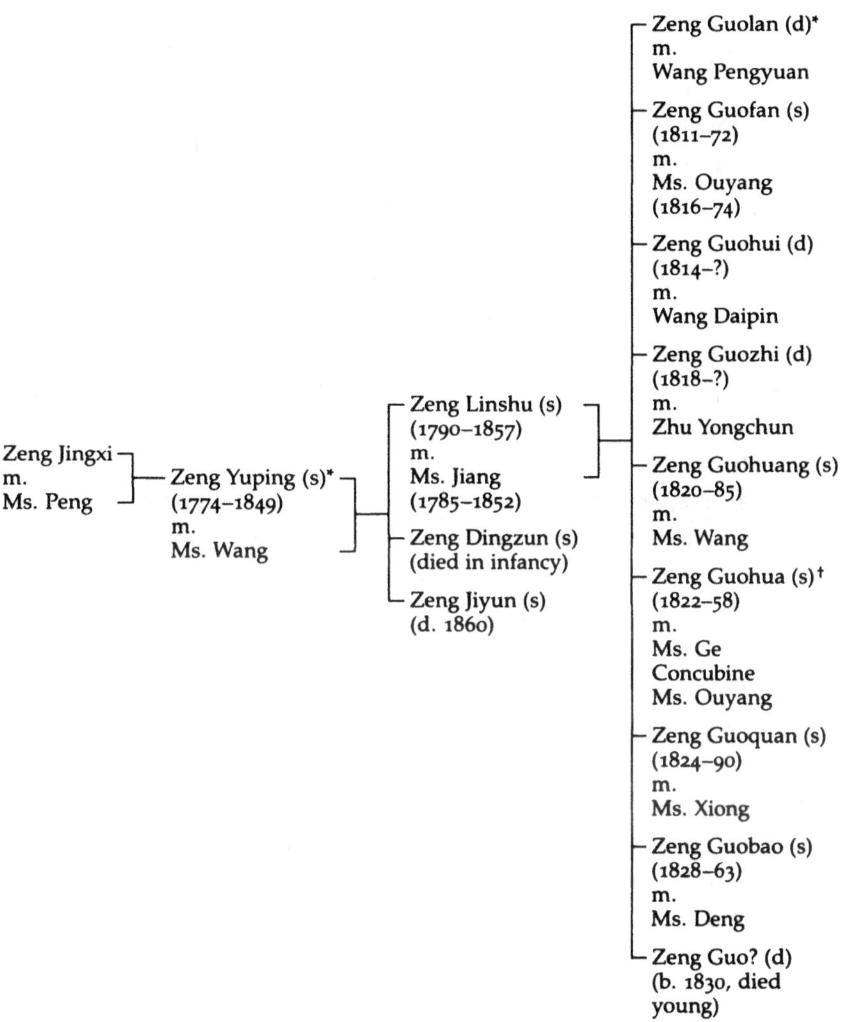

Sources: Nie Zeng Jifen, "Chongde laoren ziding nianpu"; Arthur W. Hummel, *Eminent Chinese of the Ch'ing Period;* Zeng Guofan, *Zeng Wenzhenggong quanji, wenji, nianpu;* Jian Yuwen, *Taiping tianguo quanshi.*

*s = son
d = daughter

†Given in adoption to uncle Zeng Jiyun.

well over a thousand miles. It was a difficult trip. We were frightened many times along the way by the sounds of fleeing troops. Mother was exhausted. My eldest brother, Zeng Jize (1839–90),[7] lost his footing and almost slipped into the water. Fortunately, Uncle Muyun saw him and pulled him back to safety.

After we arrived in Xiangxiang we lived in the Golden Hall, a residence built by my grandfather, Zeng Linshu. His father, Zeng Yuping (1774–1849),[8] had lived in a residence called the White Jade Hall in the countryside of Xiangxiang District. When the family property was divided, fertile lands went to his oldest brother. Zeng Yuping did not contest this; as a result, all he inherited was the White Jade Hall and unproductive land in various other places, which he gave to Grandfather's younger brother. Grandfather built the Golden Hall as a separate residence.

In February 1853, the Taiping siege of Changsha having been lifted, Father, in response to an imperial edict, set about training the Hunan Braves (the famed Xiang Army),[9] who ultimately were victorious over the Taipings. In November he received orders to lead his forces eastward against the Taipings, who had established their capital at Nanjing in 1853, and then attacked westward into Hubei. In February of the following year, Father led a flotilla northward from Hengzhou on the Xiang River against the Taipings who were advancing southward from Hubei into Hunan. Later that summer forces under Father's command expelled the Taipings from Hunan and continued their advance northward, seizing the Taiping stronghold at Wuchang in Hubei at the confluence of the Han and Yangzi rivers in the fall of 1854.

Meanwhile, in October 1854, Father declined an imperial appointment as governor of Hubei, but he continued to direct the struggle against the Taipings under the title of vice president of the Board of War.[10] In 1855 he led his forces eastward into Jiangxi. Uncle Zeng Guoquan (1824–90),[11] having passed the metropolitan examinations in the civil service, also took command of militia units battling the Taipings. The following year, 1856, Father's forces fighting in Jiangxi were reinforced by units under the command of Uncle Zeng Guohua (1822–58).[12]

In 1854, while Father was leading the struggle against the Taipings in

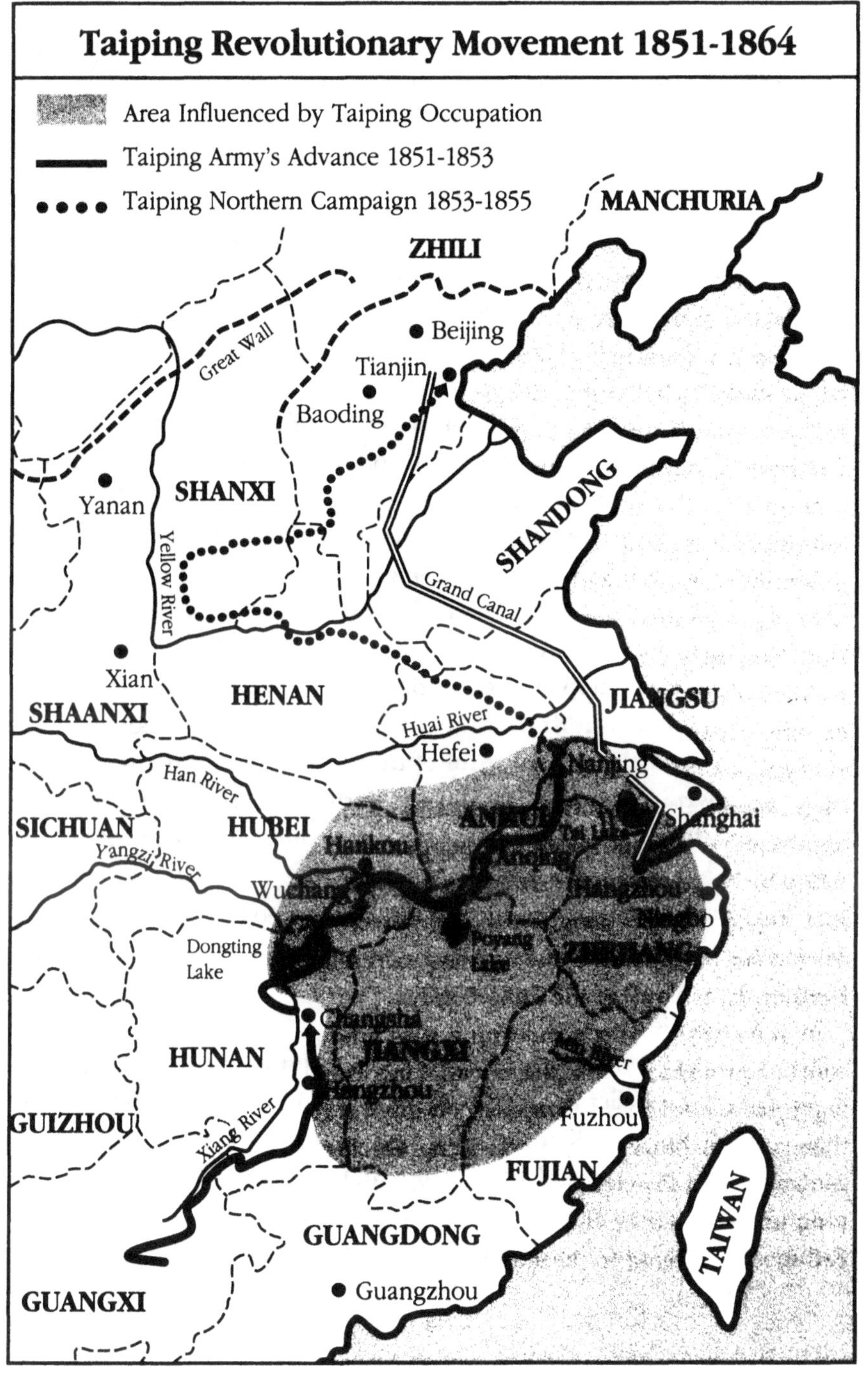
Taiping Revolutionary Movement 1851-1864
Area Influenced by Taiping Occupation
Taiping Army's Advance 1851-1853
Taiping Northern Campaign 1853-1855
MANCHURIA
ZHILI
Beijing
Great Wall
Tianjin
Baoding
Yanan
SHANXI
Yellow River
SHANDONG
Grand Canal
Xian
HENAN
SHAANXI
Huai River
Hefei
Han River
SICHUAN
Yangzi River
Dongting
Lake
HUNAN
Xiang River
GUIZHOU
Fuzhou
FUJIAN
TAIWAN
GUANGDONG
Guangzhou
GUANGXI

Hubei and Jiangxi, I left my parents' home and went to live as the adopted daughter of Father's youngest brother, Zeng Guobao (1828–63).[13] He and his wife, Madam Deng, had no children of their own, so, following the customary practice for childless couples, they adopted Jiqu, the son of my father's brother Zeng Guohuang (1820–85).[14] Since Zeng Guobao and Madam Deng also wanted daughters, they asked to adopt my fourth sister, Jichun, and me. Madam Deng moved us from the Golden Hall to the town of Zitian to be closer to her mother. From then until I was eleven I was raised in their home.

When my grandfather Zeng Linshu died on February 27, 1857, my father and Uncle Zeng Guoquan resigned their commands and hurried home to Xiangxiang to mourn. Father had been directing operations at Ruizhou in central Jiangxi, and Uncle Zeng Guoquan was at Ji'an, about a hundred miles to the south. Both had to journey approximately two hundred miles westward to reach Xiangxiang.

Another tragedy befell our family that year when Madam He,[15] the first wife of my brother Jize, died in childbirth while residing in the Golden Hall. Strangely, her mother also had died there; the house acquired somewhat of a reputation for misfortune. When Uncle Zeng Guoquan's wife became pregnant, she was fearful of dwelling there. Consequently, she engaged a wizard[16] to exorcise the evil spirits that seemed to inhabit the place. My father was at home at the time, mourning and feeling especially depressed and melancholy. He happened to be dozing during the day when he heard the disturbance created by the exorcist. Father upbraided him angrily. Before long, in the winter of 1857, Uncle Zeng Guoquan moved his family to the manor house across from the Golden Hall at the head of the valley[17] of the Zeng family.

In June 1858 Father's mourning was interrupted by orders from the court to provide relief to the imperial forces battling the Taipings in Zhejiang. He set out from Xiangxiang on July 13, again entering Jiangxi. Later that year, in November, Uncle Zeng Guohua fell in battle at Sanhe in central Anhui Province. His forces suffered a crushing defeat from Taiping units under the command of Chen Yucheng (d. 1862).[18] In July 1859 Father was ordered to the southwest province of Sichuan to block an anticipated Taiping offensive. His orders were changed en route, however, and he stopped at Wuchang, where he began planning for the recovery of Anqing, the strategic river port in Anhui Province held by the Taipings since 1853. He was encamped in Anhui in early 1860 when he received the news that his uncle, Zeng Jiyun (d. 1860),[19] had died at the ancestral home in Xiangxiang. Unable to leave his command, Father requested forty days' leave for mourning but returned to his duties before a month had passed.

Shortly thereafter an edict named him acting governor general of the Liangjiang provinces (Jiangxi, Jiangsu, and Anhui). He then moved his headquarters to Qimen in southern Anhui; from there he could direct the attack on Anqing. On August 10, he was confirmed as governor general of the Liangjiang provinces and imperial commissioner for the suppression of the Taipings.

In September 1860, when news reached Father's headquarters that British and French forces pressing for treaty revision had invaded north China and occupied Beijing, he petitioned the court for permission to advance on the capital. However, the initiation of peace talks leading to the conclusion of the Beijing Conventions made the presence of his forces in Beijing unnecessary; he was instructed to remain in Anhui.

This was a dangerous time in Father's military career. His headquarters at Qimen was under constant attack by superior Taiping forces throughout the autumn and winter of 1860–61 until he was relieved by Hunanese units commanded by Zuo Zongtang (1812–85).[20] Then, in September 1861, units commanded by Uncle Zeng Guoquan recaptured Anqing from the Taipings, and Father shifted his headquarters to that city, whence he would launch his attack on the Taiping capital, Nanjing, several hundred miles downstream.

It was more than three years since the emperor had summoned Father from mourning in Xiangxiang to renew the struggle against the Taipings. During those years our family had strengthened ties with other gentry families in Hunan through the second marriage of my brother Jize, in 1859, and the marriage of three of my older sisters in 1861 and 1862. Jize's second wife, Madam Liu, was the daughter of the renowned Hunanese military leader Liu Rong (1816–73),[21] who had fought for many years at Father's side.

My oldest sister, Jijing,[22] married Yuan Yusheng of the Xiangtan District of Hunan in late 1861. Yuan was the son of Yuan Fangying, a holder of the *jinshi* degree (1845) and a former district magistrate of Songjiang in Jiangsu. But the younger Yuan was neither a scholar nor a gentleman. My sister endured his arrogance and ill manners, but within a decade she succumbed to illness.

In March 1862 my second oldest sister, Jiyao,[23] married Chen Songsheng of the Chaling District of Hunan. He was the son of Chen Yuandui, who had passed the civil service examinations and obtained the *jinshi* degree in 1838, the same year as Father. Later he served as a magistrate at Ji'an in Jiangxi and at Chizhou in Anhui before falling in battle against the Taipings. The younger Chen was a person of perverse disposition and straitened finances. Although my sister's life with him was difficult, she felt deeply for him and did not complain.

In May of the same year, my third sister, Jichen,[24] married Lo Yunji. His father was the famed anti-Taiping leader Lo Zenan (1808–56),[25] who rose from a government student to receive the highest imperial recognition for his personal qualities of character. He later served with Father as a leader of the Hunan Braves, distinguishing himself in battle and earning an appointment as taotai of the Ningbo, Shaoxing, and Taizhou Circuit in Zhejiang, with the additional title of financial commissioner. But he was mortally wounded in combat with Taipings in 1856. Jichen's marriage to the son of Lo Zenan was also an unhappy one. She had a domineering mother-in-law who bade her scour the chamber pots and do the bidding of the servant girls.

When Father learned of the treatment that his daughters Jijing and Jichen suffered in their husbands' homes, he expressed his deep concern, but there was little he could do to improve their lot. He did, however, urge Jijing's husband, Yuan Yusheng, to mend his ways. He also asked my brother Jize to try politely to help Yuan overcome his failings. Father further counseled Jichen to suffer patiently the harsh treatment of her mother-in-law. I will say more about their married lives and about my fourth sister's marriage as well. Unfortunately, they all had unhappy lives with their husbands.

On March 7, 1862, my adoptive mother, Madam Deng, died during an epidemic which ravaged the countryside in Xiangxiang. I then moved back to the Golden Hall to be with my natural mother, Madam Ouyang, in the household of my father. Early in 1863 my adoptive father, Uncle Zeng Guobao, also passed away at his military encampment in the Congyang District of Anhui, having taxed himself physically beyond endurance.

When I returned to my father's home in 1862, I began my formal education. My brother Zeng Jihong (1848–81),[26] and I studied with a schoolmaster, Mr. Deng Yinjie. At first I attempted the *Lunyu* (The sayings of Confucius),[27] but, fearing that I would be unable to master these, I changed to the *Youxue*, selections from the *Liji* (Book of rites) *Chuli shang* (Summary of the rules of ceremony, part 1),[28] a text that assumes that learning begins in the second decade of life. I didn't understand the importance of diligence in the classroom; consequently, my accomplishments were very limited. Subsequently, when schoolmaster Deng Yinjie's son joined the class, my studies were terminated because he was not of our family. I spent my time instead making shoes and stockings with my sisters, for Mother, despite her aristocratic background, was very frugal and employed few servants.

Our family was reunited at Father's headquarters in Anqing in 1863. On November 10, Mother and her sons, daughters, daughter-in-law, and grandchild set out from our home in Hunan to the governor general's residence in Anqing. My second sister, Jiyao, was the only one of the children who did not accompany her. Escorting us on the journey were the schoolmaster Deng Yinjie and my mother's brother, Muyun. My brother Jize had preceded us to Anqing. The family traveled in Father's personal launch prepared specially by Admiral Peng Yulin (1816–90).[29] The four bulkheads were spread with white silk on which Admiral Peng himself had painted plum blossoms. The launch's decorations and furnishings were far superior to those of ordinary vessels. On the stern was a tower from which one could look into the distance. It was called the first ship of the Yangzi. Along the way we saw the scenery at the Yueyang Tower overlooking the northern shore of Dongting Lake and Huanghe (Yellow Crane) Tower[30] in the mountains near Wuchang in Hubei. As they came into our field of vision we admired them, but we were unable to go ashore.

In Anqing, the former residence of Taiping general Chen Yucheng—also known to the Taipings as Brave Prince and to his enemies as the four-eyed dog—was Father's temporary headquarters. Within the headquarters the women's quarters had only a single courtyard. In front was an official personnel office, in the rear a courtyard, and on the left side there was some vacant land. Father made a minor addition of three rooms in order to house his two daughters and their husbands separately. Furthermore, he made separate doors so that entry and exit were by different paths. When Father arrived in a new place he liked to make a planting of bamboo, so there was bamboo surrounding this building. He also liked to construct observation towers from which one could look into the distance. Consequently, he added a small tower atop the three rooms. Moreover, each evening he climbed the tower atop the main building and prayed to heaven. No incense and joss sticks were set out. There was simply a ceremonial cushion for kneeling and nothing more. The cost of all repairs and rebuilding came from Father's official salary. He did not use cash from public funds.

When Mother brought the family east to Anqing from our native place in Hunan, only one old woman servant accompanied her. Mother paid her eight-hundred cash each month. My oldest sister, Jijing, who had married into the Yuan family, had one young maidservant. My third sister, Jichen, who had married into the Lo family, had none. The heavy work in the house was done by my mother's servant. In Anqing we purchased a maidservant, paying more than ten strings of cash for her. When Father learned of this he rebuked us sharply. So we presented her to the Guo family,[31] who later were related to us through the marriage of their daughter to my brother Jihong. Father's governance of the household was thus austere and frugal. My sister-in-law and sisters dared not have a maidservant or the old woman dress their hair.

When I was young, I was bothered with head lice; therefore, I kept my hair short. I was eleven before I began letting it grow. Because my hair was short and I was young, the old woman called Ding dressed my hair. When I was twelve, the gathered topknot was popular. One had to wrap the hair around a wire frame. I heard of this style and wished to imitate it, but I made the topknot too large. Father saw it and jokingly said, "I must call the carpenter and have him enlarge the frame of the main gate so that you can walk through." He was usually solemn with his sons and daughters; however, he occasionally made jokes. Once he said to my mother, "Our youngest daughter looks like the Buddha Amitabha."[32] In the Xiangxiang patois looking like the Buddha Amitabha means appearing to be a little simple-minded.

Although I was only a small child when I was at the governor general's residence, like my older sisters I never set foot outside the gate. However, from the observation tower I was able to see the processions going forth on stilts to welcome the local gods, and I also learned something of the conditions in the city.

On July 19, 1864, Nanjing was recaptured. Father went east to inspect the troops and then returned to Anqing. On October 1, 1864, the whole family set out for Nanjing. We moved into the governor general's residence on October 10. When the Hunan Braves retook Nanjing, they searched for and captured the remnants of the Taiping forces and burnt their dens. The great mansions, for the most part, were reduced to ashes, as, of course, was the Palace of the Heavenly King in which the Taiping leader, Hong Xiuquan (1813–64),[33] had resided. However, because General Chen Yucheng (Brave Prince) had died previously, his palace was empty and thus was spared. Therefore, Father used it temporarily as the governor general's residence. Later, when Li Hongzhang (1823–1901)[34] became acting governor general of the Liangjiang provinces in 1865, he lived in the newly built Jiangning prefectural residence.

At home, Father always regulated our behavior closely in accordance with the rules of ritual. I recall when we entered the Nanjing governor general's residence we had not yet completed the mourning period for Uncle Zeng Guobao, who had died the previous year. I wore a lined jacket of blue wool and yellow silk trousers sewn with green lace, bequeathed to me by my deceased sister-in-law, Madam He. Father saw this and criticized it as being extravagant in a time of mourning. So I hurriedly switched to a pair of green trousers belonging to my third sister. These trousers were also bequeathed by Madam He.

Father also insisted on the strictest standard of frugality. The women in the family handed down and used among themselves the things that my sister-in-law had bequeathed. It was not easy to buy things in the countryside then, and Madam He's things were insufficient for our use. I recall when Jiyao, my second oldest sister, was preparing to marry; she had a gold earpick weighing seven-tenths of an ounce and worth twenty-odd strings of cash. One day it was stolen; mother was so upset that she didn't sleep for several nights, worrying that her daughter would have no ornament to adorn her head in her husband's home.

On January 3, 1865, Jiyao and her husband arrived in Nanjing from Changsha. Since our female servants were inadequate for our needs, my mother engaged an old woman named Hou from the Refugee Bureau at a monthly wage of eight hundred cash. When Tao Zhu (1779–1839)[35] was Liangjiang governor general (1830–39), this woman had entered service as a wet nurse for his son. Later, the Tao family sought refuge from the Taipings in Hunan. The old woman's husband and children were lost in the confusion brought about by the war. After the rebels occupied Nanjing, the city underwent a lengthy siege by imperial troops. The old and the weak in rebel-controlled areas were gradually released and dispersed, and Uncle Zeng Guoquan established the Refugee Bureau to accommodate them. That is how it came into existence.

When our family eventually returned to Hunan, the old woman Hou was unwilling to accompany us, so we recommended her to Li Hongzhang's mother. Subsequently, when Li Hongzhang was acting Liangjiang governor general, she was still alive and in sound health. Moreover, she had accumulated some savings and purchased ground for a grave for herself. She reckoned that to have served in the residence of the Liangjiang governor general thrice in one lifetime was indeed her good fortune.

While Father was in the military he never built a domicile for himself. However, during the reign of Emperor Xianfeng (1851–62) he constructed a study, called the Siyun Hall,[36] at our home in Hunan. The Hunan custom when putting the roof on a new building is to recite a few phrases to celebrate the raising of the main beam. The workers praised Father, singing with a Xiangxiang accent, "The Liangjiang governor general is too small. You must go to Nanjing and be emperor." For "small" this Hunan popular saying used the word for "delicate." One can see the general ignorance of the country people at that time.[37]

Each time Uncle Zeng Guoquan retook a great city from the Taipings he reported the victory, requested leave, and returned home for a stay. He brought misfortune on himself by his efforts to acquire real estate. In 1859 he built an impressive new home modeled after the architecture of an official residence. The front entrance was like those in government offices, and there were several gates. The local people were rather free with their remarks about it. When Father heard of it, he sent instructions to tear it down. I can still recall the ridgepole on the roof of the theater that was part of this residence; it was a blue ceramic floral pattern of curved lines that had been fired in Jiangxi.

Father did not buy land or residences, but in 1855, Uncle Zeng Guohuang bought land for Father in Hengyang on the Xiang River, about one hundred miles south of Changsha. In 1867 he had a building, called the Fu Hou Hall, erected on this land at a cost of seven thousand strings of cash. Father chided him for doing this. Although Uncle Zeng Guoquan's and Father's circumstances were different, they were alike in that neither was conceited because of his fame.

When Father served as an official in Beijing his income was small. Each year he scrimped in order to send money to his parents, though the amount was very small. While he was commanding the Hunan Army, he sent them only ten or twenty taels a year. By the time he had achieved success and a distinguished position, his father, Zeng Linshu, had already passed away. Therefore, Father no longer sent funds home. When he was governor general of Zhili (1868–71), he accumulated twenty thousand taels from his salary.

In 1865 the Nian rebels still ravaged north China. In May, the commander of the imperial troops, Prince Senggelinqin (d. May 14, 1865),[38] suffered a crushing defeat at Caozhou in western Shandong Province and died a hero's death. The court ordered Father to lead troops to north China to pacify the Nian. He set out on June 18. When the time for Father to depart arrived, my sister Jichen availed herself of an auspicious day to take the son she had borne in the governor general's residence on April 13 back to Hunan. Her mother-in-law, a ferocious and stern woman, was the concubine of Lo Zenan. My sister was reluctant to go, and as the time for parting drew near she was ever sorrowful and loving. When Father came from the governor general's residence to board the ship, the infantry and naval forces of the whole city fired salutes to send him off. The noise was piercing and kept on without end. My sister's child became sick with fright. After they boarded the boat, the illness worsened, and they had to return to the governor general's residence. Cures proved ineffective and, in the end, the baby died.

In May 1866, while Father was encamped with his troops at Xuzhou in northern Jiangsu directing operations against the Nian, the family began the journey from Nanjing to return to our home in Hunan. Among the family members was my new sister-in-law, Guo Yun (1848–1916),[39] a woman of the Guo family of the Qishui District of Hubei. She had married my brother Jihong on May 15 of the previous year at the governor general's residence in Nanjing. By the time we left Nanjing, Uncle Zeng Guoquan had reentered civil service as governor of Hubei. He asked Mother and the family to stay at Wuchang and pass the summer at his residence.

On September 18, Guo Yun gave birth to my nephew Guangjun in the Duogui Hall of the Hubei governor's residence at Wuchang. In the child's first month we began the journey back to Hunan. Guangjun grew in wisdom and learning. Encouraged by his mother, in 1889, at the age of twenty-three, he passed the civil service examinations for the highest degree: a distinction never achieved by his father, who died in 1881 discouraged by his lack of academic success. Guangjun was inducted into the Hanlin Academy in 1889, where he became the youngest member of that distinguished body.

On November 30 my fourth sister, Jichun, married into another Guo family of Xiangyin in Hunan. The sedan chair bearing the bride was dispatched via boat. My mother personally accompanied her to the home of the groom, returning in three days by boat to Xiangxiang. My sister's husband, Guo Yiyong,[40] was the oldest son of Guo Songtao (1818–91),[41] who in 1876 became China's first minister to a Western nation, ambassador to the Court of St. James's. The younger Guo had native intelligence and was accomplished intellectually, but he died when he was only twenty-four years old. After my sister married, she and Guo Songtao's concubine could not get along with each other. My sister's daily fare was brown rice and turnips. Guo's concubine was stingy and did not give Jichun her monthly expenses of one string of cash. One can imagine how difficult Jichun's life was.

Jichun's difficulties were in part the result of Father's frugality and his expectations of others in the family. Earlier, when Uncle Zeng Guobao died, he left an estate worth more than seven thousand taels. Uncle Zeng Guoquan supplemented this to make ten thousand taels and gave orders to give my fourth sister and me one thousand taels each. Father, however, had personally written out directions that when a daughter was married, the dowry should not exceed two hundred taels. In 1859, when his army was encamped in Jiangxi, he wrote in his diary on August 22: "This morning I dispatched Pan Wenzhi and two senior attendants with a letter to my family and two hundred taels: one hundred for Zeng Jize's wedding and one hundred for the wedding of my niece Wushi,[42] one roll each of flowered satin and corded silk material to make clothing for Zeng Jize together with silk linings and two twelve-foot lengths of material, one broadcloth suit material and one camlet skirt material, to make clothing for my niece Wushi together with silk linings."

When Mother gave my fourth sister in marriage, she limited the dowry out of respect for Father's wishes. When Uncle Zeng Guoquan heard of this, he was aghast, saying, "How can there be such a thing?" But when he opened up the dowry chest and inspected it, he believed it. He repeatedly sighed, lamenting the situation. He knew that it would be very difficult for this amount to suffice. Consequently, he presented my sister with another four hundred taels.

Throughout his life Father was scrupulously incorruptible, and he insisted that family members also refrain from accepting even small favors.

As a consequence, Mother never acquired the precious gifts that were the customary perquisites of the wives of high officials. Once, however, I recall that the wife of Admiral Huang Yisheng (1818–94)[43] very much wished to have my mother become her adopted mother. She presented Mother with a pair of green jade bracelets and a pearl. One year on Mother's birthday she gave her a reeled pongee bed canopy. Mother kept it and used it as part of my dowry. I have used it right up to the present, and it has not worn out.

Although Father insisted on frugality in his family, he provided generously for the welfare of deserving officials and their families. In 1861, the wife of the old scholar Shao Weixi (1810–61)[44] of Hangzhou, capital of Zhejiang, had fled with her children to Shanghai to avoid the rebels. Shao remained in Hangzhou and gave his life in defense of the city. When Father heard of this, he dispatched the steamship *Weilingmi* to bring Mrs. Shao, her two sons, and a married daughter to Anqing. Each month he gave them twenty taels for food and lodging. Later, when Mrs. Shao and her oldest son died, her second son and son-in-law accompanied their bodies back to Zhejiang. Mrs. Shao's daughter remained alone in Anqing. Father then directed Mrs. Shao's daughter to acknowledge our mother as her adopted mother, and she came to live temporarily in the governor general's residence. This daughter had a gift, a pearl, which she had hidden in her clothing when she fled Hangzhou. It was subsequently presented to Uncle Zeng Guoquan's wife, who also had a pair of pearl flowers linked with gold which had been presented to her by officers under her husband's command after they left the service. These things were precious. In addition to this, our family had stored away china and curios that included all types of jade bottles and precious ornaments, extraordinary things rarely seen. In the summer of 1930, a fire in the Changsha Gunpowder Works reached the family residence and destroyed most of them.

November 6, 1867, was Father's fifty-seventh birthday. He was encamped at Zhoujiakou in eastern Henan directing the campaign against the Nian when he received orders to return to his former post as governor general of the Liangjiang provinces. Though we did not then realize it, age and the responsibilities of high office had already taken a heavy toll on Father's health. He would be with us for only a few short years. This year also marked the passage of other happy milestones for our family: my maternal grandparents entered their eightieth year and their great-grandchild passed the first year of life. We sponsored a theatrical performance for the people of our district to celebrate our good fortune.

TWO ZENG GUOFAN'S FINAL YEARS (1868–1872)

Father arrived in Nanjing and resumed his duties as governor general of the Liangjiang provinces on April 10, 1867. A year passed, however, before the family came from Hunan to join him there. Meanwhile, Jize's wife gave birth to his second daughter at our home in Hunan on March 2, 1867. My other brother, Jihong, who at age twenty-one was already serving in the prefectural office in Nanjing, was stricken with smallpox. After he recovered, in the winter of 1867, he returned to Hunan.

In the fall, Father's sister-in-law, Madam Zeng Guohuang, took her son Jiqu (who had been adopted into the family of Uncle Zeng Guobao at the same time that I was) to study with a tutor at the Nanjing governor general's residence. Jiqu's wife and child accompanied him. His education had been neglected from his youth. Now, in addition to studying with tutors, Father required Jiqu to compose a letter to his family every five days and submit it for review. Late in 1868, Jiqu returned to Hunan. He later served for many years as an official in Guangdong.

In April 1868 we came east from Hunan to Nanjing, and on April 20 we moved into the new governor general's residence. Since we were all living under the same roof, Father took this opportunity to teach us diligence, frugality, and early rising and to ensure that we learned to sew, cook, and work hard; he personally admonished us and was not at all liberal or indulgent. He frequently would say that there is a limit to one's good fortune and benefits. If we squander them in our youth, then as old people we will experience hard times. All men should do more things that benefit others—not just those things which are our duty. When I recall what I have accomplished in life and the benefits I have had, I can see that they have all come about from this basic teaching. As I write, women's education is being modeled on the West; it is aimed at enjoyment and views extravagance and indolence as natural. The influence this has had on society and the nation can already be seen. Therefore, I am respectfully publishing this work schedule, which Father gave us, in the hope that it will contribute to the education and revitalization of our people:[1]

Time	*Type of Work*	*Specific Tasks*
After breakfast	culinary arts	make ordinary dishes, pastries, wines, sauces, etc.
9:00 A.M.–1:00 P.M.	make clothing	spin cotton, twist thread
After the noon meal	detailed work	fine needlework, embroidery
5:00 P.M.–11:00 P.M.	rough work	make men's or women's shoes, sew clothes

He accompanied it with the following instructions:

> In our family the sons must do four things: reading, classical study, calligraphy, and composition; none can be neglected. The women must cook, make clothes, and do fine and rough work. None of these can be neglected. I have taught this for years, but it still has not become a set pattern. Henceforth, every day I will personally inspect your accomplishments in the tasks that I have set for you. Culinary arts will be inspected daily. Making of clothing will be inspected once in every three days. I will inspect the thread you spin and the balls of yarn you have twisted. I will inspect the fine needlework and embroidery every four days; rough work, once per month. Each month you must complete one pair of men's slippers. There will be no inspection of women's slippers.[2]

Father directed his daughters-in-law, the wives of his brothers' sons, and me to follow this schedule. My married sisters were also expected to follow it from the day they arrived in our home. It was based on the idea that in China, in olden times, women who developed literary skills often tended to be vapid and spurned hard work. He exhorted us further with this poem:

If a family is diligent, it will prosper.
If a person is diligent, he will be strong.
If one can be both diligent and thrifty
Then one's fortunes will never decline.
July 13, 1868

Even now as I recall these words written to me more than half a century ago, I am struck by their applicability. My family had dwelt in the countryside of Hunan for generations, deep in the mountains, far removed from the river. The area was unrefined; the people were hardworking and simple. My father traveled north and south. He personally observed the dissolute and empty ways of the cities, and he was quick to perceive the troubles that lay ahead. Although Father was immersed in the responsibilities of high office, he had a deep-seated fear that his family members would become infected with extravagant and indolent ways; he made up his mind that eventually he would return again to the countryside to live in order to keep up the family traditions of industry and frugality, tilling the soil, and learning.

While we lived in Nanjing Father required us to learn how to prepare delicacies for banquets, but he always dined alone in his study; however, on New Year's Eve his sons and nephews joined him for a banquet. Mother brought me, my sisters-in-law, and the other women of our family to eat with her in the main dwelling. Exotic delicacies or roasts were strictly prohibited at our table. The staff also observed this; it became an established custom. Ordinarily, when entertaining guests, we only had such things as sharks' fins cooked in soy sauce and sugar, strips of cuttlefish, and bean curd soup.

In 1868, Guangxuan, the oldest of Jize's two daughters, was pledged in marriage to Li Youxian of Hefei, nephew of Li Hongzhang. Her prospective husband's family wanted her to be educated. This resulted in another opportunity for me to further my formal education. Jize gave Guangxuan instructions daily on the Ming and Qing versions of the *Tongjian gangmu*

CHART 2
Children and Grandchildren of Zeng Guofan and Madam Ouyang

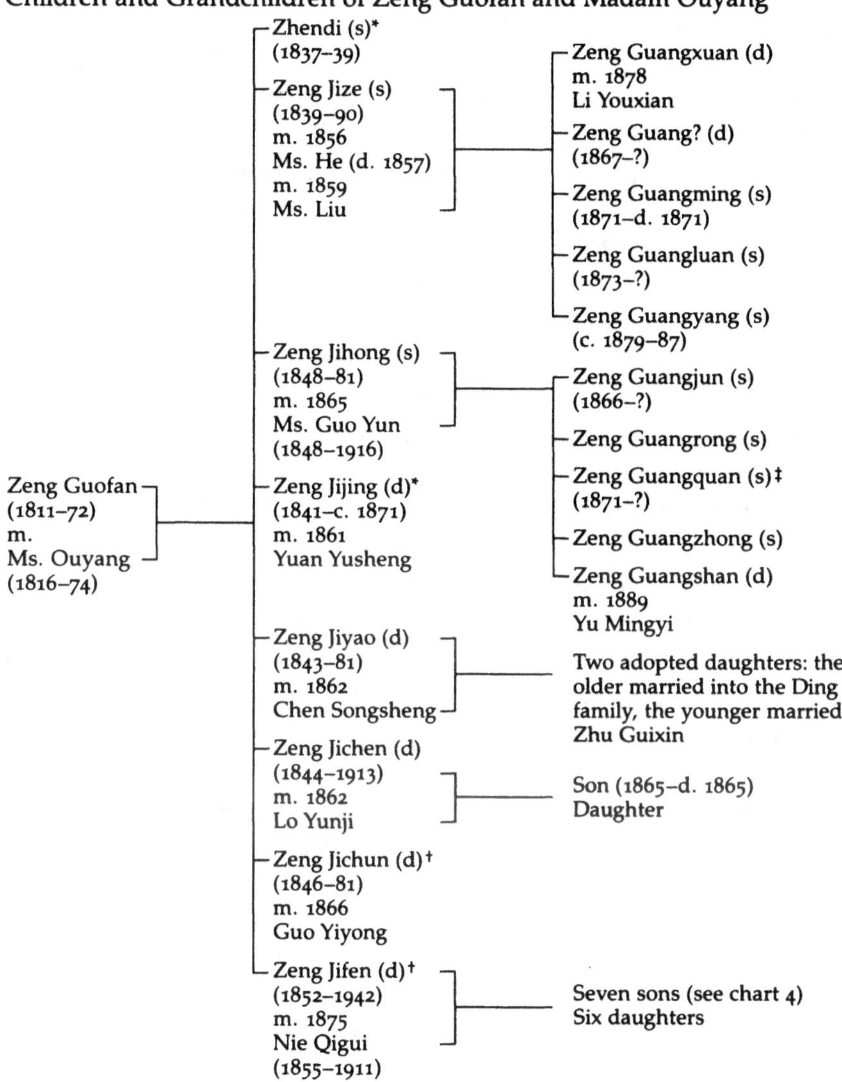

Sources: Nie Zeng Jifen, "Chongde laoren ziding nianpu"; Arthur W. Hummel, *Eminent Chinese of the Ch'ing Period;* Li Yuning, *Jindai zhonghua funu zixu shiwenxuan;* Li Enhan, *Zeng Jize de waijiao;* Liu Kwang-Ching, "Cong Zeng Guofan jiashu shuoqi," 11–12.

*s = son
d = daughter

†Given in adoption to Zeng Guobao (1854) until their adoptive mother died in 1862.

‡Given in adoption to his uncle Zeng Jize

(Selective mirror of history) and the outlines of the official dynastic histories,[3] and I listened in on them. Later on, when Jize no longer had the leisure for teaching, I went over the readings myself. Furthermore, while we were in the governor general's residence, Father had a ship's hall built. In it was a model globe more than six feet in diameter that had been made at the arsenal.[4] We children gained a general understanding of geography from it. My brother Jihong had a talent for mathematics; he instructed me in traditional Chinese algebra, right triangles, and finding squares and cubes, what is now called algebra and geometry.[5] I was quite able to grasp it. Jize first taught me the abacus. From this I learned arithmetic calculations. The arithmetic that we employed at that time still followed the old methods, not those used today. Jihong's wife, Madam Guo, also frequently followed along with the discussions. The joy of learning I experienced at that time was the greatest I have known.

It was from about this time also that the health problems that beset our family commanded an ever greater share of my interest. In Nanjing, behind the newly built governor general's residence, Father had planted a vegetable garden. When the vegetables were ripe, he told us to gather them and prepare cooked dishes. One day in late summer, I picked a cucumber and prepared it for eating. Mother ate excessively of it and developed severe gas pains. She took medicine for a long time but did not get better. Then she seemed to have a parasite in her eyes, which resulted in a loss of vision in her right eye. It became difficult for her to move around. The next year, after we moved to Zhili, she went to Dr. Hao in Baoding who performed acupuncture on the left eye. His technique was wanting; consequently, she lost the vision in that eye as well.

On December 17, 1868, Father, having received orders transferring him to the post of governor general of the metropolitan province of Zhili, set out for the north. We remained temporarily at the Nanjing governor general's residence because Mother was suffering from severe coughing and shortness of breath; Jize also stayed to attend her. In the winter we moved into the Jiangsu Provincial Examination Hall.

On May 1, 1869, we accompanied Mother to the governor general's residence in Zhili. We went east by boat from Nanjing to the Grand Canal and then north to Qingjiang in northern Jiangsu, where we changed to carts and continued north. It was very hot and dusty. By the time we reached the governor general's headquarters at Baoding in central Zhili most of us were sick. Mother traveled either in the sedan chair or in an official carriage. The rest of us rode in mule carts, shaking and jiggling. It was unbearable.

Mother spoke often of the time she accompanied Grandfather Zeng Linshu to the capital in 1840. On that trip they encountered a harsh winter, severe cold, and short days. One maidservant, carrying a small child, rode in a mule cart. Often it was after dark when they arrived at an inn. Then they were up before dawn. They warmed themselves with their own breath and patted quilts up around their heads. Gradually they turned to ice. The children whimpered and cried out endlessly. Sometimes both mothers and children cried. The bitter conditions of that journey were still vivid in Mother's memory. This trip was much more bearable.

In Baoding, Jize was stricken with dysentery. He was treated incorrectly and developed a stomach ailment. Most of my nieces and nephews were sick also. Mother's health continued to decline. In the autumn and early winter of 1869 she suffered from an inflammation in the head and coughing. It was December before she began to improve.

On June 21, 1870, the people of Tianjin in eastern Zhili rose up in protest against the abuses of the French Catholic missionaries in that city. A violent confrontation between the French consul, M. Fontanier, and Liu Jie, the prefect of Tianjin, led to rioting which resulted in Fontanier's death, the death of twelve French missionaries and their Chinese servants, and the destruction of church property.[6]

Father received an imperial edict to conduct an investigation into the cause of the incident. At that time he was suffering from a loss of vision in his right eye and recurring bouts of dizziness; he was unable even to get out of bed. He had requested two months' leave; however, when he received the orders he reacted immediately, without regard for his personal comfort. Recalling his earlier encounters with danger and adversity, he vowed to give his life if need be. First, for two days after receiving the edict, he personally wrote out his final instructions; then he set out on the mission.

In August, while Father was still conducting the investigation in Tianjin, Governor General Ma Xinyi (1821–70)[7] of the Liangjiang provinces was assassinated by a former Taiping soldier. The court ordered Father transferred to Nanjing to fill the Liangjiang post once more. He declined vigorously, but the court insisted. Consequently, following the conclusion of the investigation of the Tianjin Massacre and the execution of those responsible for the violence, on October 17, Father went to the capital. It was also the occasion of his sixtieth birthday. In Beijing he received gifts from the emperor. Mother and we children left later from Baoding and traveled south on the Grand Canal in November. When we arrived in Nanjing, we stayed temporarily in the salt intendant's residence. Although there was a flower garden in the residence, we had to go through the place where the staff was housed in order to reach it. Because of this, we never went there.

In February 1871 my second oldest sister, Jiyao, and her husband, Chen Songsheng, arrived at our residence in Nanjing. They had set out from Hunan in the winter of the previous year; however, they encountered a fierce blizzard en route and were unable to reach the official residence before the new year.

That spring Mother suffered severely from a seasonal malady. Her legs swelled and her urine carried blood. A foreigner from the Nanjing Arsenal, Dr. Halliday Macartney,[8] administered some Western medication and she recovered.

On March 8, Jize's wife gave birth to a son named Guangming. Shortly after, on March 16, Jihong's wife also gave birth to a son. This was their third child, and they named him Guangquan. In August Guangming died. Jihong's wife felt such pity for the terrible grieving of Jize's wife that she let her select one of Jihong's sons to raise until she and Jize had a son of their own. When Jize's wife heard this, she was overcome with happiness. She asked me to tell my parents. I told Father while I was helping him to prepare for a rest in his quarters. When he heard the news, he said happily, "This prompt adopting of a brother's son is in accord with the practice in Li Hongzhang's family. Why even talk of returning him at a later date?" On January 2, 1872, when we again moved into the new governor general's residence, Guangquan was taken to the home of my brother Jize.

After we moved into the new residence Father's physical condition seemed to grow worse with each passing day. On March 2, 1872, while meeting with guests, the sinews in his feet suddenly tightened up. After a few moments he was alright again. He entered the women's chambers and spoke with his second daughter, Jiyao, saying, "I just now felt death was at hand. Surprisingly, I was able to recover."

On March 5 he went out visiting. Suddenly, he wanted to speak and could not; he seemed like one about to have a seizure. After a dose of medicine he was alright. Everyone urged him to ask for leave and rest for a while. He said, "If I request leave, when will there be an end to it!" Moreover, he asked Mother about the circumstances of his father's death. She told him that Zeng Linshu had died on the fourth day of the second month (of the lunar calendar). When she finished speaking, he said, "I will meet death unexpectedly on some other day. It couldn't happen on the same day."

In the second month on the fourth day (of the lunar calendar), Father sat for a while in the women's chambers after eating. He tasted cut oranges my sisters and I had brought in. Then he went for a stroll in the large garden on the west side of the official residence. After walking throughout the entire garden, he wanted to climb the tower but could not do so because the construction was not complete. He strolled for a long time. Suddenly, his feet kicked forward repeatedly. Jize, at his side, asked, "Do your shoes feel uncomfortable?" He replied, "My feet feel numb." Hastily Jize and an orderly, who had been following them, supported him under the arms. Gradually, he lost the power to walk; by then he was already having spasms. They quickly called for a chair in which they supported him, raised him up, and brought him into the drawing room. The household gathered around, but Father was not able to speak again. He sat still for about forty-five minutes, and then he died. During his suffering, my second sister cut a piece of flesh from her arm for him to eat, in the belief that it would revive him, but it was to no avail.[9] It was the fourth day of the second month, March 12, 1872, between 7:00 and 9:00 P.M.

PART TWO IN THE HOUSE OF MY HUSBAND (1872–1911)

The second phase of Confucian womanhood, service to one's husband, began for Zeng Jifen after the death of her father in 1872. If the first phase of her life was dominated by the powerful personality of Zeng Guofan, her marriage in 1875 to Nie Qigui, scion of a prominent Hunan gentry family, opened opportunities for Zeng Jifen to assert her own personality. Nie was by no means the dominant figure in his household that Zeng Guofan had been in his. But Mrs. Nie continued to show an unwavering adherence to Confucian values and principles of behavior, the stamp of her paternal upbringing.

Some of the same influences that shaped her earlier life are manifest in the second stage. The observance of ritual, which regulated every aspect of life in her father's family and in the officialdom that surrounded it, was of singular importance to Zeng Jifen as she entered married life. Although she continues to allude to ritually determined practices, gradually human experiences rather than the formalities of life loom more important as she recalls her days as wife and mother. Her sagacity, insight, and capacity to inspire family members seem to have brought her a leadership role in the family comparable in importance to that of her husband's. Nie was energetic and in many respects an able official, but he was not the legendary Zeng Guofan. Freed from her father's iron hand, Mrs. Nie wielded considerable influence in the "women's world" of the late nineteenth century. Not only Mrs. Nie but also her mother-in-law, Madam Zhang, with whom she seems to have enjoyed a certain mutual respect, were adept at brokering influence and even funds to salvage the family fortune and official position. Nie Qigui, who rose to govern three provinces although he never passed a civil service examination, owed much to his spouse's family connections and her ability to manipulate.

Governor Nie Qigui

Still, as a wife and mother, Mrs. Nie was not principally a power broker or a manipulator. She remained intensely interested in things that affected the human condition: the welfare and education of family members, the traditions and popular beliefs that guided life, and the knowledge of sickness and medicines. In all of these fields her words display open-mindedness and the capacity for intellectual and spiritual growth. She advocated Western education for her sons. She openly admired the achievements of Western medicine.

Although Mrs. Nie was adept at the use of power and displayed the capacity for growth, these years were not the prelude to a personal struggle for emancipation. She was ever conscious of the role assigned to her in the hierarchy of the Confucian family. She reminds her readers of the pitiful lives endured by her sisters. She accepted the fact that a boorish husband or tyrannical mother-in-law was the tragic but unchangeable fate of some women. The family remained always most important for her, more important than the happiness of any single member, be it mother, wife, or anyone else. Thus we read her account of the twists and turns of fate and the power brokering that brought the family through scandal and near financial ruin in 1895; but we hear not a word of China's crushing military defeat by Japan, which, in that year, nearly toppled the empire. An unshakable faith in the family; her iron-willed commitment to industry, frugality, and virtue inherited from her father; and the open-minded acceptance of new ideas and new forms of learning seem to have enabled Mrs. Nie to guide the family from its elite status in the old imperial society into the rapidly changing economic and social milieu at the end of the century, and eventually to a position of influence in the emerging bourgeois society of the early twentieth century.

THREE MY MARRIAGE AND LIFE IN HUNAN (1873–1881)

My marriage was settled in 1869. I still have the matchmaking letter written by Uncle Zeng Guoquan. The reply to betrothal after gifts were sent to our home and all other such matters were handled by him. I originally intended to be married into the Nie family in 1872. At the time, my prospective husband, Nie Qigui (1855–1911),[1] was with his father, Nie Erkang, an official in the southern province of Guangdong. On March 18, Nie Qigui set out on the journey to Nanjing to become a son-in-law in our family. After arriving in Shanghai, he heard the news of Father's death and wired his family in Guangdong to ask whether he should continue to Nanjing or return to Guangdong. (At the time, it cost four dollars for each character in the telegram. That is almost forty times greater than today.) Their reply ordered him to continue as planned to Nanjing to console our family and pay his respects to my mother.

When Nie Qigui arrived in Nanjing, he lodged at the official residence of Jiangsu's financial commissioner, Mei Qizhao,[2] who was a good friend of the Nie family and ours. After a brief stay in Nanjing, Nie returned to Guangdong. A small steamer dispatched from the financial commissioner's office brought him to Jiujiang on the Yangzi at the northern end of Poyang Lake. There he changed to a small vessel and then followed overland routes to Guangdong. Nie's mother, Madam Zhang (1828–1911), had not been told the news of Father's death. She supposed that I was arriving as the new bride of her son, to be welcomed formally into the family. When Nie arrived, his father told her, saying, "Governor General

Zeng has died. They have not had the wedding." From that moment he was unable to speak again. He never recovered. Just three days after Nie arrived in Guangdong, his father passed away. It was July 4, 1872.

At the end of May 1872 we returned to Changsha for Father's funeral. A special imperial edict directed us to enter the city. Since there were no lodgings in Changsha, we stayed temporarily in the Zengzi Temple.[3] Jize then purchased a residence at Hongjiajing, the former abode of the Lao family then owned by Mr. Liu Yiqi. In June we bore Father's coffin to a temporary grave site at Jinpenling outside the South Gate. After the burial we went to the new residence to live.

Jize took care of Father's last wishes. He declined funeral donations and accepted only the funds Father's disciples and fellow officials of long standing collected to publish a complete edition of his writings.[4] There was some excess, which Jize added to what was left from Father's salary. It came to just enough to purchase some land and buildings.

When Father was alive, family members received monthly expenses of two strings of cash. At that time, although prices were low, we never had enough money. We could buy no luxuries; indeed, we dared not. When Mother occasionally summoned an old woman who sold wares to our residence, Father upbraided her. Other purchases were out of the question. When Jize took charge of family affairs, he used some of the savings that Father had accumulated to buy land and residences. Each month Mother received an allowance of twelve Hunan taels. My two sisters-in-law each got ten, which had to cover the expenses for the children of both their houses, since there was no separate allowance for them. I and my two brothers each received six taels per month. The wages of the male and female servants of each house were not included in this. Their wages were disbursed separately by the countinghouse, together with the monthly expense money.

In the summer of 1873, while my future mother-in-law, Madam Zhang, was still mourning, she bought a boat and, bearing her husband's remains, returned to his native place in Hunan, passing through Guangxi Province and Yongzhou Prefecture in southern Hunan. Four months elapsed before she reached Hunan. Her husband had served the government in various places for many years, but he had never bought real estate in Hunan. Since she had heard that his native Hengshan was not an easy place in which to reside, she went directly to Changsha.

Madam Zhang was born and grew up in Beijing, and she spoke the Beijing dialect. Moreover, as a child she had been afflicted with a slight loss of hearing. So when she arrived in Hunan and spoke with friends and relatives, she frequently had difficulty with the Hunan accent, which resulted in misunderstandings. My brother Jize went to visit her as a member of a family soon to be related by marriage. Jize spoke the Beijing dialect well, and this delighted Madam Zhang. Consequently, she asked him to look for a residence for her. He rented the Huangniduan residence, which he had purchased, to my future in-laws for fifty strings of cash per month. Approximately one year later, he sold it to Madam Zhang for the original price he had paid for it, slightly more than four thousand taels. When I was married, Madam Zhang had a bridal chamber built in the rear courtyard as an addition to the house; it was more than fifty feet across.

At the time that Jize sold the residence to Madam Zhang, he composed this verse:

Looking out into the distance from this house,
One can see the clouds drifting o'er the southern peak of Mount Heng.[5]
The family holds to ritual and righteousness in all ways;
It will be large and its descendants will make great contributions.

He fashioned a wooden panel bearing this inscription and hung it over the main gate.

In October 1873 Jize's wife gave birth to a son, whom they named Guangluan. In the future he would inherit the title his father had inherited from Zeng Guofan. My second eldest brother, Jihong, suggested that he take back Guangquan, the son he had earlier given to Jize for adoption, saying that they should not confuse the lineage of the oldest son with that of a younger son. Jize refused, saying that Father had previously given instructions distinguishing the two lines. How could Jihong still talk of doing otherwise?

My wedding date had been set after the mourning for Nie Erkang ended on October 7, 1874.[6] But Mother passed away on September 23, 1874. She was fifty-nine years old. That winter we also entered the national mourning for Emperor Tongzhi (r. 1862–74). At the time, Madam Zhang's wish was to bend the mourning rules a little and, after one hundred days had elapsed following my mother's death, have a small sedan chair, borne by two men, come to carry me back to the Nie household.[7] When I heard of this, I objected strongly. Consequently, it was agreed to hold the regular ceremony the following year.

On December 13, 1874, we moved Father's grave to the southern slope of Mount Fulong at Pingtang in the Shanhua District west of the Xiang River.[8] Our mother's casket was interred there with his. Uncle Zeng Guoquan selected the grave site through geomancy.[9] In their later years, Father and Uncle Zeng Guoquan had agreed that if Father died first, Zeng Guoquan would determine the grave site through geomancy. If Zeng Guoquan died first, then Father would make the inscription for his memorial tablet.[10]

On October 22, 1875, I was married. One year had elapsed since Mother's funeral. In accordance with ritual practice, the period of mourning prescribed for an adopted child after the death of the child's natural parent was reduced from the usual three years (for a natural parent) to one year.[11] Since I had been adopted by Uncle Zeng Guobao in my youth, the time was then right for me to be married. However, it was not yet one year since the national mourning period for Mother (calculated from the date the court held ceremonies for her) had begun. Therefore, there was a ceremonial procession but no instrumental music. Since my brothers were still in mourning, my cousin Jiqu, the one also adopted by Uncle Zeng Guobao, brought me to my husband's family home.

A traditional belief passed down from generation to generation says that if a new bride is menstruating when she enters her husband's home, it is an omen of misfortune and decline. This has been known in north and south for a long time. On the day I was married it happened that I was menstruating but forgot about this omen. Subsequently, when the bride and groom bowed to heaven and earth in the wedding ceremony, I remembered it and silently prayed, "If this omen proves to be true, I pray that I alone may suffer the dire consequences. Do not cause the Nie family to feel its devastation." Only after I reached mid-life did I reveal this to family members. Until then, I worried about it secretly.[12]

My dowry included the one thousand taels Uncle Zeng Guobao had left to me. When Father died, each of his daughters got one thousand taels. When Mother passed away, each received an additional eight hundred taels. With interest this came to roughly three thousand taels. The wealth that I brought to my husband's home through inheritance was greater than my sisters had brought to their marriages. I felt guilty because of Father's instructions and warnings that his daughters' dowries should not exceed two hundred taels. This money was deposited in the Qianyi Bank, operated by Mr. Zhu Yutian. Mr. Zhu became very wealthy through his skill in handling money. During the Tongzhi, Guangxu, and Xuantong reigns (1862–1911), he was the acknowledged leader of Changsha commerce. I placed the receipts for my deposits in a small box and made entries in a new account book. This account book had many volumes. I used these funds for many years but did not use them up. Jize checked everything over carefully.

At that time, the usual practice was to have eight garments in the bridal chest. Because my wedding date had been postponed several times, all the garments had been made and then altered three times. Prior to my marriage, my sister Jiyao was in the provincial capital. She personally checked my marriage garments and the rest of my trousseau when she returned to visit our parents' home. The leather from Hunan used to make the bridal chest was inferior, and today the clothes are all moth-eaten. However, the bed that I used was made by a craftsman from Suzhou under the direction of the engineering bureau that built the new Liangjiang governor general's residence. It was decorated with gold lacquer and delicately carved, ornate and beautiful. We showed it to artisans in Hunan, but they all declined to attempt such a task. Even today, it is in my Hunan residence.

The groom's gifts, which the Nie family sent to me at the time of betrothal in 1872, included a pair of green jade bracelets. My father-in-law, Nie Erkang, had bought the jade in Guangdong for eight hundred taels. He had an artisan make a pair of bracelets, but they were small. Neither my mother-in-law, Madam Zhang, nor any of the other women in the family could put them on, so he did the expedient thing and used them as a betrothal gift. Father-in-law had predicted that someone who enjoyed good fortune would be able to wear these bracelets. When I put them on, they fit my wrist perfectly. However, it was not good jade. Today their color is faded.

Madam Zhang's family was originally from Anxiang District in Hunan. Her grandfather served as an official at Jinzhou in Fengtian Prefecture in the northeast. After he died, his sons observed the mourning rites and then lived in Beijing rather than at their home in Hunan. When she was growing up in Beijing, Madam Zhang showed ability and intelligence. She managed the family home, met guests, and took care of family affairs single-handedly. She dressed like a man and was straightforward and unrestrained. There was no boudoir manner about her.

Her future husband, Nie Erkang, had had difficulty with the triennial spring examination for the highest civil service degree, but he stayed on in Beijing with an official appointment. After his first wife, Madam Gan, passed away, he sought a second wife. The matchmaker forwarded a betrothal document stating Madam Zhang's birth date and related information. Nie Erkang at first was quite disinterested. He instructed his older brother, Chunfan, to withdraw him from marriage negotiations, but Chunfan neglected to forward the withdrawal. A long time passed before Nie Erkang discovered this. He was concerned because it had been such a long time and he had not made his decision known. Finally, he found it too difficult to decline, so he did the upright thing and extended an offer of marriage.

When they were married, their mutual respect was strong. Nie Erkang immediately put his wife in charge of household affairs and withdrew from social activities with his friends. Freed from distractions, before long he was successful in the spring examinations; he obtained the highest civil service degree and, in 1853, was inducted into the Hanlin Academy, the highest academic recognition accorded to civil service graduates. From that time on the family prospered. Because of Chunfan's role as intermediary and since he had no children of his own, we subsequently gave our son Qichang to be adopted as his heir.[13]

The Nie family, from the time of the Southern Song dynasty (1127–1279), resided in Qingjiang in Jiangxi Province. At the beginning of the Qing dynasty (1644–1912), Nie Yingchan, of the thirteenth generation, moved to Hengshan in Hunan Province. In the fifteenth generation, Nie Jimo (see chart 3) resided in the Hengshan District and was highly respected. He was skilled in the practice of medicine and had established his own pharmacy. Often he went to the prison in the district magistrate's office to treat the prisoners. In old age he remained vigorous. The district magistrate bestowed an honorary title on him, but he declined it and continued his activities as before, unceasingly. Jimo's son Nie Tao achieved the highest civil service degree in 1737 and was named district magistrate of the Zhenan District in Shanxi Province. Jimo sent letters of instruction on the administration of government to his son in words that were profound and far-reaching. They are included in the *Jingshi wenbian* (Documents on statecraft).[14] Nie Jimo lived to be ninety-three years old.

Nie Tao died when he was seventy-eight. His grandsons Nie Gaomin (Jinbu), Nie Jingmin (Xinru), and Nie Xianmin (Rongfeng), the sons of Nie Zhaokui (see chart 3), passed the civil service examinations one after another and served in departments of the six boards in the imperial government in the early years of the Jiaqing reign (1796–1820). Their names were well known in southern Hunan at that time. Nie Erkang was Nie Tao's great-grandson, the son of Nie Zhenmin. Though Nie Erkang was inducted into the Hanlin Academy in 1853, he did not pass the special examinations for Hanlin compiler and was sent to Guangdong as a district magistrate. There he presided over busy cities and served as magistrate of Gaozhou Prefecture. He was appointed an expectant taotai.

The busy cities of Guangdong were considered difficult to govern, but Nie Erkang was diligent and sympathetic to the people's grievances. He heeded their cries and showed his brilliance. The official documents of Gangzhou (*Gangzhou gongdu*) and other books[15] he published were assembled through a lifetime of effort. When I married into the family, it was already too late to see him.

Madam Zhang's disposition was stern but enlightened. When my father-in-law died, he left savings of sixty thousand taels. Aside from that there was no property. After returning to Changsha, my mother-in-law

CHART 3
Ancestors of Nie Qigui

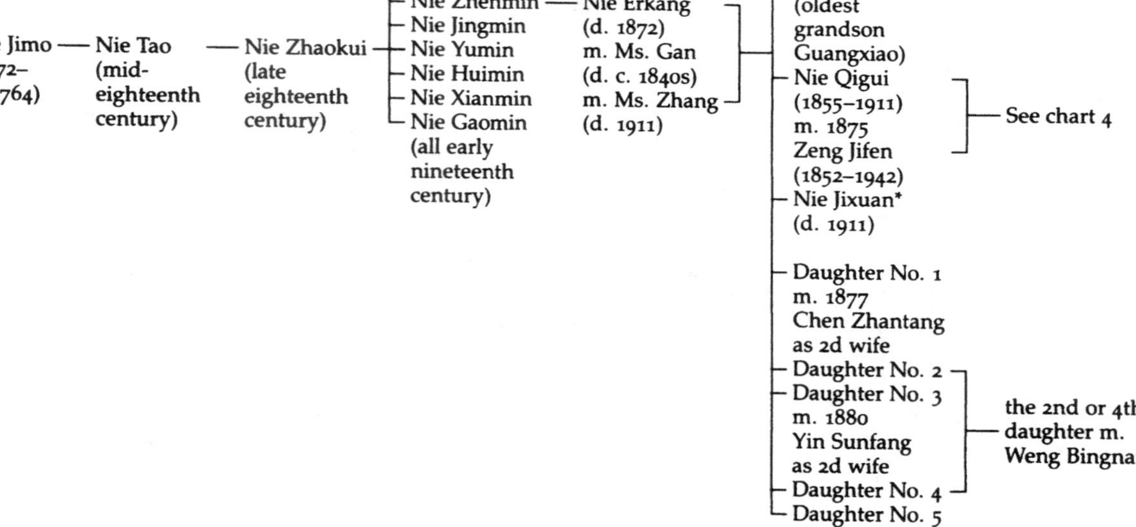

Sources: Nie Zeng Jifen, "Chongde laoren ziding nianpu"; Nie Qijie, "Chongde laoren jiniance," 283–84.
*Posthumously adopted Nie Qijun (1906–?)

bought land and residences, gave three daughters in marriage, and acquired two daughters-in-law. She personally managed all this. Although she was not literate, no one dared try to deceive her. If tenants sought rent relief in hard times, she usually rebuked them and refused. My husband tried to find ways to agree to their requests. Though he would not openly agree, he would help them clandestinely from his private funds. Madam Zhang rarely had harsh words or angry looks for me.

On September 24, 1876, my oldest child, Qibin, was born. His pet name was Quan'er. At the time, my husband was at home and our life was uneventful. Fortunately, he had a position as assistant in the Yunnan Likin Bureau[16] to which Liu Changyou (1818–87),[17] governor general of Yunnan and Guizhou provinces, had appointed him. The monthly salary was only fifty taels, and our costs for entertaining had to come from this. Because we received a monthly allowance of only two strings of cash from my mother-in-law, we could not afford to engage in social activities. Usually there was not even enough to meet our daily needs. We relied on the interest from my dowry to make up the difference.

Members of my father's family held shares in the Yuzhen Bank of Changsha. The manager gambled and drew on bank funds to cover his losses, and the Zeng family deposits were completely consumed. The bank was involved in lawsuits continuously from 1876 down to the winter of 1880. Madam Zhang had deposits of more than seven thousand taels that she (like other depositors) could not withdraw. At the time, she had two old women servants, Bai and Dou. Both were northerners. Old woman Dou had been my husband's wet nurse and had been with Madam Zhang for years. The money the two servants had accumulated was also in the bank, having been personally deposited for them by my husband. When Madam Zhang was unable to withdraw her money, she rebuked the bank manager bitterly and threatened to bring the matter to court. My husband, who always treated his relatives with respect, certainly did not wish to be involved in a lawsuit that would offend his in-laws, who were stockholders in this bank. For a while he made excuses for them and evaded the issue, hoping to postpone making demands.

In 1877, the Lis of Hefei, the family of Li Hongzhang, dispatched a boat to bring Jize's oldest daughter, Guangxuan, who was betrothed to Li

Youxian, to Anqing. My second and third sisters, Jiyao and Jichen, went with her. Jiyao returned to Hunan before long. The next year Guangxuan was married. In 1880 she and her husband joined Jize in London, where he had been posted as ambassador to the Court of St. James's in 1878.[18] Guangxuan's husband returned to China alone after only a brief stay in Great Britain.

Shortly after Jize went to London in 1878, the Muslim uprisings in far northwest China ended and peace was restored to Xinjiang. The court named Chonghou (1825–93)[19] ambassador to Russia with instructions to negotiate the return to China of the Ili River valley, an area Russia had occupied during the uprisings. The Treaty of Livadia,[20] which Chonghou concluded with Russia, was rejected by the court in early 1880, and Jize was named ambassador to Russia in February 1880 with instructions to negotiate a more favorable treaty. When the international tension with Russia mounted during 1880, Uncle Zeng Guoquan was placed in command of defenses at the Shanhaiguan[21] where the Great Wall approaches the Gulf of Zhili. Jize completed negotiations for the Treaty of St. Petersburg in early 1881,[22] regaining for China much of the territory in the northwest that Chonghou had previously conceded to Russia. Zeng Guoquan was then named governor general over several provinces in this region (Shaanxi, Gansu, and Xinjiang), but he declined the appointment because of ill health. After a period of recuperation, he was appointed governor general of the southern provinces of Guangdong and Guangxi in 1882.

My sister Jiyao and her husband, Chen Songsheng, also accompanied Jize to Europe in 1878 when he was named ambassador to England and France. Chen Songsheng was narrow-minded; he rarely let my sister visit her parents' home. Their family circumstances were quite straitened because he was burdened with old debts. Moreover, the wife of his older brother, Xingsheng, had been sick for a full year, during which time Xingsheng was in the southeastern province of Fujian and no one heard from him. While he was absent his wife died, and the medical, drug, and burial bills were all borne by Songsheng. The debts were overwhelming. Our mother learned of this when she was on her way to Nanjing in the spring of 1868. Mother also knew that permits were to be issued for the transport and sale of salt to merchants.[23] Peng Yulin, a close friend of Father's, paid her a visit, following which he presented six salt permits to the Chen family. At that time the value of each was approximately two thousand taels.

Monies that the Chen family collected each year for rent were used entirely to pay old debts. When Chen Songsheng's paternal uncle—an official in Fujian—became aware of Songsheng's circumstances, he turned over twenty thousand taels in provincial revenue destined for Hunan to him to put in his bank account, temporarily, to draw interest. Songsheng and my sister were in Nanjing when Xingsheng returned to Hunan from Fujian. Xingsheng took advantage of Songsheng's absence and secretly withdrew these funds and squandered every last tael. In the summer of 1872, when Songsheng returned to Hunan, he learned of this. He was very worried and could not face his uncle. Since the funds that his uncle had lent him had to be replaced, he sold the salt certificates and received twenty thousand in payment. Still, he was only able to make up what was missing; there was no surplus whatsoever. He was as impoverished as before. All they had to live on was the twenty strings of cash he got each month from his post at the Salt and Tea Bureau.[24]

Jiyao's married life was unbearable, but she went along with the twists and turns of fate and showed no resentment. Her husband was an intolerant and impatient person. Nevertheless, when he was sick and coughing up blood, my sister supported him, treated and cared for him. She was truly able to anticipate and take care of his every need.

Jiyao was saddened throughout her life because she was unable to bear children. I am heartsick, even today, when I think of the loneliness of my sister's life, the two of them without children for such a long time. But Jiyao had a deep affection for the wife of Xingsheng. When Xingsheng's wife fell sick and was nearing death, she gave instructions that her daughter should be given to Jiyao to adopt. Subsequently, Xingsheng married again. His second wife had a daughter and that child was also given to Jiyao. So although she was unable to bear children herself, she had two daughters. The older one married into the Ting family. The younger daughter accompanied my sister and Songsheng to Europe. Jiyao died in

France in 1881, and her younger daughter's subsequent marriage to Zhu Guixin was arranged by Guo Yun, the wife of my brother Jihong.

In January 1879 my husband took a concubine of the Yang family. My mother-in-law did not know about this at first. On New Year's Eve, concubine Yang set off firecrackers in the bedroom. My husband rebuked her, and she became upset and wept. As I customarily did, I went from the front courtyard outside and returned to my quarters to go to sleep. I was at a loss what to do and could only try to ignore what was happening. My mother-in-law had previously warned us that on New Year's one must not get angry or shed tears. If one does, it will inevitably lead to three years of misfortune. The next year, our home experienced many untoward happenings. Madam Yang's temperament was obstinate and intractable. Later, my husband very much regretted having taken her as a concubine. In 1881 he had someone take her back to her home in Hengshan. Subsequently, she was married to someone else.

On November 2, 1877, I gave birth to my first daughter. Her pet name was Yingu. She was just able to walk when I was teaching her brother to recognize characters, but she knew enough to pick up the box with type characters in it and bring it to me. At birth, her left hand was clenched in a fist and would not open. I asked Yang Dating of the wound section in the Hunan Army Barracks to treat her. For a month she showed gradual improvement, but ultimately he was unable to correct the condition. In 1879 Yingu became seriously ill. My husband bore her to the temple and prayed that she might recover. He repented his sins and took an oath to do good works in the future. It was to no avail. She died during June of that year.

When the milk of my oldest son, Qibin's, wet nurse was insufficient, we engaged another wet nurse. Her whole body broke out with small sores, and when my son took her milk, this disease was passed on to him. As a result, he had an inflammation in the joints of his legs. Today this disease is called tuberculosis of the bone. At first we did not discover what he had; later, it was too much for us to cope with. Consequently, we were never able to treat it successfully. We cared for him tenderly for more than ten years, but in the end we could not save him.

My second son, Qichang, was born on August 14, 1879. His pet name was Chang'er. The next year my third son arrived under auspicious circumstances. On New Year's Eve I customarily did not stay up to welcome the new year. The New Year's Eve that ushered in 1880 was no different. I slept peacefully but dreamt that, at a certain place, a unicorn (*qilin*)[25] had been born. When I went to see it, it seemed to be a small animal in a tiny box. But my memory is very poor; I can't recall its form. After the dream, I thought to myself that this should indicate a good omen, so I consulted a book that explains dreams.[26] It indicated that there would be a name known throughout the empire. On October 8, 1880, I gave birth to my third son, Qijie (1880–1953),[27] and gave him the pet name Xiang'er, which means "child of good fortune." The wet nurse that I hired cost only sixteen hundred cash per month. After we went to Nanjing in 1881, wet nurses cost three or four taels. After the establishment of the Republic it increased to five or six yuan. In recent years it is even more costly.

In September 1880, my husband's third sister married Mr. Yin Sunfang of the You District in eastern Hunan. He later served as a district magistrate in Jiangxi.

The matter of my mother-in-law's deposits in the Yuzhen Bank in Changsha had never been resolved. Since 1876, Madam Zhang had been threatening to bring the matter to court. In 1881 my husband and I finally decided to take two thousand taels from my dowry and borrow one thousand taels that my sister Jichen, who had married into the Lo family, had on deposit in the Qianyi Bank. The three thousand taels were to be given to my mother-in-law in order to avoid a maelstrom of lawsuits. But I dared not openly say that this money had come from my family. So we tactfully asked Messrs. Fu Qingyu, Guo Songtao, and my sister-in-law's husband, Chen Zhantang, to act on our behalf as middlemen to reconcile the legal dispute. Each gave Madam Zhang one thousand taels to settle the dispute. We had relied on the interest from my dowry to meet our daily needs; now, having used part of the capital to compensate this loss, we found ourselves in difficult financial circumstances.

FOUR LIFE IN NANJING AND WAR WITH FRANCE (1881–1885)

The compensation of Madam Zhang after the failure of the Yuzhen Bank had depleted my dowry and forced us to borrow one thousand taels from my sister Jichen. She repeatedly tried to calm our anxiety over this, saying, "You may borrow my funds and I don't want interest. When you have money, then return the principal. We certainly should not become agitated and distressed over money." But I was deeply concerned about our meager family finances and our debts.

In July 1881 my husband went to Nanjing with his brother-in-law Chen Zhantang, who had married my husband's oldest sister in the summer of 1878. He had been in charge of contributions for the province of Yunnan at Changsha in Hunan but was recently appointed director of the General Bureau for Defense Planning at Nanjing.[1] After arriving in Nanjing, Nie resided in the Hunan hostel. In December I joined him with our children. At first I had been unwilling to go because he had no position and no way of providing for us. But he wrote repeatedly urging me to come. Finally, I asked my mother-in-law what her wishes were. At first she rejected the idea. Later, when my husband's oldest sister, Chen's wife, went to join her husband in Nanjing, she invited me and the children to go with her. She spoke on my behalf with my mother-in-law, who gave me six hundred taels for traveling expenses. With this I set out by boat north on the Xiang River and then east on the Yangzi toward Nanjing.

At the time, Li Hanzhang (1821–99),[2] older brother of Li Hongzhang, was governor general of Hunan and Hubei. Since there was a long-standing relationship between our family and the Lis, my husband told me to visit Madam Li at the official residence when I passed through Wuchang. When Madam Li was in Nanjing, she and my mother had been good friends, but that was ten years earlier. Many changes had occurred in the interim. Nevertheless, when she saw me, she received me with great warmth. The next day a letter appointed my husband to the directorship of the Hubei Salt Distribution Bureau. The monthly salary was fifty taels.

Governor General Li's concubine personally came to the boat landing to bid me farewell. Because our boat was so small and dingy, I begged her not to. I even had our boat moved across the river to Hanyang to avoid her. To my surprise, she still came. Governor General Li also dispatched a gunboat to send us off to Nanjing.

My sister-in-law's husband, Chen, had arranged for the Liangjiang headquarters to dispatch a tug to Wuchang to tow the boats carrying the members of our two families. Unexpectedly Zuo Zongtang, newly appointed governor general of Liangjiang, was coming east from Hunan at that time, so the tug was diverted to meet him. With Governor General Zuo's boat in tow, the tug would only take the Chens' vessel. It left our boat without a tow and departed.

At that time, steamships did not yet go into Wuchang, so I rented a salt boat that was returning empty to Nanjing and followed the Chen family's vessel. The fare was forty or fifty strings of cash. Since Madam Zhang had supplied the travel expenses, I used seventy-odd strings of cash to purchase four hundred piculs of coal, which I had loaded into the boat for future use. (At the time the price of coal was only 190 cash per picul.) When we reached the market town of Huayang in Anhui Province, our boat had the coal on board. It was not uncommon for boats carrying official families also to carry coal. If one had influence, there would be no inspection at the *likin* barrier; however, we were closely inspected and rebuked for carrying coal through a *likin* barrier without documentation. At the time, Jize's oldest daughter, Guangxuan, who had married into the family of Li Hongzhang, had returned from England and resided nearby in Anqing. When she heard of this, the Lis sent someone to intervene on our behalf, and we were allowed to proceed.

The other everyday items we had brought along for ourselves, including a sedan chair covered with blue woolen material, were judged to be alright. Altogether, we brought three male chair bearers and five or six women servants, including the old woman Duo, who had been my husband's wet nurse; three old women: Liang, Zhou, and Zhang; a wet nurse; and a maidservant. My brother-in-law Weng Bingnan and his servant also went with us. Nie's sister had married into the Weng family before I married into the Nie household. Weng later served as a district magistrate in Guangxi Province. Although the fee for the boat was not high, when we passed through Jiujiang near the outlet of Poyang Lake, we had to pay a boat tax of thirty taels. Moreover, we had to provide our own food, and this was no small expense.

When I departed the Nie family in Hunan in December 1881, I left with a heavy heart: my brother Jihong had died in Beijing the previous April. He was only thirty-four and had suffered from severe depression because of his failure in the civil service examinations for the highest degree. This tragedy was made worse in June by the death of my sister Jichun, widow of Guo Yiyong, at the provincial capital, Changsha. Then, in November, my sister Jiyao, wife of Chen Songsheng, died in France where she and her husband had accompanied our older brother Jize on his diplomatic assignment.[3] Neither of my sisters had experienced the joy of giving birth. In that year I lost three of my generation. I was forever saddened by this.

My third sister, Jichen, who had lent us the funds to compensate part of Madam Zhang's losses in the Yuzhen Bank, was worried that my constitution was not very strong and that I would probably follow my sisters to an early grave. Jichen's own life was plagued with misfortune also. Her mother-in-law treated her shabbily. In the countryside where they resided, it was difficult at times to find servant women, so Jichen washed her own personal clothing and dishes. Although her mother-in-law had a maidservant, the maidservant did no work for my sister. On the contrary, Jichen's mother-in-law let the maidservant do as she pleased but scolded and humiliated Jichen at will.

Jichen gave birth to a son who did not survive. After that, she had only one daughter, so her husband bought a concubine. Relations between husband and wife were not harmonious. My brother-in-law, Lo, later went away in search of employment. When he sent for his family, my sister directed his concubine to go instead. In 1888, he died at Qinzhou in southwestern Gansu Province. Fortunately, he had begotten a son by his concubine who, though still unborn at the time of his death, would continue his family line. This truly was the result of my sister's wisdom. Although my brother-in-law really did not like that concubine, my sister had insisted that she go to him.

After I arrived in Nanjing at the end of 1881, we lived in the Hefei Examination Hostel in Madao Avenue. My husband's advancement as an official had been slowed by his failure on the district civil service examinations and family circumstances that prevented him from accepting overseas assignments. He had planned to join my brother Jize abroad in 1880, when Jize was named ambassador to Russia, but at the time, our brother-in-law Chen was transferred, and it would have been a hardship for the family for both to leave at one time. So Nie didn't go. Then, in early 1882, he received telegraphic orders transferring him abroad, but because of his mother's advanced age and my pregnancy, which prevented me from going with him, he again did not go. Guo Songtao, former ambassador to Britain and France, had considered Nie for this post over and over again. I still have his letters on the subject. In Nanjing, however, my husband's career took a turn for the better thanks to the close relationship that developed between him and Governor General Zuo Zongtang of Liangjiang.

Nie first met Governor General Zuo in Nanjing in late 1881. Nie, just twenty-seven, had recently been named director of the Hubei Salt Distribution Bureau. Zuo asked him if the one named Nie Jimo, the author of "Jiezi shu" (Letter of instruction to my son),[4] was of an early generation of his family. Nie answered, "He is a very remote ancestor." Zuo asked, "Are you able to recall that text?" Nie replied, "I am." Zuo said, "I first read this text twenty years ago in the *Huangqing jingshi wenbian* [Documents on statecraft]."[5] With a deep sigh of admiration he added, "To this day I can still recite it." Then he recited several paragraphs of the text. Nie corrected the mistakes in the places where Governor General Zuo's memory failed him. The governor general admired this, saying, "Not to forget one's ancestors is admirable." He then invited Nie to stay and dine with him and told him to come back and visit often. Each visit they ate together.

In the spring of the next year, 1882, Nie was appointed deputy director of the Liangjiang Office of Military Affairs,[6] referred to today as the Chief of Staff's Office, an agency for military planning. After the pacification of Xinjiang in 1881[7] there were no military operations for several years; nevertheless, Zuo Zongtang advocated military preparedness. He established the Office of Military Affairs within his headquarters and spent several hours there each day. He took his noon meal there together with the director and deputy director. The breadth of Zuo's learning, the farsightedness of his military strategy, the diligence with which he managed administrative affairs, and the insight with which he chose people all were unequaled.

The delicacies on his table frequently included dog meat. One day he transferred a piece of dog meat to Nie's bowl with his chopsticks. Nie took an opportunity to put it on the table surreptitiously. Governor General Zuo saw him and promptly said, "This is lamb from a well-known place. The taste is superb. Why don't you eat it." Nie replied, "I always abstain from beef and dog meat and dare not." Zuo laughed and assented.[8]

About the same time, my husband accompanied Governor General Zuo to the provinces to inspect troops. I checked his uniforms and put them in order. In going upstairs many times, I disturbed the child I was carrying in my womb. I took frequent doses of medication to prevent a miscarriage, and the problems stopped temporarily; but, on August 1, I finally miscarried.

Only two weeks previously, on July 15, 1882, we had moved from the Hefei Examination Hostel to lodgings in the Tang *heting*, the house of the Tang family on the shore of the Qinhuai River.[9] It was already into the second year since my husband had come to Nanjing and secured an official post. Our sole support was the fifty taels per month from the Hubei Salt Distribution Bureau. Although Nie did not want me to do so, I mentioned our plight to Governor General Zuo Zongtang's daughter-in-law. About the beginning of 1883, Nie received an appointment as deputy director of the Jiangnan Arsenal in Shanghai,[10] China's largest defense industry, supervised and controlled by Governor General Zuo.

When Nie went for an interview with Governor General Zuo, there were several people being interviewed together. All had obtained appointments to what, at that time, were regarded as lucrative posts. When they left, Zuo saw them out but kept Nie for a few moments. He said to him, "Today everything is happy for you, isn't it? People of your generation seek office for its rewards. But you are different, you can take great responsibility. Force yourself to do it." For his whole life Nie felt profound gratitude for Zuo's recognition and encouragement.

Director Li Xingrui (1827–1904)[11] of the Jiangnan Arsenal petitioned Governor General Zuo asking that Nie not take up his post in Shanghai, that instead he be given his salary without having to perform any duties. Zuo refused to do this. Furthermore, he directed Nie to proceed to his new post without delay and rush to produce one hundred light artillery pieces for shipment to Nanjing within a fixed time limit. As a result, Nie was unable to return home to pass the (lunar) New Year with us in early February 1883.

When Director Li was accused of financial irregularities at Jiangnan, Governor General Zuo secretly directed Nie to investigate this and report to him. Nie then appointed a person to look into it confidentially. This person reported that the accusations, for the most part, were based on firm evidence. Nie included the evidence in a report to the governor general. He completed the draft and then destroyed it. He prepared another draft which for the most part covered things up and cleared Li's name. Subsequently, Li left his office in order to mourn the death of a parent. He stayed in Shanghai afflicted with a malady of the feet. Nie went to see him from time to time and never bore a grudge over the former affair.[12]

Meanwhile, hostilities broke out in 1883 between French and Chinese forces in Vietnam, a Chinese dependency, as China attempted to check the spread of French colonial control. In the summer of 1884, French naval units threatened the south China coast. Governor General Zuo, who had been called away from his post in Nanjing in 1883 to quell an uprising in Shandong, was summoned to Beijing in June 1884 and placed in charge of military affairs for the empire. In August he was named imperial high commissioner for the southeastern province of Fujian, where the French were attacking.

In December 1883, several months after the birth of my son Qiwei on August 26, I moved with the children to Shanghai to join my husband. Meanwhile, Uncle Zeng Guoquan was appointed governor general of the Liangjiang provinces, replacing Zuo Zongtang, but Zeng Guoquan did not arrive in Nanjing to take up his post until early 1884. By then I had already left for Shanghai with the children; it was too late for us to see him.

Pan Jingru,[13] who succeeded Li Xingrui as director of the Jiangnan Arsenal, left when Uncle Zeng Guoquan came as governor general of the Liangjiang provinces. Pan was succeeded by Zhong Yungu.[14] But Zhong's leadership did nothing to improve public sentiment about mismanagement of the arsenal. Consequently, Nie was promoted to director. Earlier, when Nie was appointed deputy director, his monthly salary was only 50 taels, the same that he had received at the Hubei Salt Distribution Bureau. After Pan left, it was increased to 150 taels. When Nie was promoted to director, it was finally increased to 200 taels.

While Zuo Zongtang was Liangjiang governor general (1882–84), he not only treated my husband as one of his own children, he also was concerned about me and asked that I pay him a visit. In the winter of 1881, I visited him when he was in temporary residence at the Liangjiang headquarters. When I arrived, I got out of the sedan chair at the main hall and crossed the several courtyards before reaching the women's quarters. Zuo happened to be away on official business. I had not been there since 1872, when I accompanied my father's casket from this same residence. I contemplated the present and recalled the past with deep feeling; hundreds of emotions crowded into my heart. Afterward, though Governor General Zuo frequently asked about me, I was unwilling to go there. When he understood my feelings, he directed that the central gate be specially opened so my sedan chair could go straight through to the third hall. On my next visit, I dismounted there and met him. After we exchanged greetings, Governor General Zuo said to me, "Was your father born in 1812?" I replied, "In 1811." He said, "In that case, he was one year older than I. You should consider me the younger brother of your father." Then he showed me around the official residence. He sought out my bedroom of ten years ago. I respectfully confirmed that it was mine.

Later, when Uncle Zeng Guoquan came to Nanjing, Governor General

Zuo said to him, "My youngest girl already considers my home to be her girlhood home." He used the term for "youngest girl" that is used in the Hunan dialect. He was, of course, referring to me.

In August 1884 the French fleet attacked in the outer harbor at Fuzhou and sank several Chinese warships.[15] The warship *Yangwu* returned fire with several salvos.[16] Although the *Yangwu* was ultimately sunk, the French admiral, Courbet, was struck by gunfire from our forces and died in action. The French carefully concealed this information; China knew nothing of it.[17] At the time, telegrams were arriving daily from headquarters of the Northern Fleet saying that the French were about to occupy the arsenal. The alarm spread, and personnel fled in great confusion. Former director Pan Jingru moved his home to Suzhou. Deputy Director Cai Eryuan[18] moved to the International Concession. Countless others moved to the International Concession or to Ningbo about one hundred miles south of Shanghai. Some were robbed of their possessions while fleeing.

An old woman who sold pearls and jade had left a jade hair clasp with me. When she heard the news, she came hurriedly to get it before fleeing. She said that the French would attack the arsenal on the next day. Although I knew what this would mean, I remained calm, trusting the will of heaven. One day shortly after that, my husband said to me quite unexpectedly, "I have arranged for a boat. You should make a quick selection of our valuables and check our luggage. Prepare, in case of emergency, to take the children, the maidservants, and old women aboard this boat and seek refuge in Songjiang."[19] "What will you do?" I asked. "I have the duty to defend the arsenal. I cannot leave," he replied. I told him, "I have never regarded my own life as important. If we are to die, let us die together. There is no need for me to leave." He chastened me, "Although you do not fear death, how will it be for the children if we both perish?"

What he said was correct, of course. I couldn't suppress my tears. So I quickly made preparations but did not actually board the boat. Time passed and we never received an official report warning us that the arsenal would be attacked. Meanwhile, my mother-in-law heard rumors of the danger in Shanghai and, knowing that I was pregnant, in early autumn sent a servant to escort us back to Hunan. By that time the French had begun peace talks,[20] so I remained in Shanghai.

FIVE LIFE IN SHANGHAI AND FINANCIAL RUIN (1885–1895)

After the war, life in Shanghai was more tranquil. There was, however, no shortage of relatives and friends who visited us at the arsenal. On February 20, 1885, my daughter Qide was born. In April my brother Jihong's widow, Guo Yun, came to Shanghai from the governor general's residence in Nanjing where she resided with Uncle Zeng Guoquan. Tang Haiqiu, acting Shanghai taotai, made arrangements for us to use a house belonging to the foreign firm of J. J. Bucheister Company.[1] I took the children and went for a stay of ten days, during which time I was able to attend the theater and to travel around the International Concession. Then, in August, Madam Zhang went to Nanjing from the family residence in Hunan to see her oldest daughter, whose husband, Chen Zhantang, had just been named taotai in Taiwan. We later received Madam Zhang in Shanghai for a short visit. In 1886, Chen, who held the rank of senior secretary in the imperial government, purchased a post as taotai on Taiwan for my husband.

In Shanghai I spent most of my time within the confines of our official residence at the arsenal, venturing forth only rarely. There was no thoroughfare from the arsenal, which was situated on the west bank of the Huangpu River south of Shanghai, northward to Xieqiao near the West Gate of the Old Chinese City,[2] a distance of more than two miles. The thoroughfare from the arsenal north to the Small East Gate of the Old Chinese City was built by the arsenal's Artillery Division[3] commander,

Yang Jinlong, at my husband's suggestion. On my occasional social outings, I had first to take a sedan chair to Xieqiao and then change to a horse-drawn carriage. The Yongni Opera House, which I frequented, was operated by the actor Xiang Jiuxiao. The theater had only one electric lamp. It cost two yuan to use it each evening. The rest of the lamps were gas. I also recall going to the circus in the Hongkou section of Shanghai north of Suzhou Creek.[4] The price of a single ticket for a box seat was two yuan. I was bewitched by the beauty and variety of it all. It was truly a rare spectacle.

Fifty years have passed from then until this writing. Countless changes in social customs and material culture have taken place. One example is the way attitudes toward games of chance have gradually evolved. My father, Zeng Guofan, detested things used in gambling such as cards and dice. He once went to my brother Jihong's room and saw bone dominoes on the table; he took them away from him without hesitation. When Father mentioned this to my mother, she told him that ivory dominoes could tell one's fortune; but Father did not believe in fortune-telling.[5] When his brother Zeng Guohuang went to Nanjing, Father gave the dominoes to him. Later, in Baoding, my brother Jize acquired a set of Chinese chess[6] pieces with lions on them with which he played chess on New Year's Day. Recently, in Shanghai, I had an artisan make a similar set. Even to this day, on New Year's Day our family always plays chess with the children. There is not much won or lost, but it is lively and thoroughly amusing. I have never engaged in other forms of gambling.

After I returned to Hunan, mahjong became popular.[7] In recent years women can't seem to get along without it. Also, there is little else for old people to do to pass away the time other than play mahjong. I was not naturally inclined this way. When I was in my father's house, I learned to play Chinese chess, and that was all. My brothers took great delight in it, and I also enjoyed it. Now that I am old, when I have nothing to do, I often play one or two games by lamplight.

Changes in traditional methods of spinning also began to take place about this time. In the countryside near Shanghai, a great Buddhist fair[8] was held to sell various types of farm produce. I heard that there were treadle-operated cotton spinning wheels with three wooden spindles there. We had a small hand-operated spinning wheel in our home in Hunan, but I had not brought it to Shanghai with me. So I had someone purchase one for me at the fair, and I asked a local worker to instruct me in spinning. But I was not able to learn how to spin really well on three spindles. For a long time I could spin only on two. Every night after the evening meal I spun one or two ounces of cotton. When I had spun several pounds of yarn, I used it to fasten together cloth woven by a local person to make two or three bolts of nankeen. This wheel is now in our Hunan home.

In July 1886 Jize was summoned to Beijing to be assistant director of naval affairs[9] with the rank of junior vice president of the Board of War. He passed through Shanghai in November and stayed for a while at the official traveling residence of the governor general. He had been abroad for eight years. Though he was just forty-six years old, his cheeks sagged and the hair on his temples was sparse. When he discovered that our home was still in straitened circumstances, he gave us one thousand taels as a present.

Jize's wife accompanied him to Shanghai with their second son, Guangyang, who was then eight years old. He was a very bright child. In England he had suffered with intestinal ulcers. He underwent surgery but did not fully recover. When he arrived in Shanghai, his flesh was emaciated, the incision was draining pus and blood, he was unable to extend his legs, and his fever was constant. Mr. Liu Kangsi urged us to ask the noted doctor Ma Peizhi of Meng He, the medical center in northwestern Jiangsu,[10] to treat him. If Dr. Ma was to attend to Guangyang, we would have to fetch him in a small steamer. At the time, the only small steamer to be had was at the arsenal. Jize, however, did not want his son to take any more Chinese medicine. Just then, though, Jize was called off to Nanjing to see Uncle Zeng Guoquan. Thereafter, my sister-in-law personally asked my husband to send the arsenal steamer to fetch Dr. Ma. Jize was unaware of all this. The boy took the medication prescribed by Dr. Ma and the fever subsided.

When Jize returned to Shanghai from Nanjing and learned what had happened, he bowed and asked my husband to take care of everything for him because he had to go immediately to Beijing in response to his orders. He left his family in Shanghai for medical treatment. Dr. Ma continued to treat the boy and there was steady improvement. Gradually he was able to stand and also to ride a tricycle. In January 1887 we took a photograph; he was pudgy and cute. In February or March, however, Guangyang was careless about something he ate or drank. He developed severe diarrhea, more than fifty attacks in one day. Alas, we could not save him.

I helped care for him during his illness and, as a result, developed night chills. During March and April I contracted very severe malaria. My husband wired the governor general's residence in Nanjing to have Dr. Zhu of our native Xiangxiang District in Hunan come to treat me. Dr. Zhu ground fluid from Korean ginseng[11] and brewed a medicine which he gave to me. A month passed before I began to improve. When the illness was at its worst, the fever did not subside day or night, and I feared that I would not recover. So I talked with my husband and drafted my final instructions. I made general arrangements for the care of my sons and daughters after my death. My oldest son, Qibin, who was eleven and suffered from a chronic illness, overheard us talking and cried pitifully. My husband scolded me sternly for speaking so carelessly.

In late summer 1887, after my recovery, Uncle Zeng Guoquan's second daughter-in-law, my sixth sister-in-law,[12] came to Shanghai for a holiday and invited me to go to Nanjing. And so, in October, I took my children to Nanjing for a reunion with their relatives. The women's quarters in the renovated governor general's residence were approximately eighty feet across. There were five rooms in the rear on the east and three in the rear on the west. Originally, these three rooms were prepared to be the groom's quarters for my marriage. On this visit, I resided in them. Zeng Guoquan had arranged things for us, and the preparations were lavish. I recalled that in the past fifteen years I had been there three times, and I was overwhelmed by the myriad emotions that welled up in my heart.

Originally, I had intended to remain in Nanjing long enough to see Uncle Zeng Guoquan off to the capital and then return to Shanghai. But when he had traveled as far as Qingjiang[13] in northern Jiangsu, he received an edict canceling his scheduled imperial audience. He actually had not been happy about going, and his mood improved after he returned to the Nanjing governor general's residence. When he saw that I was about to leave, he insisted I stay longer. Consequently, I remained in Nanjing another month before returning to Shanghai.

Later, Uncle Zeng Guoquan came to Shanghai on a tour of inspection. When he visited the arsenal, a banquet was held. Following his orders, it was in our residence. Zeng Guoquan said, "I am on a diet. I will only eat a little broth and boiled cabbage. I require nothing else." Our children then paid their respects to him. When he saw them, he was very pleased, saying, "When I was preparing for the examinations in the Xiangxiang District, the examination candidates wore long gowns of blue linen and short woolen jackets. You are just like that generation of young scholars. You enjoy the simple life, so you can dine with me." Just then they were changing clothes, and my husband went around searching for the small ceremonial cap worn by a "junior guardian of the heir apparent"[14] for Uncle Zeng Guoquan to wear. But he laughed and said, "No need for that." While speaking he took an old melon skin cap from his sleeve and stuck it on his head. Today I still recall how insufferably dirty and worn his hat was. It was clear that Zeng Guoquan was not fastidious about his everyday clothing and food.

When we lived at the arsenal, Mrs. John Fryer and I enjoyed each other's company from time to time. Mr. John Fryer (1839–1928)[15] was then an editor and translator of new books at the arsenal. His wife was refined and sincere, and we got along very well. She told me everything about her way of doing things. At that time Western women placed great emphasis on household handicrafts. Later, I taught what I had learned from her to many in Hunan and Shanghai. When Mrs. Fryer saw the cotton spinning wheel I had purchased, she told me that the hand-operated machines in America were constructed very similarly to those in China.

As a result of my contacts at the arsenal, I felt that foreign languages and science were important fields of knowledge. Consequently, I directed my two sons, Qijie and Qichang, to study English with Mrs. Fryer daily. Since they still had to study Chinese, they could not devote themselves wholeheartedly to English until after 1898 and the beginning of educational reform.[16]

Our family finances did not improve during our years in Shanghai.

Although my husband's salary as director of the Jiangnan Arsenal was two hundred taels per month, all our household supplies were purchased on the local market. We took nothing from government stores. Since Shanghai was at the crossroads of north-south commerce, the arsenal was a very busy place. As I have mentioned, there was no lack of visitors, some seeking employment. All we could do was give them a little help with their traveling expenses; this came out of our own pocket. By the time we left the arsenal we had suffered losses totaling more than ten thousand taels, which we were not able to recoup until the early 1890s after my husband was named Shanghai taotai.

In the eight years that we were at the Jiangnan Arsenal, the deficit that existed when my husband assumed office was eliminated. At the end of his tenure there was a surplus of more than 100,000 taels.[17] Shao Youlian (d. 1901),[18] Shanghai taotai, reported my husband's success to Zeng Guoquan, who was still governor general of the Liangjiang provinces, in very laudatory terms. Uncle Zeng Guoquan decided to submit a secret memorial to the throne, in 1889, recommending that my husband be appointed taotai and that he remain in Jiangsu pending an assignment to office. This memorial was also given to the Grand Council[19] to be placed in the records. As a result of this recommendation, my husband was summoned to Beijing for an imperial audience.

Jize was in the capital at the time. In honor of the occasion, he painted a scene of mountains and a river at dawn on a silk fan, inscribed a poem on it, and presented it to his brother-in-law. The poem read as follows:

When the morning sun has just risen from the shore into the heavens,
I still can vaguely see the shadow of the misty moon.
The heavens are covered with various-colored cloud formations
An extremely beautiful vision.
Now I try to use my brush to describe these natural conditions for you.
I hope that what you do
Before long will be like the brilliance of the sun breaking through
The clouds that cover the heavens.
I give this to you to send you on your way.
I repeat the four lines of the poem of farewell three times.[20]

May heaven protect you everywhere
And may your wishes be fulfilled.
This poem I have written and given to you.
It expresses my intense interest and very deep hidden meaning.
Take it and return; it can serve, as Bao Zhao's letter from Dalei did,
To tell of the beauties of nature.[21]

My brother Jize's high hopes for my husband's career were soon realized. Early in 1890 my husband was named taotai of the Su-Song-Tai Circuit, or Shanghai taotai, and superintendent of the Shanghai Customs.[22] The incumbent, Gong Zhaoyuan,[23] left to be provincial judge of Zhejiang. My husband's name was originally tenth on the list for this position. Because of Uncle Zeng Guoquan's memorial recommending him, he was selected and appointed—passing over the others.

Several years earlier, in 1885, my husband had consulted Li Xiao'an, a fortune-teller from the southeastern port city of Ningbo, to tell his fortune year by year. Li had said that my husband would have an imperial audience in 1888 and, in 1890, just after the Beginning of Spring,[24] he would be confirmed in the most desirable and lucrative post in the southeast. My husband was appointed to the post of Shanghai taotai on January 30, 1890, just one day after the official Beginning of Spring on the solar calendar. This was indeed marvelous.

Nevertheless, these were difficult times for me. My son Qikun, our seventh child, had been born on October 12, 1888. By early 1890 I was in my thirty-ninth year and expecting my eighth child. Since I had given birth too often, I took a dose of musk to abort the pregnancy, but it had no effect. Then I had frequent disputes with Qikun's wet nurse. I became so agitated that I developed a toothache. I dared not take medicine to cool me down, so I gave birth prematurely on March 19, 1890, to our son Qixian. Because of this, his body was weak and thin at birth.

A few days earlier, on March 12, my brother Jize had died in Beijing. My husband, fearing that I would be further grieved, kept me from seeing the papers where I could learn of Jize's death. When I searched anxiously for the papers, my husband had the newspaper office make a revised copy solely for the purpose of showing to me. Jize's early death at age fifty-one was a great loss to China. There were those who said he had died young because of his unwise reliance on Western medication.

I had great faith in the efficacy of Chinese medicines. As a young woman I had learned something of how to mix them and began distributing remedies to those in need. During my mother's final years, when she was often sick, I mixed medicines and tonics for her. I would consult the *Yanfang xinbian* (New compilation of effective medication),[25] a compendium on the Chinese pharmacopoeia for home use. If it was inconvenient to fetch a doctor or if medication was ineffective for a long time, this volume could be helpful. The first edition quickly sold out, but it was republished in Changsha between 1846 and 1847. For the past few decades almost every home has had a copy.

In 1874, when my mother was seriously ill, I made a vow to distribute medicine to the needy if she recovered. At that time I began making pills of ageratum, sweet dew tea, and all-purpose ointment with cinnamon, a remedy handed down through the family of Commander Zhang Shaotang of Nanjing. Moreover, in the summertime I bought cholera medicine and distributed it to the needy. While we were in Hunan, my husband developed throat symptoms. He puffed medicinal powder made of crystalized melon and recovered. Then I made this medicine, but I changed it and used crystals of bitter melons. Furthermore, my dragon and tiger pills helped many with mental disorders. Later, I also cured Shao Youlian, a close family friend of my husband. Thereafter I frequently made medicines and gave them to people.

In April 1890 we moved into the official residence of the Shanghai taotai and welcomed my mother-in-law, Madam Zhang, to come and live in our care. Two years earlier my husband had gone to Hunan for his mother's sixtieth birthday celebration, bearing scrolls inscribed with couplets from her many well-wishers. On May 7, 1890, we celebrated her sixty-second birthday in Shanghai with an operatic performance and a banquet.

While Madam Zhang was at the official residence, she came to realize how frugal I had been over the years. She saw that my husband and I still wore clothing from the early years of our marriage. When my sister-in-law, Jize's wife, returned from abroad, she brought back woven woolen garments and lace made with fine thread. Such things were rarely seen at that time. I inquired as to how they were made and obtained several items from her. She showed me, but I was too pressed for time to complete them. Later, whenever I had the leisure, I created new garments based on these. I made a suit of woolen clothing by hand for my husband. It was sewn very carefully, but I relied largely on memory when making it and my memory was not good. When the garment was completed, the length was not uniform. Over the past fifteen years, I had also made seasonal clothing for the children, but I had no time to worry about whether or not I had clothes for myself.

After the mid-autumn festival (September 17) in 1891,[26] Madam Zhang decided to return to Changsha; she felt she needed to look after the family property in person. While she was at the official residence in Shanghai, my husband provided her with a monthly stipend of three hundred taels. When the time for her departure drew near, she gave instructions to her son, saying, "After I return to Hunan you must continue to send three hundred taels to me monthly. I will secure property and build houses for you." My husband followed her instructions and sent the money. She bought two residences for us, one at Liuyangmen and one at Lexintian. However, in addition to the monthly stipend, we sent funds regularly, totaling thirty or forty thousand taels, for the costs of construction.

In 1891, a wave of resentment toward Christian missions spread through the Yangzi Valley.[27] An incident involving French missionaries that occurred in the city of Wuhu in eastern Anhui in 1891 could not be resolved locally. My husband, in his capacity as Shanghai taotai, discussed this with the French consul in Shanghai and reached a settlement.

During the time my husband was Shanghai taotai, and even after he left that post, I continued to bear children. My daughter Qichun was born on May 9, 1891. On August 31, 1892, I gave birth to twin girls. The weather that summer was extremely hot. To cool off I reclined on the floor close to a basin of ice; moreover, I ate cold dishes. As a result, I was stricken with diarrhea which developed into dysentery and damaged the fetuses. Consequently, I gave birth prematurely in the seventh month. When they were first born the twins were still alive, but they died before a month had passed. The second twin was already beyond saving at birth. After the birth I was again sick with fever. Mr. Zhao Chongshan examined and treated me. I was a long time recovering. Twenty-one months later, on June 14, 1894, I gave birth to my daughter Qipu.

The specter of early death seemed to haunt our family. On April 7, 1892, my firstborn, Qibin, died. He had been sick from his fourth year, but he had a generous nature and was a model of sensitivity and considerateness for his brothers. The medical treatment was wanting. His life dragged on for thirteen years, but in the end he died. On Qibin's deathbed, his father faced him and promised, "You are my firstborn son. In the future, the first son born to one of your brothers will be your heir." On October 20 we transported the casket in which his body rested from Shanghai back to Hunan and buried it peacefully.

In the winter of 1893, two of my sons—Qichang, the oldest surviving son, and Qijie—returned to our family home in the Hengshan District of Hunan to take the district-level civil service examinations. When Qichang was small he was frail and frequently ill. I had secretly vowed to the god of Mount Heng,[28] in the Hengshan District, to make a pilgrimage to the mountain if my son were spared. So I asked Qichang to take this opportunity to fulfill my promise to the god of the mountain.

Our two oldest sons' marriages were also settled by 1893. The Zuo family of the Xiangyin District of Hunan had proposed betrothal of a daughter to Qichang. The Xiao family of the Taihe District in Anhui also sought to join our family in wedlock. They had been salt merchants in Yangzhou[29] in Jiangsu Province, where they had resided for many years. Madam Xiao was of the Wang family of Changsha and wished to betroth her daughter to the son of a Hunan family. I asked my mother-in-law and consulted the popular Hunan deity Ding Xiang Wang[30] before sending a betrothal gift. In 1896, Qichang married a daughter of the Zuo family. In 1900, the birth of his son Guangjian, who was adopted posthumously by his Uncle Qibin, marked the beginning of a new generation of the Nie family. Qijie married a daughter of the Xiao family in 1898.

In late 1893 my husband was appointed to the post of provincial judge in Zhejiang Province; however, we did not immediately leave Shanghai because of a shortage discovered during the turnover of funds to the official named to succeed him as Shanghai taotai. Meanwhile, in 1894, on the recommendation of Governor of Taiwan Shao Youlian, my husband was

CHART 4
Children of Nie Qigui and Zeng Jifen; and Nie Qigui and Concubine Zhang

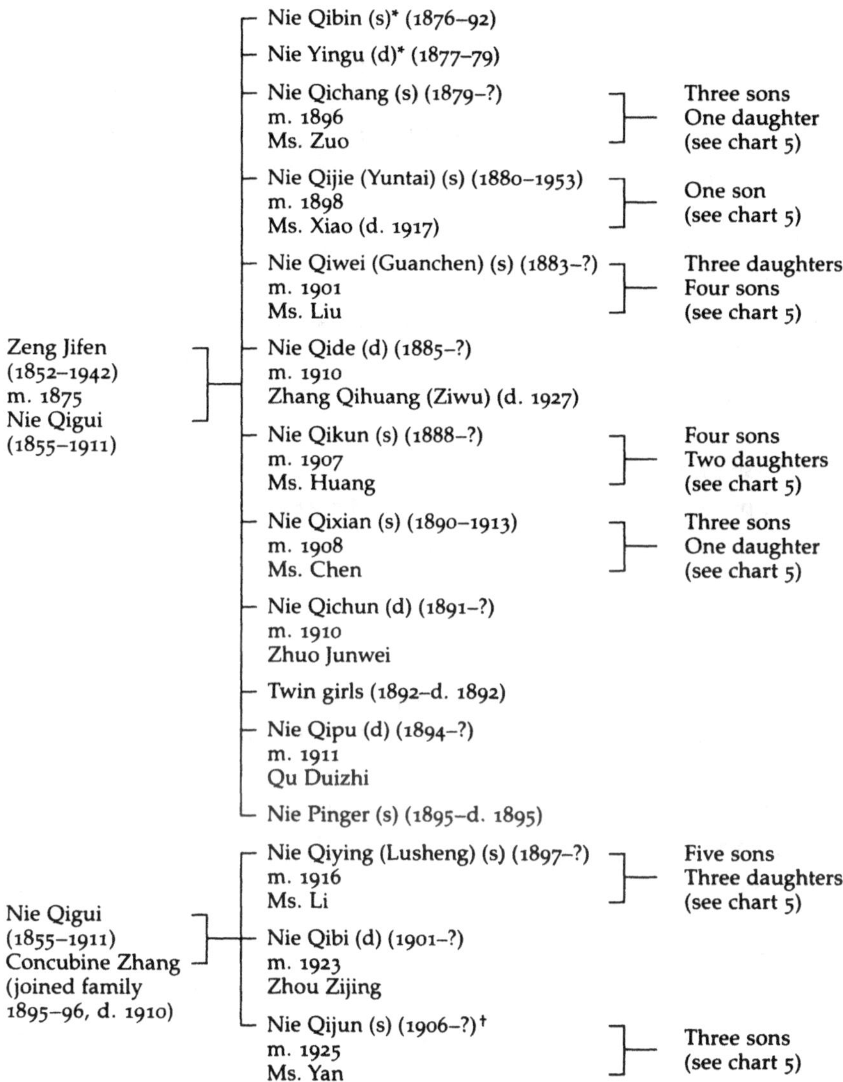

Sources: Nie Zeng Jifen, "Chongde laoren ziding nianpu"; Marie-Claire Bergere, *The Golden Age of the Chinese Bourgeoisie;* Howard L. Boorman and Richard C. Howard, eds., *Biographical Dictionary of Republican China.*

*s = son
d = daughter

†Given in adoption in 1911 to Nie Qigui's deceased younger brother Jixuan.

appointed to a position in the Taiwan Grain Tribute Bureau. He held this important post from the beginning of the war with Japan in 1894 until early 1895; because of this, his assumption of the provincial judgeship in Zhejiang was further delayed.[31] On August 13, 1894, however, we moved from the Shanghai taotai's residence to new quarters in Jiangxi Road.

When my husband first received his appointment as Shanghai taotai in 1890, two accountants as well as footmen and doormen were continued in the posts they had held under the previous taotai, Gong Zhaoyuan. All were experienced under the previous administration, so no major changes were made. My husband was new in office; moreover, he was of a good and generous disposition. Therefore, he did not place great importance on personal wealth and did not think to make a careful check of everything. In 1894, when he turned over the office to his successor, he discovered a shortage of more than 800,000 taels. His successor, Huang Zuluo, pressed anxiously for payment and checked everything carefully. Only then did they discover that when Nie accepted the office there was already a shortage of 200,000 taels. Xu Zijing, the accountant for the previous incumbent, had managed the transition in 1890 when this shortage occurred.

The previous year I had had an opportunity to observe the luxury in which the accountant Xu Zijing lived. In the winter of 1893, when the son of Governor Shao Youlian of Taiwan was married, Shao entrusted Xu to handle all the arrangements. Shao's bride was of the family of Li Hongzhang's youngest brother's wife. My husband had been the intermediary for this marriage; therefore, I was invited to attend the wedding in company with the honored relatives. It would not have been right for me to decline. There, I saw Xu's concubine, called his "upstairs wife," who entertained guests. She wore a court necklace and embroidered jacket, and her whole person dazzled with gems and diamonds. I heard then that the gold, jade, pearls, and malachite she wore were worth more than 20,000 taels. Later, when Xu's accountability for the shortage had been established, he surrendered a steam vessel, the *Feijing*, worth more than 100,000 taels, along with four stems of jeweled flowers, a pair of jeweled bracelets, a jeweled lotus flower, many precious objects of chrysoprase strung into a long string, and a string of eighteen cornelians, altogether valued at 10,000 taels. We eventually liquidated these things in Li Hongzhang's bank and handed over the funds to my husband's successor. They were all fine, perfect gems. At that time the price of gems was low; by later inflated prices they might have been worth ten times as much. Though they were stored in my wardrobe for several months, I never took them out and tried them on.

When my husband took the post of Shanghai taotai, he began making regular deposits of funds into a separate account for me. He said that this money was to pay back the funds from my dowry that had been given to my mother-in-law after the failure of the Yuzhen Bank. I told him from the beginning, "As husband and wife we should seek to have a common purpose. I do not consider individual wealth important." When he prepared to leave the post of Shanghai taotai, there were more than eight thousand Shanghai taels in my account.

These funds were used to help offset the shortage. We also sold gold objects of mine. The amount realized was far less than we needed, so we pledged stocks and other things to get cash in order that my husband might transfer the seals of office. The debts we incurred from this were not repaid in full until 1910. My husband became so nervous that he spat up blood and suffered from nosebleeds. Though he was finally able to turn over the office, he incurred the wrath of his successor. My husband even reached the point where he requested removal from office so he could clarify responsibility for the missing funds legally and settle the matter with his successor.[32]

SIX END OF A DYNASTY: REBIRTH OF A FAMILY (1895–1911)

Over the next decade and a half (1894–1911) our family at first prospered as my husband served with distinction in one provincial post after another. Ultimately, however, he left office the victim of accusations by jealous colleagues and undiscerning censors. A timely decision to commit our resources to industrial development in the private sector and our son Qijie's talent for management eventually enabled us to recover our fortunes and find a new future.

Toward the end of February 1895 we left Shanghai, traveling aboard an ordinary boat to my husband's new assignment as provincial judge of Zhejiang Province. On February 25 we took up residence in the provincial capital, Hangzhou, at the southern terminus of the Grand Canal. I was then heavy with child. My son Ping'er, our thirteenth child, was born four months later, on June 20, but survived only until September. After the death of Ping'er, Madam Zhang, a woman from the Xinchang District, Shaoxing Prefecture in Zhejiang, joined our household as a concubine, with the title *shuren*, official consort of the third rank.[1] She later bore two sons and a daughter.

In September we also sent our second son, Qichang, who was then in his seventeenth year, back to Hunan in the company of his father's fifth sister to marry a woman of the Zuo family. The marriage took place on January 8, 1896. We expected that Qichang and his new bride, along with my mother-in-law, would come from Hunan to join us at the official residence in Hangzhou in March 1896. But Qichang and his wife did not arrive until February 1897, by which time my husband had been transferred to Jiangsu. My mother-in-law joined us in Jiangsu in April 1897, having made disposition of her property before leaving Hunan.

In April 1896 she divided the assets her husband, Nie Erkang, had bequeathed and the land and residences she had acquired over the years. She drew up a document prescribing the division, which read as follows:

> Your father died while serving in eastern Guangdong and we returned to Hunan. His personal wealth, accumulated during his official career, was not great. Because I was careful, we had plenty and I was able to purchase homes and land. Now I am approaching seventy and my vitality is waning. I find it difficult to manage. Therefore, I propose to distribute the dwellings and real estate among family members.
>
> The rents in grain from these lands total seven thousand piculs. My oldest son, Nie Boyuan, and each of my two other sons are to receive rent income of fifteen hundred piculs. The dwelling at Huangniduan was acquired by the main branch of the family. It really should be divided equally in three shares. However, I fear that if brothers live together, it will be difficult to maintain harmony. Therefore, it shall revert entirely to Boyuan. The dwelling on the main street of Liuyangmen was purchased with funds given to me each month by Nie Qigui, hence it shall revert entirely to him.
>
> The brothers Boyuan and Qigui will both have residences, but Nie Jixuan will have none. Therefore, he will receive an additional five hundred piculs of grain rent above the fifteen hundred so that he may purchase a dwelling for himself.
>
> Two thousand piculs remain beyond what has been alloted. I will retain this to supply day-to-day requirements for food, clothing, and the like. The living expenses of my fifth daughter will also come from this until I die. Then, five hundred piculs from the rents that I have kept and two thousand taels of mine are to be given to her. The remaining fifteen hundred piculs in rents shall be retained as a fund for the main branch of the family.

The same year that my mother-in-law drew up her will, she became ill. She dreamed that Luzu,[2] one of the Eight Immortals, gave her a long gown with the character *shou*, for long life, embroidered on it eighty times. It was repeated twice under the lapels. She understood this to mean that she would live to be eighty-two. When she passed away in 1911, she was eighty-three.

In October 1896 my husband was assigned to a new post, financial commissioner of Jiangsu Province at the provincial capital of Suzhou. In the winter of 1896–97, in Jiangsu, he developed scabies over most of his lower body. Several of our sons came down with measles; others in the family suffered from ailments of the throat. Fortunately, they all responded well to treatment and recovered. In November, I was stricken with stomach pains, a hardening of the spleen, and a loss of appetite. Mr. Lin Boying diagnosed this condition and treated it successfully; however, it was more than fifty days before there was improvement and the symptoms began to disappear.

While we were in Zhejiang, my husband had also served as acting provincial financial commissioner on two or three occasions, in addition to his regular post as provincial judge. The superintendents of the Imperial Manufactories,[3] where silk and other items for use by the court were produced, received their funds from the office of the financial commissioner. It was customary for the financial commissioner to deduct a fee from this allocation. My husband never did this, not in Zhejiang nor subsequently while he was financial commissioner in Jiangsu, where the Suzhou manufactories were funded through his office. The various superintendents of the manufactories who held office during his tenures as financial commissioner all regarded him with the utmost respect and appreciation for this.

In 1897 our son Qikun, age nine, was betrothed to a woman of the Huang family of Pingxiang District in Jiangxi. Huang Aitang, of this family, had served as a district magistrate in Shanghai, where he and my husband had been closely associated. Madam Huang brought her daughter to Suzhou and we were able to meet her. Ten years passed before they were married.

On April 7, 1898, we celebrated my mother-in-law's seventieth birthday. Several weeks later, on April 24, our son Qijie married a woman of the Xiao family. My husband had to be in Shanghai when the wedding took place.

That year, in July, an international dispute arose over the Siming Hostel, a residence for people from the city of Ningbo that was located in the French Concession in Shanghai. Soldiers from the French Concession were preparing to take down the perimeter wall of the hostel to make way for the construction of a road in the concession. When Ningbo merchants and other residents of Shanghai from Ningbo heard of this, they staged protest demonstrations and strikes. The French landed marines and artillery. A dozen protesters were killed and more than thirty were injured. The crisis grew worse, and the Shanghai taotai was unable to calm the situation. Liangjiang Governor General Liu Kunyi (1830–1902)[4] then requested the throne to dispatch my husband to Shanghai to handle the negotiations in his capacity as provincial financial commissioner.[5]

In the autumn of 1899, my husband served as acting governor of Jiangsu. When the news reached us that Prince Pujun[6] had been named heir apparent, we knew that the Empress Dowager (1835–1908)[7] was determined to dethrone Emperor Guangxu (1871–1908).[8] My husband received orders to go to the capital for an imperial audience. I was very upset by this for it was unclear just how far the turmoil at court might go. But he went to the capital as directed and received further orders to meet with Robert Hart (1835–1911), superintendent of the Imperial Maritime Customs,[9] to discuss increasing tariffs and eliminating the *likin*.[10] While he was in the capital he stayed at Taiji Chang, the former residence of my older brother, Jize. The next year, during the Boxers' siege of the legation quarters in Beijing, this house was looted and burned by soldiers of the Gansu Army of Dong Fuxiang (1839–1908).[11]

At the time that my husband went to Beijing, Jize's second daughter was taken ill, so I stayed behind to look after her. During that time, when I had nothing else to do, I would occasionally linger about the jewelry shops and purchase some pieces of green jade. I bought a pair of chrysoprase bracelets for my mother-in-law, which subsequently—by the terms of her will—were given to Qiying (the oldest son of Nie's concubine, Madam Zhang) to send as a betrothal present to the daughter of Li Hanzhang.

As the situation in the capital worsened, I grew more anxious for the safety of my husband. I read the paper daily and knew that conditions at court were deteriorating day by day. I feared there would be a great disaster while my husband was still there. I worried constantly; then, on

January 31, 1900, the lunar New Year, while I was watching the children play, I suddenly threw up several mouthfuls of blood. I had never had this problem before; after I received medical attention it did not recur.

In February, my husband ventured out on the streets of Beijing. His horse was startled, upsetting his carriage, and he was run over. Fortunately, he was wearing heavy clothing, which protected him, and he suffered no injury.

Nie returned to his post as financial commissioner of Jiangsu in May 1900 and again served as acting governor. When the antiforeign and anti-Christian Boxer Uprising threatened to spread into the Yangzi Valley, he issued strict orders to his subordinate units to use every means to protect Christian churches, to prepare ground and naval units, and to suppress the anti-Christian secret society known as the Red Gang[12] at Changzhao and the smugglers on Lake Tai on the Jiangsu-Zhejiang border. Because of these actions he was able to conclude an agreement with the foreign consuls to protect the southeastern provinces from invasion by foreign forces.

By the time the expeditionary force—comprised of troops from the eight nations whose interests in China had been harmed by the Boxers—reached Beijing and lifted the Boxers' siege of the foreign legations, it was August 1900. The Empress Dowager had moved the court west, temporarily, to Xi'an. While the tribute grain sent annually from Jiangsu Province to feed the officials and garrisons at the capital was en route, instructions were received to redirect the shipment to the court's temporary location.

That winter my husband was named governor of Hubei Province; however, within ten days of this appointment he was transferred to the governorship of Jiangsu. Meanwhile, on November 4, 1900, the wife of our second son, Qichang, gave birth to our first grandson, Guangjian; he was adopted as the son and heir of our oldest son, Qibin, who had died in his youth without issue.

We spent most of 1901 at the Jiangsu governor's residence in Suzhou. In the fall our fourth son, Qiwei, brought his bride, a daughter of the Liu family of Xiangxiang District of Hunan, to the governor's residence. Her father was Liu Zi,[13] second grade viscount and financial commissioner of Shanxi.

Before the year ended, my husband received orders transferring him to the governorship of Anhui Province. We traveled in three ordinary boats from Suzhou to Shanghai and then by steamship up the Yangzi to Anqing, the capital of Anhui, where we stayed temporarily in the provincial mint[14] until we could move into our official residence.

In 1902, while residing at the governor's mansion in Anqing, we received a written proposal of marriage for our daughter Qipu from the Qu family of the Shanhua District of Hunan. Qu Hongji (1850–1918),[15] the prospective bridegroom's father, was then serving on the Grand Council. The proposal stated the exact date and hour of the birth of his son Duizhi.

At about the same time my mother-in-law left our residence in Anqing to return to our native place in Hunan. Qiwei and his wife accompanied her on the journey. After her arrival in Hunan, my mother-in-law fell sick. My husband requested leave from his official duties so that he could return to Hunan to be with her. The concubine Madam Zhang and Qichang and his wife accompanied him to Hunan to assist in caring for his mother. My husband arranged for a Mr. Li of Yangzhou to treat her. After she recovered, my husband returned immediately to Anqing, accompanied by his son Qiying and our grandson Guangjian. The rest of the family remained in Hunan.

The following year, 1903, in the summer, my husband was named governor of Zhejiang Province. However, he stayed on temporarily in Anqing at the urging of Zhang Zhidong,[16] the governor general of the Liangjiang provinces (which included Anhui), and gentry from Anhui. In September, he proceeded to Nanjing to proctor the provincial examinations and then went on to his new post in Zhejiang. The examinations and the educational system were changing; new areas of learning were becoming known.[17] That same year our son Qichang went to Beijing, where he took the examination for a special course in economics for which he had been recommended by Governor General Cen Chunxuan (1861–1933).[18] Several years later, in 1906, his brother Qiwei went to Japan to study.

I again encountered foreign learning in 1903. In June, I read a work on home economics, *Jiazhengxue*, by the Japanese writer Shimoda Utako (1854–1936).[19] I was very pleased with it. There were some parts, however, that seemed slightly at variance with conditions in China. Therefore, I made some carefully considered changes to make it suitable for Chinese readers. I had my sons Qichang and Qijie and my niece's husband, Liu Shoulin, prepare the printing blocks of the final version at the governor's residence in Anqing.

In 1904 Qichang arranged a permit for us to buy land in Nan Subprefecture on the shore of Dongting Lake. Over the years the water in the lake and river had gradually receded in a southward direction. As a result, in the districts on the shore of the lake in Hunan Province, land had emerged from the marshes. The Colonization Bureau[20] issued permits and recruited people to cultivate this land. Our family secured more than six thousand acres of shoreline property at a cost of more than three thousand strings of cash; however, we were without the wherewithal to construct the dykes that were necessary before the land could be brought under cultivation.

The following year, we returned to Hunan for a visit. My mother-in-law, Madam Zhang, was anxious about the collection of rents, funds, and other business matters pertaining to the main branch of the family. She wished to hand over management to our family, so she had my husband draw up a document specifying the details. There were lands, with annual rents in kind of twenty-five hundred piculs of grain, valued at twenty-eight thousand taels. In addition, there were twenty-two thousand taels in cash on hand, making a total of fifty thousand taels. Her income from this was to be three hundred taels per month beginning from January 9, 1906.

In 1905 my husband encountered serious difficulties in carrying out his official duties as governor of Zhejiang. Twice he submitted memorials requesting permission to retire in order to care for his mother, but he was not permitted to do so. In September, Censor[21] Yao Shu secretly prepared and submitted charges that my husband had favored the appointment of personal friends to official positions and had overextended the operations of the provincial mint.

What had happened was this: Taotai Liu Gengxin was originally director of the provincial mint. Under his management operations showed no improvement, so my husband appointed a new director, Taotai Zhu Youhong. After Zhu took over, profits in the mint exceeded 100,000 taels. Nie commended his achievements and, in an extraordinary move, appointed him acting grain intendant. Some of the profits from the mint should have been returned to the governor's office, but none were. Instead, they were all retained and used for sending students overseas and for funding the Commission for Army Reorganization.[22] Others in the provincial government received nothing and were disappointed. Their jealousy gave rise to hate. Moreover, at the time, there were unemployed taotais and prefects whom my husband had removed from office. They resented him deeply and conspired with the censors to impeach him. An edict directed the Tartar general of Fuzhou to investigate the charges and make a report. Although the investigation found nothing irregular, the court believed the charges brought by my husband's subordinates, and he was directed to vacate his office. In October we traveled by ordinary boat to Shanghai; from there we caught the steamer *Jiangxin* to Hankou and then returned to Hunan, where we took up residence at Lexintian.

Important family milestones marked the passage of the next few years. On October 28, 1906, the concubine Madam Zhang bore another son. In that same year my husband took a second concubine, Madam Zhu, who held the title of *ruren*,[23] consort of the seventh rank. In March of the following year, 1907, our son Qikun married a daughter of Mr. Huang Chengxuan of the Pingxiang District in Jiangxi. Huang was salt and tea taotai[24] of Sichuan; the marriage was celebrated in the official residence in Sichuan. In the summer they returned to Hunan. On March 22, 1908, our sixth son, Qixian, married the daughter of Mr. Chen Naihan of Changsha. Mr. Chen had previously served as taotai of the Hangjiahu Circuit[25] in northern Zhejiang. On April 19 my mother-in-law celebrated her eightieth birthday. We had a dramatic performance and hosted a banquet in her honor.

At that time in Hunan, the cost of each day's performance by a theater troupe was only twenty-odd strings of cash. If the troupe gave a special performance for a high official or a birthday celebration, the gratuity was two hundred cash. In the old days in Xiangxiang District, in the first month of the new year, when we celebrated the Lantern Festival,[26] we always had a dramatic performance. My uncle Zeng Guohuang particularly delighted in these and frequently summoned the performers to our home. It cost no more than a few strings of cash.

At that time, many homes in the countryside worshiped Guanyin,[27] the goddess of mercy, and musical performances were often staged to fulfill vows made to her. These plays always included the *Tale of Xiangshan*,[28] performed with wooden puppets. A day's performance then cost several hundred cash. When I was a child, I greatly enjoyed watching these.

In 1908 an opportunity arose to recoup the financial losses we had sustained in 1894. In that year, when my husband left the post of Shanghai taotai, we borrowed to cover the huge shortages in the reserves resulting from peculation by the accountant, Mr. Xu. Thereafter, our family accountant, Mr. Tang Kuisheng, managed to recover some of the stocks that Mr. Xu had acquired, among which stocks in the Hong Kong and Shanghai Banking Corporation and the Kaiping Mines[29] were foremost. In addition to this, he sold the steam vessel *Feijing* and a dock that Mr. Xu had purchased and replaced some of the missing funds. Then there was 54,000 taels worth of stock in the New Huaxin Cotton Mill, an enterprise capitalized by merchants and officials.[30] This was actually worth nothing because it had not paid dividends for several years.[31] In 1904, Mr. Tang asked our family to take over management of this enterprise jointly with him, but my husband declined because he felt it would not be fitting for him to manage a commercial enterprise while occupying an official post. Mr. Tang then leased it himself and asked our son Qijie to be the director.[32] The name was changed to the Futai Company. In one year there was a surplus of 100,000 taels.

Before long, Mr. Tang died. A relative of his, Mr. Tang Zhixian, then asked Qijie if our family would enter into joint management with him and direct operations because Mr. Tang's bereaved survivors were not up to the responsibility. He pleaded with Qijie and made a lengthy supplication. Finally, it was agreed that the Tang family would provide 40 percent of the operating capital and our family would bear 60 percent. Qijie would be general manager. The lease on the Futai Company was originally for six years. This was shortened to four years; it expired in 1908. The original stockholders could not cover the liabilities; so they discussed it and decided to sell the plant. Our family put up 325,000 taels and purchased it.[33] We changed the name to Heng Feng.[34] This was all done by Qijie and Qiwei, after securing the approval of their father.

Our family did not have this huge sum of money, but we saw the hope of future development for the enterprise and couldn't bear to see it slip away, so we borrowed the necessary funds. Qiwei handled this matter when he and I came to Shanghai with my daughter Qide, in May 1908, to purchase things for my daughters' dowries, since the time for them to marry was drawing near.

After my husband retired from official life, the savings from his salary were not great and there was also the large debt he had incurred to purchase the plant; the burden was onerous. Fortunately, the cotton mill improved steadily. We were just able to keep the business going in those days, but the amount spent for building dykes for the land reclaimed from the lake in Hunan was considerable. Moreover, the Great China Cotton Mill[35] established by Qijie in 1921 suffered business losses. We felt the effect of this very severely. The Heng Feng plant was repeatedly expanded and repeatedly contracted external debts. As of this writing (in 1931), we have been unable to pay them back completely. This was the fortune of my family over the past twenty years.

The years from 1909 until the Revolutionary party overthrew the imperial government in early 1912 were a time of many changes in our family: more grandchildren were born (see chart 5); we were exposed to new aspects of foreign cultures; our daughters married into prominent gentry families. Then, on the eve of the revolution, my mother-in-law and my beloved husband both succumbed to a fatal illness.

In 1909 we engaged Mr. Yin Hebai to instruct our daughters in painting. Later, the concubine Madam Zhu also studied with them. Mr. Yin had previously been a retainer in the official residence of my father; he later became the leading photographer in Hunan. My brother Jize had studied sketching with him and had given him his first camera.

In February 1910, our oldest surviving daughter, Qide, married Zhang Qihuang (1877–1927),[36] a native of Lingui District in Guangxi who held the *jinshi* degree. He served as magistrate of the Zhijiang District in Hunan and was well known as an official. My nephew Yu Shoucheng, who served as a taotai in Hunan at the same time, knew Zhang, and he served as a middleman between Zhang and our family. My husband had also heard of Zhang's accomplishments as an official. He respected him and praised his great talent. Consequently, in the previous winter he had sent Zhang a goose as a betrothal present. A month later our daughter Qide and Zhang were married; husband and wife went together to his post in Zhijiang.

In March of that same year we gave our second-oldest surviving daughter, Qichun, in marriage to Zhuo Junwei of Fujian Province. His father, Zhuo Zhinan, served as taotai in Hangzhou while holding the rank of assistant department director in the imperial government. My nephew Guangzhong, Jihong's son, was the go-between and arranged the betrothal. Zhuo came to Hunan and was married at our home.

Two months after the wedding my son Qiwei, my daughter Qipu, and I went to Shanghai. My new son-in-law, Zhuo, and Qichun accompanied us. We found my son Qijie and his wife both ill. Though their condition gradually improved, Qiwei was taken ill in May from the heat and humidity. He was treated by Dr. Xia Yingtang and responded well. In mid-September Qijie, his wife and son Guangkun, my daughter Qipu, and I visited an exhibit of the Society for the Encouragement of Industry in Nanjing.[37] It was well organized and very extensive in its coverage.

On September 28 my husband's concubine Madam Zhang died. A letter arrived informing me of this just as we were about to begin traveling. So Qijie escorted me back to Hunan.

In January 1911 we gave our daughter Qipu in marriage to Qu Duizhi. His father, Qu Hongji, resided in Changsha. Earlier, when we promised our daughter to the Qu family, my mother-in-law had expressed her strong approval. She was anxious to witness the ceremony. Before the wedding date, she went to our prospective son-in-law's home to look things over.

In one year we had given three daughters in marriage. We were all exhausted from the arrangements and the anxiety. Shortly after Qipu's marriage, my mother-in-law was taken sick. First it was only a cold, but it became more serious over the New Year and, on February 16, 1911, she passed away.

Because of the great number of people in the family and the turmoil that surrounded her death, we did not settle the division of rents and grain belonging to the main branch of the Nie family until the spring of 1913. Our branch of the family made disposition of these assets, which consisted of lands producing rents of twenty-five hundred piculs of grain and the income from this, which, with accumulated interest, totaled forty thousand taels.

My husband had attended his mother day and night. The temperature in the sickroom was very high, and on his frequent trips in and out he caught a cold, which developed into a fever. Moreover, while his mother was nearing death, he was often unable to control his grief. He became more distressed day by day. On March 2, his breathing was blocked by phlegm and he lost consciousness. He succumbed very shortly following the death of his mother. In a little more than ten days I experienced two great losses. I was shocked and saddened. To this day I shudder at the thought of it.

My husband's younger brother, Jixuan, grieving for his mother and brother, died on March 31, 1911. Since his widow had no children, we gave the child Qijun, the offspring of my husband and his concubine, to be Jixuan's adoptive heir, and Qijun took the place of his son at the funeral.

When my husband's posthumous memorial to the court became known, we received an edict awarding a great ceremonial offering on his behalf. His name was published and given to the State Historiographer's Office for inclusion in the Biographies of Filial Sons.[38] Furthermore, we were awarded a tablet to be placed over our door extolling filial piety.

PART THREE IN THE HOUSE OF MY SON (1911–1942)

Mrs. Nie began her life as a widow—the third and final phase of Confucian womanhood—in 1911 amid the armed uprising that brought two thousand years of imperial rule in China to an end. Late in that year she left her ancestral home in Hunan for the security of her son's home in Shanghai, where the family-owned cotton mill was situated. Although she was no stranger to the bustling, treaty-port life of Shanghai—having dwelt there with her husband from 1886 to 1895, this time she came not as the wife of a prominent imperial official but as the mother of one of China's new elite, a cotton entrepreneur whose fortunes were waxing with the new bourgeois economy.

In the second decade of the twentieth century, Mrs. Nie, now in her sixties, found herself no longer at center stage in the drama of family life. During the final decade of dynastic decline the principal roles in the family had shifted to the next generation—to Qijie and his direction of the family business undertakings. The Nies prospered in these years in part because of the direction in which Mrs. Nie earlier had steered the careers of her husband and her sons, and also in part because of family members' industry, ingenuity, respect for education, and public-spiritedness—values Mrs. Nie exemplified to the younger generations.

Her concerns gradually focused on the growth of the family and the personal development of its members, her own spiritual life and that of her widowed son Qijie, and the changes in Chinese society that she viewed from her vantage point as an octogenarian. These and other aspects of Chinese culture are recorded on the final pages of her autobiography. The professional affairs of the male leaders of her household now figure less prominently in her recollections. The summary report of her final decade of life, compiled and edited by her son-in-law, reveals an old woman

Mr. Nie Qijie

whose values remained remarkably unshaken through nine decades of life in a society undergoing constant upheaval. Her life's achievements resulted from the practice of the Confucian virtues taught by her father and the open-mindedness and sagacity required by a new age, qualities that remained with her to the end, bringing tranquillity and purpose to her final years.

SEVEN **WIDOWHOOD (1911–1942)**

Revolutionary activity began in Changsha on October 22, 1911. We left the city a week later, on October 29, by boat, bearing my husband's body to its final resting place in the Imperial Fields at Tangping in the district west of the river.[1] Qixian preceded us and made the necessary arrangements. Afterward, Qijie stayed on in the countryside to supervise the work on the tomb while Qixian and Qikun returned to Changsha to attend to our family's interests. In December, their wives joined me and the Qu family (my daughter Qipu's in-laws) aboard the steamer *Yuanjiang* which was bound for Shanghai for repairs.

In Changsha, the Revolutionary party[2] looted to secure military supplies. Many were forced to turn over their savings. Our family, however, had suffered financial setbacks over the years and had nothing deposited in the banks in Changsha. Still, having to face this turn of events and hurry through the burial of my husband so we could leave for Shanghai was very upsetting.

When we reached Wuchang, the city was under heavy bombardment from Hanyang, and Wuchang was returning the fire. Shells were flying across the river, but the *Yuanjiang* steamed peacefully beneath the gunfire. That night we berthed at the Riqing Company pier in Hankou. The sound of gunfire continued throughout the night like fireworks exploding on New Year's Eve. Shells ignited a fire in the buildings of the China Merchant's Steam Navigation Company in Hankou.[3] Flames illuminated the sky.

In 1912, following the abdication of the emperor and the establishment of a new government, Qixian played a crucial role in the struggle between the Revolutionaries and the Constitutionalists[4] in Changsha. He led Zhang Qihuang's Nanwu Army[5] back from Jianli in Hubei to Changsha, where the Forty-ninth and the Fiftieth regiments of Revolutionary soldiers were just about to lay siege to the residence of the Constitutionalist military governor Tan Yankai (1879–1930).[6] The Nanwu Army prevented them from doing so. Governor Tan subsequently named Qixian to command his garrison troops, a position of great trust.

Later, Qixian's influence proved very helpful to our relatives. Guangxiao, the oldest grandson of my late husband's older brother, Boyuan, came under suspicion by the new regime and was very nearly executed. The concubine of my nephew Qixun was imprisoned for smoking opium. Both escaped more serious punishment and were released through Qixian's intercession.

In 1912 we took up residence in Shanghai on Qianji Li in Xihuade Road. The number of people in our household increased steadily as friends and relatives descended upon us. We then built another home in Weisai Road. Today, it is the Eastern District Primary School operated by the Shanghai Municipal Council.[7] We moved into our Weisai Road residence in October 1913.

Though my husband went early to his grave—in his fifty-seventh year—during my years as a widow in Shanghai his descendants multiplied, married, and produced new generations as the older ones passed away. In the first years of the Republic, seven more grandchildren were born (see chart 5).

Not long before our sixth son, Qixian, succumbed prematurely to a fatal illness, his wife gave birth, on July 13, 1913, to their fourth child, a boy. Qixian had been very conscientious about everything he did; he incurred the dislike of some because of this. Tragically, he was only twenty-three when he died. In the year and a half prior to Qixian's death, he and my son-in-law Zhang Qihuang struggled to make the wetlands reclaimed along the shore of Dongting Lake productive. My husband acquired this land in 1904, but dykes had to be built before it could be brought under cultivation. My husband's intention had been to provide a means of livelihood for many peasants and to produce great quantities of grain. Who would have thought that such a huge investment would result in nothing? Yet, in ten years there had been absolutely no harvest. Qixian and

Qihuang labored unceasingly to ensure that my husband's efforts were not in vain. After Qixian's death, Qihuang raised several large loans. Finally, he was successful: after 1916, we began to see abundant harvests. Our family paid back the loans one by one. My husband's hopes and dreams for this land were finally realized.[8]

In 1917, Qijie served as vice president of the Chinese Commercial Mission to the United States.[9] The following year, he organized the Chinese Cotton Mill Owners' Association of Shanghai.[10] After World War I, the board of directors of the Shanghai General Chamber of Commerce opened its membership to cotton mill owners; Qijie was among the first to join. In 1920, when the chamber was torn by factionalism between radicals and conservatives, Qijie stepped in and mediated.[11] He was subsequently elected president of the chamber, an office he accepted reluctantly and held for only one year before tendering his resignation.

In March 1916, Qiying, the son of my husband and his concubine Madam Zhang, married the daughter of Li Hanzhang,[12] older brother of Li Hongzhang. Shortly after the marriage they went to the United States, where their first two sons were born in 1917 and 1918. After returning to China in 1919, they had six more children (see chart 5). When Qiying and his family returned from the United States, my grandsons Guangjian and Guangkun both left China to continue their studies in America.

On the day that Qiying's first son was born in the United States, I was grieved by the death of my daughter-in-law, Qijie's wife. She had been wise, loving, and loyal to our family. Unfortunately, she was not strong. After joining the family she was often ill. Finally, she succumbed to one of her many ailments.

In April 1918 Mr. Qu Hongji, my daughter Qipu's father-in-law, passed away. Earlier in the spring of that year, Mr. Qu and his wife and I went to Hangzhou where we visited the various scenic spots at West Lake.[13] Qijie and my oldest granddaughter accompanied us. Thirteen years had elapsed since my husband and I left Zhejiang in 1905. While he served there, we had visited West Lake in an official capacity; however, we could not go about leisurely taking in everything as we wished. This time, in a wheeled cart and casual clothing, we went about freely and thoroughly enjoyed ourselves.

Nineteen eighteen was my sixty-seventh year. My children and grandchildren were grown, and family business monopolized my life; however, I was hard put to look after everything. As a result, on New Year's Eve 1918, I distributed our property among family members.

My conversion to Christianity several years earlier profoundly influenced the allotments I made at that time. In February 1915 Qijie, his wife, and I were baptized in the Methodist Episcopal Church on Kunshan Road in Shanghai. I had been introduced to the doctrines of Christianity several years earlier, in 1910, when my daughter Qijun and I went to Shanghai to visit Qijie and his wife, who was ailing. While I was there, my niece Jirong invited me to go with her to Hangzhou, but I did not. However, she came frequently to visit me and explained the truth of Christianity to me. I began to understand it and gradually developed the will to follow this teaching. After I returned to Hunan, I sometimes spoke about it with friends and relatives. When I returned to Shanghai in 1911, I felt that world affairs were worsening because men were so absorbed in the pursuit of pleasure. If one would save men's hearts from such temptations, then one must begin by loving others as oneself—thus strengthening and increasing one's faith. A decade after our conversion, we began holding weekly family worship services, during which Qijie would preach.

Guided by the principles of my new faith, I divided the land and property my father-in-law, Nie Erkang, had left and the family assets—real estate, stocks, and cash—that my husband had accumulated over the years into ten equal shares. Earlier generations of my family always gave to the poor. When my husband was alive, we made numerous contributions and performed works of charity. I was, of course, familiar with the Christian doctrine that enjoins us to love all men but, first of all, to help the needy and assist those in distress. Therefore, following the biblical prescription to donate one-tenth of one's wealth, I designated one-tenth as a fund to support charitable works. The annual interest was to be used to make contributions to the church and to various disaster relief efforts. The capital was not to be used unless there was absolutely no alternative, in the hope that the good deeds and virtues of our ancestors could be perpetuated.

I designated two-tenths to the main branch of the family for my own financial support; the cost of social activities in the main branch of the family was also to come from these funds. I gave half a share to my oldest grandson, Guangjian, the adopted heir of my oldest son, Qibin, who had died in his youth. (I am saddened as I think of his death.) Since my son Qijun had been given in adoption to his father's younger brother, Jixuan, Qijun had productive land coming to him from his grandfather in that branch of the family. Therefore, I gave half of one share to him.

Each share was valued at more than eighty thousand taels. Stocks in the cotton mill made up most of this; real estate was next. The liquid assets were almost all offset by debts of the various branches of the family. We then drew up a document in nine copies dividing these assets. My six sons and two grandsons, Guangjian and Guangyao (the oldest son of my deceased son, Qixian), each held one copy. Following Guangjian's death in 1926, I determined to use his half share to establish an educational fund for my husband's sons and grandsons. If one of the family members was really in need, he or she could secure assistance from this fund; however, the funds must be properly managed. I also donated the real estate on Peikai'er Road in Shanghai to the Shanghai Municipal Council to establish a public school, which, following the Western practice, was named the Governor Nie Public School.[14]

By the 1920s, Qipu had moved to Beijing with her husband and the second generation of our descendants began to marry. On May 16, 1922, my granddaughter Guangzhao, daughter of Qichang, was married to Cao Mingxian. Cao had studied in the United States, where he received a master's degree in engineering. At the time they were married, he was employed as a teacher in the Nanyang School.[15]

Qibi, the daughter of my husband and his concubine Madam Zhang, married Zhou Zijing of Nanjing on June 24, 1923. He was formerly an instructor at Jiaotong University,[16] later dean, and most recently head of the Engineering Research Institute in the graduate school. He was talented, industrious, and sincere and followed a simple way of life. My son Qijie discussed Zhou's suitability as a husband for Qibi with me, and we decided on the marriage.

The following year, in April, Qijie's son Guangkun married a woman of the Liu family of Lujiang District in Anhui Province. She was the grand-

CHART 5

Grandchildren and Great-grandchildren of Nie Qigui and Zeng Jifen, and Nie Qigui and Concubine Zhang

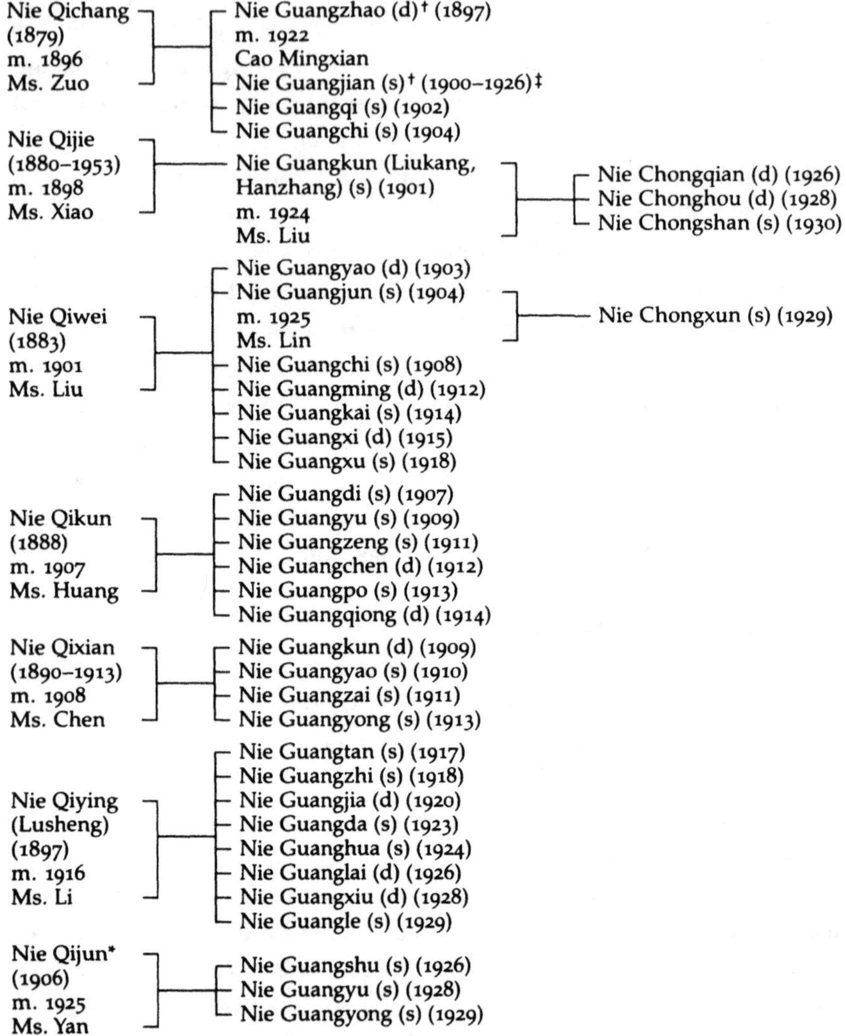

Sources: Nie Zeng Jifen, "Chongde laoren ziding nianpu"; Marie-Claire Bergere, *The Golden Age of the Chinese Bourgeoisie*.

*Given in adoption in 1911 to Nie Qigui's younger brother, Jixuan.

†s = son
d = daughter

‡Given in adoption to his deceased uncle Nie Qibin.

daughter of Liu Bingzhang (1826–1905),[17] former governor of Jiangxi and Zhejiang provinces and governor general of Sichuan, and the daughter of Governor General Liu's son, Liu Tiqian. Our first great-grandchild, a girl, was born to Guangkun and his wife in March 1926. By 1930 I had another great-granddaughter and two great-grandsons (see chart 5).

Meanwhile, on July 31, 1924, the concubine Madam Zhu succumbed to tuberculosis. She had begun coughing up blood in the fall of 1910. Though she recovered, thereafter she had frequent attacks. Each time she recovered, until, finally, one attack proved fatal. Following my husband's death, I had asked her, "Since you are so young and have no children, you certainly are not obligated to stay with our family. I could have your older brother choose a spouse for you." But she did not wish to leave. Moreover, she held strictly to prescribed behavior: she would not go out walking without a companion. When she died, since she had no children of her own, I told my sons to honor her as a concubine mother. Qijie escorted her coffin to Hunan. She was buried by the side of my husband's tomb at Tangping.

In May of the next year, 1925, Qijun, the youngest son of my husband and the concubine Madam Zhang, married a daughter of the Yan family of Lianping District in northeastern Guangdong. She was the granddaughter of Yan Zhongji,[18] the former financial commissioner of Shaanxi and Zhejiang. Qijun's wife subsequently bore three sons.

In December 1925 Qiwei's oldest son, Guangjun, married a daughter of the Lin family of the He District of Guangxi. She was the granddaughter of Lin Zhaoyuan (d. 1886),[19] the former governor of Guizhou, and the daughter of Lin Shitao,[20] a compiler of the Hanlin Academy. In August 1930 she gave birth to our fourth great-grandchild, the second great-grandson (see chart 5).

During 1926, my oldest grandson, Guangjian, died. He was the second child and the oldest son of Qichang. When Guangjian was two years old, he had been given in adoption as an heir to his deceased uncle Qibin, our first son. Guangjian had been ill for some time, and the doctors found his condition difficult to treat. On October 4, 1926, we moved into a new residence in Liaoyang Road. We built this residence because the house in Weisai Road was too large and the various branches of the family could not live together at one place. Qikun and Qiwei and their families had their homes elsewhere, but the rest of the family now dwelt in the four buildings that formed the new residence. On the morning that we moved in, I went to see Guangjian. His mind was alert and he said, "It is rude of me not to rise when you come to see me." I never thought that he would actually die less than half a day after we were in our new home. He was gifted intellectually, but also very practical. He had worked hard on the business of the lands in Hunan reclaimed from the lake. Early in the summer, despite his illness, he had made a trip to Hunan to look after things. Now, after all, he was gone. What a pity.

News reached us in the summer of 1927 that our oldest son-in-law, Zhang Qihuang, husband of Qide, had died in battle. Since 1911 he had given every moment of his time to national affairs. Most recently he had been engaged in planning and operations at the military headquarters of Wu Peifu (1874–1939)[21] at Hankou. Regrettably, because of his unyielding attitude and outspoken manner, he incurred the dislike of many. When Wu Peifu's army was defeated by the Northern Expeditionary Forces[22] of the Guomindang, Qihuang lost his life, felled by sniper fire, in the Deng District of southwestern Henan at Goulinguan. It was autumn when his remains were brought south. That winter we selected a grave site, through divination, on the plateau of Qigan Shan near Suzhou. During his lifetime Qihuang helped his family, relatives, and friends. He was an ardent bibliophile but did not pursue any productive enterprise.[23] After his death, Qide was disconsolate and penniless. Consequently, I set aside a monthly stipend for her to help raise and educate her children.

In March 1928 the wife of my husband's brother Jixuan turned sixty. I sent Qijun (her adopted son) and his wife and child to Hunan to pay our respects. In April we received her in Shanghai to live temporarily. On May 14, 1930, she passed away while still in Shanghai. Qijun bore her coffin back to Hunan. The burial was delayed because the geomantic alignment of the grave site was obstructed. After the burial took place, we heard that the Communists were approaching the provincial capital, Changsha,[24] so Qijun was instructed to escort his father's fifth sister from Hunan to Shanghai to avoid the anticipated disturbance. Many others came to Shanghai with them. Later, they returned to Hunan in groups.

Because there continued to be frequent disturbances in Hunan, Qijun's fifth aunt stayed on in Shanghai. She was sincerely respectful of family and friends. Never having married, she cared for her mother, Madam Zhang, throughout her life. Her nature was humane and compassionate. She fasted from meat for long periods, made offerings to the Buddha, and lived very frugally. Although her inheritance was small, her help to the needy and to her kinsmen was very generous.

I have never been one for ostentatious displays on birthdays. When I passed my seventieth year on May 6, 1921, Guangjun, the oldest son of my brother Jihong, sent a letter of congratulations from Hunan. Friends and relatives came to pay their respects; they wished to have a stage performance and a celebration, but I refused to allow it. In 1931, when I passed my eightieth birthday, friends and relatives again wanted to have a celebration, and again I refused. When the day arrived we had some plain food prepared for guests, and nothing more. Nearly all of my children, grandchildren, and great-grandchildren—more than eighty people in all—were present. On this occasion I recalled and wrote down what I had witnessed over the past eighty years in the evolution of women's hairstyles, women's apparel, cuisine, and transportation.

There is a great deal that is of interest in the evolution of women's hairstyles. It is a pity that in my early years I was shut away deep in the women's quarters. My experience was extremely narrow, and I am not able to generalize beyond those things that I personally saw or heard. Generally, during the Xianfeng (1851–61) and Tongzhi (1862–74) periods, women coiled their hair at the back of the head and elongated it. It was something like the way women wear their hair in the north China countryside today. It required a rigid form inside the hair. The place where the hair was bound together was decorated with red thread and made secure with a flat hair clasp.

When I was seven or eight years old, I saw a hairstyle, in my district, called the "cow's horn." It was said to be popular in Baoqing Prefecture of Hunan. Wood was used to fashion the horn. It was painted black, and the hair was twisted inside. The horn protruded above the top of the head four to five inches, and a swallow's tail, made from a horse's tail, trailed on the neck. Today this coiffure is considered unsightly. Those that I have seen recently in the nearby countryside are somewhat shorter, about two to three inches in height, and not very pointed. They are similar to the silver ingot style (see drawing) and are also artificial.

Later, in other areas, the fashionable hairstyles were the silver ingot, the Yangzhou laurel blossom, and the *pingsantao*. All had swallow tails. The important thing about these was that they created a false impression and did not allow the hair to be natural. This was in the Tongzhi period and earlier.

In the Guangxu period (1875–1908), the so-called *baba* was popular. One wound the hair in two or three coils, and the center protruded. Three hair clips were placed next to each other evenly in a row. No effort was made to create a contrast among the coils.

Unmarried women combed their hair into a knot, sometimes to one side of the head. Some wore two knots, one on each side. Sometimes the forehead was covered with short hair, which was referred to as "bangs." After 1900, both young and older women wore hair on the forehead. They controlled it with a small comb, which gave it a bouffant appearance.

After the outbreak of the revolution in 1911, young women generally abandoned their old hairstyles. Some arranged their hair in the form of a snake; others imitated Japanese styles. There was great popular enthusiasm for the dazzling new styles. This continued through 1914, when there was a renaissance of the old styles. First there was the butterfly, then the chrysanthemum heart, the coiled queue, the abalone, the S, the horizontal S, and, most recently, the fan style. All were coiffed on the back of the head.

About 1926 or 1927, women started bobbing their hair. The young women and daughters-in-law in our family, one by one, bobbed their hair. The way this caught on was something we could not foresee at the time.

When I was young, clothing styles were simple and unadorned. This was especially the case in my family. As I have mentioned, one garment was sometimes handed around among my sisters, aunts, and sisters-in-law. My father detested showy things and gave written instructions forbidding us to wear jackets with broad lace borders and skirts with multicolored floral patterns. Styles we consider obsolete today were regarded as chic in those days. When my brother Jize returned to China

1. I saw this when I was eleven or twelve. Artificial hair is twisted and worn on top of the real hair. In the middle there is also a long tress. The center is tied to the real hair.

2. This knot is artificial. The real hair is twisted inside. In the middle, the core of the knot is real hair tied in a long bundle.

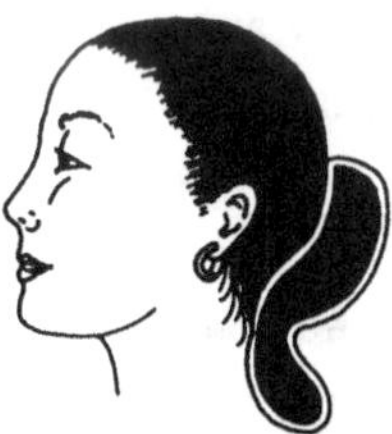

3. This is the Yangzhou laurel blossom style. Using black wool one wraps around fine wire and twists it into various flower patterns. Inside there is a liner of stiff paper. The swallow tails are, for the most part, made from horse tails. Most have real hair in the inside.

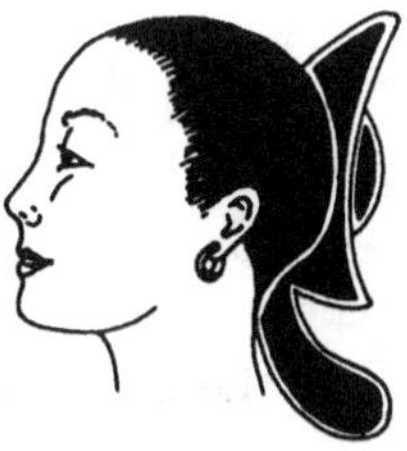

4. This is the silver ingot style.

5. This is the lion looking at the Yangzi. These two styles were seen in Anqing. The knot was real hair. The swallow tail was made from horse tails.

6. In the north they called this the *pingsantao*. For the most part they used real hair when fixing it this way. It was seen in both north and south. In the north some wove in horse hair.

after serving abroad as a diplomat, he gave me foreign material. It cost several yuan per foot. But I personally never bought such costly material. Even today it is rare for anyone in our family to wear clothing made of material costing four or five yuan per foot.

After 1900 the atmosphere was more open. Men and women both preferred high collars and narrow sleeves. Formerly sleeves were from eighteen to nearly twenty-three inches wide. At this time, they were cut down to a few inches. Western personal attire—such as woolen jackets with lace and filigree buttons—was popular, and the former practice of rolling the sleeves up horizontally was discontinued.

The symbols of rank of the imperial era could no longer be displayed indiscriminately. Although imperial rank had been conferred on the concubines in our family, we did not permit them to wear vermilion skirts. Other families did not even allow concubines to wear plum-colored outer jackets or red embroidered shoes. Our family was quite indulgent in this matter. After the revolution there was no resumption of spot checks (*fangjian*) on clothing.[25]

In the early years of the Republic, high collars concealed the jowls. The styles were not attractive, but they did not reveal the figure. Nine or ten years later, the popular *qipao*[26] was not as unsightly as shorter garments nor as inconvenient as the long skirt. Now, I have never been opposed to a nice way of dressing, but the *qipao* barely covers the knee, the sleeves don't reach the wrist, and the neck and the elbow are exposed. I really don't take any pleasure in looking at this sort of thing.

I have also witnessed dramatic changes in tastes in food and drink over the past several decades. Take banquets, for example; as I noted previously, when Father was alive we were not allowed roast meats. In those days, when officials entertained, roast meats were almost always served in great quantities. Not until after the establishment of the Republic was this practice entirely eliminated.

Though the conventions governing dining changed, the number and variety of dishes and the extravagance and artfulness of preparation surpassed earlier times. In my native province of Hunan in the last years of the Qing dynasty, a banquet of sharks' fins cost only ten strings of cash and was regarded as very lavish. During the Changsha rice riots in April

1910,[27] Lai Chengyu, taotai of the police force, rebuked the Tianrantai Tea Shop for selling tea for one hundred cash a bowl, which is evidence of the extravagance and affluence that prevailed early in this century; however, what was considered extravagant then is hardly worth mentioning today. Today, tea in a first-rate teahouse is at least one jiao (a tenth of a yuan) per bowl.

In the early years of the Republic, we lived in Shanghai. A shark's fin banquet was no more than about eight yuan. In recent years, one can't begin to think of having such a banquet for less than sixteen yuan. In affluent homes it is often the case that one banquet can cost several hundred yuan. People don't consider this unusual. I believe in halting this pointless waste.

When entertaining friends or relatives, I seek to please their tastes and try not to be too austere; this is the middle way.[28] My personal expenses for ordinary dishes vary from time to time, based on the availability of foodstuffs. Still, when I serve more at certain times, it costs no more than a few yuan. For many years I have eaten no meat on New Year's Day. In recent years, on my birthday I have eaten only vegetables. I am satisfied that I have virtually eliminated waste and excess. But when I entertain, I fear that I am insufficiently attentive to my guests. I never set out lavish meals to entertain them; I rarely even add an extra dish. Fortunately, my friends and relatives know of this and are generally forgiving.

Although changes in the means of transportation have not affected life as directly as have the changes in clothing and cuisine, the old society in which our family lived has been transformed by changes in transport and traffic. Formerly, as the wife of an official, I rarely ventured out, and when I did I was always accompanied by attendants. After returning to private life, we had our own sedan chair. In Hunan it was commonplace for three men, the so-called three kidnappers, to bear a sedan chair. Since we moved to Shanghai, we have kept a horse-drawn carriage. In Shanghai there has been automotive traffic since 1914 or 1915; however, when I go out, I still travel in a horse-drawn carriage. The horse is natural power; there is no reason to abandon its use in favor of gasoline, which expends the energy of millions for the momentary enjoyment of a single person. At present, China has no prospect of opening oil wells. Why should we contribute great sums of money to the foreign powers to indulge personal tastes for travel? I am old. If I have occasion to travel, it is not urgent and there is no need whatsoever for haste. Furthermore, recently the traffic congestion in Shanghai is growing worse. There is not a single street that is entirely safe. Therefore, I prefer to seek tranquillity and eschew haste.

EPILOGUE

Qu Duizhi

Seeking tranquillity and eschewing haste were appropriate sentiments for Mrs. Nie to express in concluding her autobiography in 1931, her eightieth year. In the decade that remained to her she lived quietly in Shanghai, leaving the city only twice. She went calmly to her final rest while Shanghai was under Japanese occupation in 1942.

Following her instructions, her son-in-law Qu Duizhi, husband of Qipu, recorded her autobiographical data in chronological format and punctuated the text. Two editions were published prior to her death. Qu then appended a synopsis of his mother-in-law's last decade of life. The original autobiography together with this document and memorial essays contributed by her sons were republished following her death. Brief as they are, Qu's words tell us of Mrs. Nie's unflagging commitment to traditional values, now reinforced by her new Christian faith, and her remarkable ability to achieve tranquillity in the midst of turmoil.

After my mother was eighty years old, her spirit remained strong. Her daily activities followed a fixed schedule. In the morning she arose and took something to drink and some food at her bedside. After her morning ablutions she had breakfast, leftovers from the evening meal. Then she read a chapter from the Bible and, kneeling over the back of a chair, prayed to heaven for a few moments. Afterward she wrote or read the newspaper. There were many requests for her to write, in response to which she wrote good wishes or proverbs. She always drew her words of wisdom from Zeng Guofan's poem *Hate Not and Seek Nothing* (*Buzhi Buqiu Shi*).[1] When she was in her ninety-first year, she could still make a brush stroke with disciplined structure and perfect proportion. Those who saw it marveled at this unusual talent.

She took a brief nap after lunch. When she got up she attended to clothing materials, medicines, tonics, and such things. She personally operated the sewing machine and made clothing to distribute to the needy. Each year she mixed medicines according to prescriptions, some of which she drew from her accumulated wisdom; others she got from shops; still others she had acquired through inquiries and then recorded for future use. Each time she heard of a prescription being passed around she recorded it and waited for investigations and studies to confirm its efficacy. If she heard that friends or relatives were sick, she either presented them with medicine or told them of a prescription. She evaluated their progress for ten years. After dinner she played a game of chess with family members or, if she felt like it, chatted a while and then went peacefully to sleep.

Her teeth were always very strong. In her later years, she frequently ate bread, butter, and millet gruel. She selected foods that were warm and soft, and took only a little. Although her food tasted the same year in and year out, it didn't bother her. The cook she employed was old and not adept at seasoning food. Family members sometimes could not bear to eat what he prepared, but Mother was always forgiving.

In the spring of 1933 she visited Beijing, the old imperial capital (1421–1928). She had not set foot in the city since she left eighty years before, as a child. She had long wanted to go there. At this time, transportation was swift and secure, and she reckoned her spirit and physical mobility were still up to a long trip. So she made arrangements with the Yu family, the in-laws of Zeng Jihong's daughter Guangshan, for the Yu and Zeng families to go together. Mother had not seen old friends and relatives in the north for many years. The reunion was very happy. She stayed in the residence of my family for about a month, and then returned. In 1936, she traveled in Nanjing to view the development of the new capital (1928–37). She stayed at the home of the Zhuo family and had a visit similar to her Beijing trip.

In 1937, war broke out in Shanghai. The Liaoyang Road residence was directly in the field of fire, but Mother did not accept the idea of moving lightly. Only when the fighting could no longer be avoided did she accede to family members' requests to move her residence to Jubolaisi Road in the western district. She had to move in a hurry and could not take her possessions with her. Afterward, when we checked the household property, everything was gone. She took all this very calmly. What was lost was lost. She was not one to cry over spilt milk. When the landlord demanded that we vacate the Jubolaisi Road residence, we moved again to rented quarters at 2028 Jing'ansi (Bubbling Well) Road. Though the rented quarters we lived in were cramped, this never bothered her. Throughout the war years she was constantly concerned about national affairs and the welfare of the people.

In the spring of 1941 she reached her ninetieth year. Even those who didn't understand such things considered this a great event in the world of men. She specially ordered a vegetarian banquet for the closest relatives, but she would not allow a congratulatory celebration. In 1942, as spring turned into summer, she was frequently bothered with coughing and spitting up and had a slight fever. The doctor examined her regularly and gave her medicine, but it had little effect. When winter came, it turned suddenly cold; she developed nephritis along with the coughing and spitting. In December 1942 her capacity to take food diminished daily. She appeared to be steadily declining in strength. We changed doctors several times and tried both Chinese and Western medicine to treat her symptoms. At first there was some improvement, but in the long run it was to no avail. On December 30, 1942, late in the afternoon, she died peacefully. She was in her ninety-first year. She had made disposition of her affairs. The previous evening she spoke to each of us with words of comfort and encouragement. Nearly all her sons and daughters, their spouses, and her grandchildren and great-grandchildren were by her side. She led a full and perfect life. Rightly, she had no regrets.

TRANSLATOR'S AFTERWORD

Will Mrs. Nie's testimony stand in the court of historical inquiry? In the main, the account of her life and the fortunes of her family correlates with developments in Chinese civilization during her lifetime. In another sense, however, the record of her life takes her readers a few steps farther along the path of historical understanding.

A central theme in recent studies of nineteenth- and twentieth-century China is continuity. William Rowe's investigation of nineteenth-century urban society in Hankow points to the comparative calm that prevailed in that city throughout a period of economic, demographic, and cultural change.[1] The late nineteenth and early twentieth centuries, an era once seen as a time of sharp departures from traditional patterns of civilization—military defeat in 1895, political upheaval in 1911, intellectual revolt in 1919—is now viewed, by some, as a time of continuous evolution of the inherited civilization. Studies that point to the continuity between the Self-strengthening era of the late nineteenth century and political and economic modernization in the early twentieth, in the words of Paul Cohen, see "self-strengthening as a stage in longer term processes that instead of grinding to a complete and ignominious halt in 1895 continue well into the present century."[2]

Chinese scholars concerned with the question of continuity in Chinese civilization from the late nineteenth to the early twentieth centuries have turned their attention to the development of capitalism. Some have observed that the government-supervised merchant enterprises initiated during the Self-strengthening movement "made it possible to begin to transform funds obtained from land rents, commercial profits, usury, and corruption into productive capital," and that this "played a principal role in promoting the development of national capitalism." One view is that among those who financed and operated the government-supervised merchant enterprises it was the merchants, rather than the officials, who emerged as the capitalists of the twentieth century.[3]

Mrs. Nie's family exemplified some aspects of this pattern. Nie Qigui invested funds gleaned from the traditional economy and his official salary in government-supervised merchant enterprises. When the opportunity arose to buy up stock in the financially troubled New Huaxin Cotton Mill, the family mobilized the risk capital necessary to do so and transformed it into a private enterprise. The Nies' official pedigree did not cramp their style as they assumed the role of twentieth-century capitalist entrepreneurs. It may have enhanced it.

Shen Chuanjing of Sichuan University has reconsidered the role of capitalist development in his interpretation of the evolution of modern Chinese society. While retaining a fundamentally Marxist approach, Shen sees the growth of capitalism as well as anti-imperialism and antifeudalism as basic impulses driving the development of Chinese civilization in the late nineteenth and twentieth centuries. The emergence of the capitalist class was linked to anti-imperialism and antifeudalism in the struggle for independence, democracy, and, especially, national strength and prosperity. This struggle, Shen observes, passed through five successive stages: the Taiping Rebellion, the Self-strengthening movement, the Reform movement, the 1911 Revolution, and the New Culture movement.[4]

Rowe's study of nineteenth-century Hankow identifies the urban elite, the incipient bourgeoisie, as an important force for social cohesion and progress during the Taiping era and the Self-strengthening years.[5] Marie-Claire Bergere's work on the Chinese bourgeoisie in the twentieth century explicates the growth of capitalism from its nineteenth-century roots well into the 1930s, emphasizing the last three stages of Shen's formulation. She observes that the new bourgeoisie—merchants and businessmen—gained prominence and influence in China only after the 1911 Revolution, though Rowe's study of Hankow notes the emerging leadership of the commercial class in noneconomic and governmental affairs throughout the nineteenth century. The Western commercial presence in the treaty ports in the late nineteenth century accelerated economic changes already under way. This, in turn, provided opportunities and incentives not only for merchants but also for gentry—officeholders and holders of civil service degrees—to invest in China's economic future. A fusion of merchant and gentry groups in business undertakings resulted. This unstable alliance, known as the *shen-shang*, or gentry-merchants, reflected the early evolving stage of Chinese capitalism and the strength of the gentry in traditional Chinese society.

The decline of government authority in the early twentieth century opened the way for increased merchant activity and influence within the alliance, but it was not until the withdrawal of the European imperialist influence in east Asia during World War I that the Chinese bourgeoisie began to flourish. This prosperity continued in the postwar years, centered in the treaty ports and the foreign concessions, where bourgeois enterprises were sheltered from the disruptive warlord fighting that plagued China's hinterlands.[6]

The transition of the Nie family from bureaucratic elite—gentry—to bourgeoisie took place within this fused social group, the *shen-shang*. The conversion of the joint government-merchant New Huaxin Cotton Mill to the privately owned Heng Feng Cotton Mill in 1908 and Nie Qijie's emergence as a cotton entrepreneur and business leader during and after World War I exemplify the gradual assumption of bourgeois functions by representatives of the bureaucratic elite. Bergere cites Nie Qijie as an example of the emergence of the new *shen-shang*, which might be termed the embourgeoisement of the Chinese gentry.[7]

Mrs. Nie does not tell her readers much about the business affairs of her family after the reorganization of the Heng Feng Cotton Mill in 1918–19. This may have been because of the disagreements among family members concerning management of the mill or the downturn in family fortunes occasioned by the renewal of imperialist competition in the Shanghai cotton industry in 1923. In any case, she never mentions Qijie's relinquishing the leadership of Heng Feng to his younger brother in 1924. This is due, perhaps, to her advanced age and growing preoccupation with internal family matters and cultural affairs. But it may also reflect her displeasure with the self-interested squabbling of the younger generation and the decline of her personal influence and government connections. After the establishment of the Nationalist government in 1928, bureaucratic controls were gradually extended over the bourgeois economy. Less than a decade after Mrs. Nie's death in 1942, the complete "rebureaucratization" of the Chinese economy under the People's Republic marked the end of bourgeois influence in twentieth-century China.[8]

If Mrs. Nie's autobiography gives us an account of her family's changing role in the Chinese elite that conforms generally to the historical record, her revelations regarding herself reveal a distinctive face in the historical crowd, a woman who clung to traditional values in a time of wrenching change. In a century when the emancipation of women was an issue of growing importance in China, Mrs. Nie had hardly a word to say on the subject, other than a few obliquely disparaging references. It was not that she was unconcerned with the difficulties that were often the lot of Chinese women. The unhappy arranged marriages of her sisters seemed tragic but unavoidable to her. Restricted educational opportunities brought her disappointment but were not a cause for resentment or rebellion. Bound feet, twelve pregnancies, and a husband with a penchant for concubines were features of traditional family life that she accepted unquestioningly, but self-induced abortion was an alternative she also felt was hers.

Where does the autobiography of such a woman fit in the complex mosaic of literature by and about Chinese women during the late nineteenth and early twentieth centuries?[9] The attraction that autobiography holds for its readers stems from the candid disclosure of individual and family matters and the personalized perspective on the times.[10] If the author is a woman, there is the further presumption that the disclosures will enrich the record of human experience and the social history of times constructed largely by male writers. Mrs. Nie's autobiography does this, but because of her conformity to traditional social norms and her high social status, she reveals less than the modern Western reader might hope for, and her disclosures and perspectives differ from those of women of her day who saw themselves as agents of change or victims.[11] Furthermore, her reserve—her Confucian sense of propriety—led her to choose the *ziding nianpu*, the chronological autobiography, a genre suited principally for historical writing rather than self-disclosure.[12] Though Mrs. Nie tells her readers less than they might hope for of her feelings and views as a woman, indirectly she probably reveals more than she intended to.

The lives of the Chinese women we meet in the biographical and autobiographical literature of the late nineteenth and early twentieth centuries usually move in one of the two broad historical currents: continuity and change.[13] Mrs. Nie's life moved in both. Her life story is a mine of information concerning a traditional Chinese family distinguished by its social prominence, affluence, adaptability, and mobility. Moreover, Mrs. Nie's life reflects the tension between values handed down through this family and the pressures of social, economic, and political upheaval, pressures she neither embraces nor dismisses. In coping with this tension she reveals intellectual acumen and emotional flexibility. Sometimes her actions belie her self-proclaimed conservatism. Often they are at odds with the familiar image of traditional Chinese women as prisoners of their families and victims of social change. Nor can her ability to cope be dismissed as the consequence of her affluent and well-connected family circumstances. Similar circumstances smothered the individuality of her sisters. But Mrs. Nie was different; she found ways to express her individuality though she would never acknowledge her desire to do so.

Li Yuning has studied the tension between inherited values and social, economic, and political change in the lives of Chinese women of the late nineteenth and early twentieth centuries. Mrs. Nie's life exemplifies what Li sees as the positive influence that the traditional values of diligence, fairness, and duty have had on women in modern China. Diligence Li defines as keeping abreast of the times; fairness, as the recognition of women's capacities; and duty, as the fulfilling of responsibilities to the family and the nation. She observes that studies of the history of women in modern China have emphasized reform and often overlooked the contributions of tradition.[14] Mrs. Nie's account of her life is a step toward redressing this historical imbalance, toward restoring tradition to its rightful place in understanding modern Chinese women.

Mrs. Nie was a positive person. She exemplifies the filial piety and moral activism of the neo-Confucian tradition epitomized by her father. For the most part, she idealized her father. She encouraged her husband, respected and admired her mother-in-law, and nurtured and guided her children. She never stepped beyond the bounds of her place in the family: still she used her personal connections to secure bureaucratic positions for her husband, her judgment and vision to prepare her sons for business opportunities, and her personal funds to shore up family resources. She transformed the traditional family into an arena where she could exert her personal influence internally and broker prestige and social status externally, all for the benefit of family members. She recorded it all in language that disguises their moral lapses and reflects favorably on all. Given that she saw Confucian filial piety and Confucian and Christian moral activism as her missions in life, the traditional family and women's role within it were very well suited for her to accomplish these ends. Further emancipation probably appeared meaningless to her.

I have noted the adaptability of the Nie family to the commercial environment of the twentieth century. It is clear, however, from Mrs. Nie's autobiography that this was change within tradition. Important values of the traditional gentry were retained and infused with new meaning.[15] Education came to concentrate on new subjects appropriate to a new stage in China's civilization. Civic responsibility and works of social welfare, long the province of the Confucian gentry, remained important functions of this new bourgeois family. Respect for the aged, frugality, preservation of traditional culture, dedication to learning, humility, humanism, and religious eclecticism—all ideals of the Confucian gentry—were among the moral principles that motivated Mrs. Nie and her family members in their new circumstances.

The May Fourth movement of 1919, China's revolution in thought and values, passed unnoted in Mrs. Nie's autobiography; and not surprisingly, for preserving inherited values, not rejecting them, was the province of this family. A rejection of these values was neither relevant nor appropriate to Mrs. Nie or her family members; they were adapting successfully to the challenges of a new era. Somehow, in China of the 1930s—a country torn by insurrection, invasion, and militarism—for many the importance of these values was lost just as the status of the bourgeoisie gave way to the bureaucrats and the soldiers. Mrs. Nie, however, remained to the end—as she remains for her readers today—an exemplar of personal cultivation in the modern tradition of Confucianism.

NOTES

Preface

1 I have identified the following editions of Mrs. Nie's autobiography: *Chongde laoren bashi ziding nianpu* (The chronological biography of a parent of great virtue, edited by herself at age eighty), with portrait and calligraphy (1931); *Chongde laoren bashi ziding nianpu* (Shanghai, 1933); *Chongde laoren bashi ziding nianpu*, rev. ed. (1935); "Chongde laoren ziding nianpu" (Chronological biography of a parent of great virtue edited by herself), published following her death in 1942, including a synopsis of the last decade of her life by her son-in-law Qu Duizhi, subsequently republished on Taiwan with other materials related to the Nie family in Nie Qijie, ed., "Chongde laoren jiniance" (Memorial volume for a parent of great virtue), in Shen Yunlong, gen. ed., *Jindai zhongguo shiliao congkan* (Collected historical materials on modern China), 3d ser., no. 22 (Taipei: Wenhai chubanshe, 1966), 307–45; "Chongde laoren ziding nianpu," in Yang Yunhui, ed., *Zeng Baosun huiyilu* (The memoirs of Zeng Baosun) (Changsha: Yuelu shushe, 1986).

This translation is based on the Taiwan reprint edition and draws on related materials from "Chongde laoren jiniance."

2 The *nianpu* (chronological or annalistic biography) first appeared during the Song dynasty (960–1278). Early chronological biographies were often catalogs of the writings of prominent men of letters arranged chronologically and juxtaposed with autobiographical data to facilitate dating and determination of the historical context of each writing. The first chronological autobiography (*zixu nianpu*) was that of the celebrated Song loyalist Wen Tianxiang (1236–83). The popularity of the chronological autobiography grew slowly until the Ming dynasty (1368–1644), when it became quite widespread. In the nineteenth century the form experienced an unprecedented surge in popularity, surpassing all other forms of autobiographical writing. In the twentieth century, after the introduction of Western autobiography and the vernacular as the literary lan-

guage, the writing of chronological autobiography declined. Through the Ming dynasty chronological autobiographies remained formal in tone, reflecting the quasi-catalog character of the *nianpu* from which they were derived. See Wu Pei-yi, *Confucian's Progress*, 32–43. Mrs. Nie's chronological autobiography reflects the formal style and literary language of earlier chronological autobiographies but introduces some materials that disclose her feelings and attitudes. It probably represents a stage in the transition toward the twentieth-century trend of writing more personally revealing autobiographies. Mrs. Nie's is a *ziding nianpu* (self-edited chronological biography), indicating that she arranged and prepared the materials but may not have personally written all of the text.

3 Kann, *Currencies of China*; King, *Money and Monetary Policy in China*.

Introduction: Cultural and Historical Setting

1 The most comprehensive bibliography of the voluminous literature on Chinese women that I am familiar with is Karen T. Wei's *Women in China: A Selected and Annotated Bibliography* (1984), which includes sections on biographies, autobiographies, and memoirs as well as works of historical perspective. See also the discussion on literature pertaining to Chinese women in the translator's afterword of this volume.

2 Mary C. Wright, *Last Stand of Chinese Conservatism*, 127.

3 Chang Chung-li, *Chinese Gentry*, 102, 122, 126.

4 Bergere, *Chinese Bourgeoisie*, 37–60.

5 Chang Chung-li, *Chinese Gentry*, 165.

6 Ho Ping-ti, "Salient Aspects of China's Heritage," 9–27.

7 Chang Chung-li, *Chinese Gentry*, 3–32, 174, 197–98.

8 Smith, *Cultural Heritage*, 46–50.

9 M. C. Wright, *Last Stand of Chinese Conservatism*, 79–84, 129–33.

10 Chang Chung-li, *Chinese Gentry*, 11–13.

11 Ch'u, *Local Government*, 107–11.

12 Ibid., 111–12.

13 Porter, *Tseng Kuo-fan's Private Bureaucracy*, 121–29.

14 Liu, *Orthodoxy in Late Imperial China*, 281–310.

15 Smith, *Cultural Heritage*, 212–13.

16 Ibid., 64–65.

17 Ibid., 216, 252–53.

18 Reischauer and Fairbank, *East Asia: The Great Tradition*, 224–25; Smith, *Cultural Heritage*, 216–17.

19 Ebrey, *Chinese Civilization and Society*, 245–48; Levy, *Chinese Footbinding*.

20 One of the five Confucian classics dating from the first century B.C. Chai Ch'u and Winberg Chai, eds., *Li Chi*, 1:202–8 and tables following 208.

21 Smith, *Cultural Heritage*, 147–49.

22 Ibid., 149–55.

23 *Ciyuan*, 363.

24 Smith, *Cultural Heritage*, 219–25.

25 Ibid., 215.

26 One of the five Confucian classics dating from the Zhou dynasty (1027–256 B.C.). Fung, *History of Chinese Philosophy*, 1:379–95; Smith, *Fortune-Tellers and Philosophers*, 93–129.

27 Smith, *Cultural Heritage*, 226, 233–35.

28 Ibid., 236, 240.

29 Ibid., 187–89, 197–200, 230–32.

30 Hook, *Cambridge Encyclopedia of China*, 140, 144; Unschuld, *Medicine in China: A History of Ideas*; Unschuld, *Medicine in China: A History of Pharmaceutics*.

31 Lin, *Importance of Living*, 248.

32 Hook, *Cambridge Encyclopedia of China*, 144, 149, 150; Huard and Wong, *Chinese Medicine*, 154–59.

33 Teng and Fairbank, *China's Response to the West*. An example of the response paradigm may be found in the popular text by Fairbank, Reischauer, and Craig, *East Asia Tradition and Transformation*, which has appeared in various revisions since the early 1960s. It should be noted that Fairbank has criticized and departed somewhat from this paradigm in his more recent formulation: Fairbank, *Great Chinese Revolution*, 41.

34 Studies by Chinese and Chinese-American scholars in Western languages that focus on developments in Chinese civilization only marginally related to China's "response to the West" include Ho Ping-ti, *Studies on the Population of China* and *Ladder of Success in Imperial China*; Chang Chung-li, *Chinese Gentry*; Hsiao Kung-chuan, *A Modern China and a New World: K'ang Yu-wei, Reformer and Utopian*; Chang Hao, "On the Ching-shih Ideal in Neo-Confucianism."

35 Fan Wenlan, *Zhongguo jindaishi*; Hu Sheng, *Imperialism and Chinese Politics*.

36 These studies differ from the studies by Chinese and Chinese-American scholars on subjects largely unrelated to the Western pressures on China cited in note 34. These works deal with subjects readily susceptible to interpretation according to the response paradigm: the Opium Wars, rationalization for reform, and intellectual change. But the extensive use of Chinese source materials seems to have led the authors to more balanced interpretations. See, for ex-

ample, Chang Hsin-pao, *Commissioner Lin and the Opium War*; Chang Hao, *Liang Ch'i-ch'ao and Intellectual Transition in China*; Y. C. Wang, *Chinese Intellectuals and the West*; Rowe, *Hankow Commerce and Society in a Chinese City*, 341–46. An even broader conceptual view of the inherent dynamism of nineteenth-century Confucianism is elaborated in the works of William Theodore de Bary: *Unfolding of Neo-Confucianism*, 1–32; and *East Asian Civilization*, 67–104. Thomas Metzger also points to neo-Confucian ideology as a source of inspiration for transformative and revolutionary changes in nineteenth- and twentieth-century China; see *Escape from Predicament*, 16–18.

37 Liu Kwang-Ching, "The Ch'ing Restoration."

38 Cohen, *Discovering History in China*, 9–55.

39 Ho Ping-ti, *Population of China*, 24–64, 270–78.

40 Smith, *Cultural Heritage*, 51–53; Ho Ping-ti, "The Significance of the Ch'ing Period," 189–95.

41 Lawrence D. Kessler, "Ethnic Composition of Provincial Leadership during the Ch'ing Dynasty"; Liu, "The Ch'ing Restoration," 409–17.

42 Ho Ping-ti, "The Significance of the Ch'ing Period," 195.

43 Jen Yu-wen, *Taiping Revolutionary Movement*; Kuhn, "The Taiping Rebellion," 264–310.

44 Chiang Siang-Tseh, *Nian Rebellion*; Kuhn, "The Taiping Rebellion," 310–16; Liu, "The Ch'ing Restoration," 456–77.

45 Chang Hsin-Pao, *Commissioner Lin and the Opium War*, 1–50.

46 Ibid., 51–217.

47 Wakeman, "The Canton Trade and the Opium War," 195–212; Fairbank, "The Creation of the Treaty System," 213–63.

48 Cohen, "Christian Missions and Their Impact to 1900," 543–90.

49 Morse, *Trade and Administration of the Chinese Empire*, 323–51.

50 Kennedy, *Arms of Kiangnan*, 25–33; Giquel, *Journal of the Chinese Civil War*; Smith, *Mercenaries and Mandarins*.

51 Kennedy, *Arms of Kiangnan*, 45–49, 53–54, 58–66, 79–87, 99–112, 123–39, 149–60.

52 Biggerstaff, *Earliest Modern Government Schools in China*, 154–99.

53 Feuerwerker, *China's Early Industrialization*, 9–12; W. K. K. Chan, *Merchants, Mandarins and Modern Enterprise*, 89–92; Kennedy, *Arms of Kiangnan*, 125–26.

54 Kennedy, "Self-strengthening: An Analysis Based on Some Recent Writing," 7–28.

55 Hsu, "Late Ch'ing Foreign Relations," 84–109; Liu and Smith, "The Military Challenge: The Northwest and the Coast," 209–11.

56 Cohen, *China and Christianity*, 63–273.

57 Hsu, "Late Ch'ing Foreign Relations," 85–88.

58 Hsu, *Ili Crisis*.

59 Leibo, *Transferring Technology to China*, 132–52; Chere, *Diplomacy of the Sino-French War*.

60 Rawlinson, *China's Struggle for Naval Development*, 129–97; Wu Hsiang-hsiang, "The Construction of the Summer Palace and Naval Funds in the Late Ch'ing Dynasty," 28–34.

61 Fairbank, Reischauer, and Craig, *East Asia: The Modern Transformation*, 469.

62 Hsu, "Late Ch'ing Foreign Relations," 101–9.

63 Ibid., 109–15, 130–41.

64 Chang Hao, *Liang Ch'i-ch'ao*, 25–34.

65 Hsiao, *A Modern China and a New World*, 193–406.

66 Chang Hao, "Intellectual Change and the Reform Movement," 318–29.

67 Esherick, *Origins of the Boxer Uprising*, 235–40, 257–313.

68 Tan, *Boxer Catastrophe*, 76–242.

69 Ichiko, "Political and Institutional Reform," 398–402.

70 M. C. Wright, *China in Revolution*, 19–21, 142–226.

71 W. K. K. Chan, "Government Merchants and Industry to 1911," 434–43; Bergere, "Chinese Bourgeoisie, 1911–1937," 724–29; Y. C. Wang, *Chinese Intellectuals and the West*, 254–79.

72 Ayers, *Chang Chih-tung and Educational Reform in China*, 196–244.

73 Huang, *Liang Ch'i-ch'ao*, 36–83.

74 Y. C. Wang, *Chinese Intellectuals and the West*, 229–54.

75 Ibid., 279–94.

76 Ibid., 294–305; Eto and Schiffrin, *1911 Revolution in China*, 153–223.

77 E. P. Young, *Presidency of Yuan Shih-k'ai*, 122–29, 138–76, 210–40.

78 Ibid., 186–92; Borton, *Japan's Modern Century*, 291–95.

79 Bergere, *Chinese Bourgeoisie*, 37–83; Chen Zhen and Yao Luo, *Zhongguo jindai gongyeshi ziliao*, 1:55–56.

80 Chow, *May Fourth Movement*, 19–83.

81 Sheridan, "The Warlord Era," 284–381.

82 Li Chien-nung, *Political History of China*, 363–67; A. B. Chan, *Arming the Chinese*, 13–17; Sheridan, "The Warlord Era," 308.

83 Chow, *May Fourth Movement*, 84–116.

84 Schwartz, "May Fourth and After," 406–8.

85 Ch'en, "Chinese Communist Movement to 1927," 505–18.

86 Wilbur, "The Nationalist Revolution," 537; Bergere, *Chinese Bourgeoisie*, 213–41; Wilbur, *Sun Yat-sen*, 96–111.

87 Ch'en, "Chinese Communist Movement to 1927," 505–26.
88 Wilbur, "The Nationalist Revolution," 527–720.
89 Eastman, "Nanking Decade," 151–60.
90 Ch'en, "The Communist Movement 1927–1937," 183–220.
91 Eto, "China's International Relations," 111–15.
92 Iriye, "Japanese Aggression," 492–504.
93 Ibid., 504–19.
94 Ch'en, "The Communist Movement 1927–1937," 220–25; Van Slyke, "The Chinese Communist Movement during the Sino-Japanese War," 610–11.
95 Eastman, "Nanking Decade," 547–57.
96 Ibid., 557–608.
97 Hsu, *Rise of Modern China*, 601–5.

Chapter One. A Soldier's Daughter

1 November 26, 1811–March 12, 1872; courtesy name Bohan, literary name Xiusheng, the first Marquis Yiyong, posthumous title Wenzheng. Imperial official, militia leader, imperial commissioner for the suppression of the Taiping Revolution, governor general of the Liangjiang provinces, and governor general of Zhili. In addition to his official positions, Zeng Guofan was well known as a neo-Confucian scholar; he was awarded the *jinshi* in 1838 and became a compiler of the Hanlin Academy. He was founder of the Xiang (Hunan) Army, architect of the Qing dynasty's victory over the Taipings, a leader of the struggle against the Nian Rebellion, and one of the originators of the Self-strengthening movement, in which he promoted military-industrial modernization and technological education. Zhu Dongan, *Zeng Guofan zhuan*; He Yikun, *Zeng Guofan pingzhuan*; Hummel, *Eminent Chinese*, 771–75; Cai, *Qingdai qibai mingren zhuan*, 1036–47.
2 Daughter of Ouyang Cangming (1787–1869) of the Hengyang District of Hunan (see note 5). Li Enhan, *Zeng Jize de waijiao*.
3 Courtesy name Zhuting, imperially bestowed title *guanglu dafu* (grand master for splendid happiness). Failed the district-level civil service examinations seventeen times before earning the first degree, *shengyuan*, in 1832, just one year before his son Zeng Guofan did. Zeng Guofan, *Quanji*, vol. 5, *nianpu*, 2–3; Jian Yuwen, *Taiping Tianguo*, 2:1039.
4 Known for frugality in managing her home. She bore nine children: five sons and four daughters. Zeng Guofan was her second child and oldest son. Jian, *Taiping Tianguo*, 2:1039; Zeng Guofan, *Quanji*, vol. 1, *wenji*, 228.

5 Courtesy name Futian, of the Hengyang District of Hunan. Ouyang Cangming was a *linsheng* (a district-level government stipendiary in the civil service system) and a friend of Zeng Guofan's father, Zeng Linshu, with whom he arranged his daughter's marriage to Zeng Guofan. In the 1860s, the court awarded him the honorary title *fengzhi dafu* (grand master for forthright service). Li Enhan, *Zeng Jize de waijiao,* 1; Zeng Guofan, *Quanji,* vol. 1, *wenji,* 243–44; vol. 5, *nianpu,* 2.

6 Not otherwise identified. Madam Qiu bore two sons and two daughters. In the early 1860s, the court awarded her the honorary title *yiren* (lady of suitability). Zeng Guofan, *Quanji,* vol. 5, *wenji,* 244.

7 December 7, 1839–March 12, 1890; courtesy name Jigang, posthumous title Huimin. Oldest son of Zeng Guofan, diplomat and imperial official. After the death of Zeng Guofan in 1872, Zeng Jize inherited the title of marquis. From 1878 until 1885, he served as China's minister to Britain and France. In 1880 he was also named minister to Russia; in that capacity he negotiated the Treaty of St. Petersburg restoring the Ili region to China. Li Enhan, *Zeng Jize de waijiao;* Hummel, *Eminent Chinese,* 746–47.

8 Courtesy name Xingang. The court conferred on him the honorary title *guanglu dafu* (grand master for splendid happiness). Zeng Yuping had three sons: Zeng Linshu, the oldest and father of Zeng Guofan; Zeng Dingzun, who died in infancy; and Zeng Jiyun. Hummel, *Eminent Chinese,* 751; Zeng Guofan, *Quanji,* vol. 1, *wenji,* 226–27; vol. 4, *riji,* 14; Jian, *Taiping Tianguo,* 2:1039.

9 Also known as the Hunan Army. Zeng Guofan recruited the Hunan Army from local defense corps in Hunan in the first half of 1853. It grew to a strength of over 120,000—including naval and cavalry units—before Zeng Guofan demobilized most units in 1864–66 following the defeat of the Taipings. The Hunan Army was provincially based and financed largely through local trade taxes known as *likin*. Wang Ermin, *Qingji junshishi lunji,* 1–302; Long Shengyun, *Xiangjun shigao.*

10 The title vice president of the Board of War carried with it no power or authority. It no doubt was awarded to Zeng on the advice of imperial officials who were apprehensive of his growing military power. Zeng, however, had declined the governorship of Hubei, a substantive and more powerful post, because he was still in the ritual three-year period of mourning following the death of his mother. The court probably realized he would decline the governorship before they offered it to him. Jen, *Taiping Revolutionary Movement,* 242–43.

11 October 12, 1814–November 13, 1890; courtesy name Yuanpu, literary name

Shuchun, posthumous title Zhongxiang. Zeng Guoquan earned the *jinshi* in 1855. He commanded the Hunan Army forces that recaptured Nanjing from the Taipings in 1864 and subsequently served as governor of Hubei (1865–67), governor of Shanxi (1877–80), governor general of Guangdong and Guangxi (1882–83), and governor general of the Liangjiang provinces (Jiangsu, Jiangxi, and Anhui; 1884–90). He died while incumbent in the Liangjiang post. Hummel, *Eminent Chinese*, 749–51; Cai, *Qingdai qibai mingren zhuan*, 1138–42.

12 Courtesy name Wenpu, posthumous title Minlie. Zeng Guohua was killed in battle at Sanhe in central Anhui in 1858. Hummel, *Eminent Chinese*, 755; Jen, *Taiping Revolutionary Movement*, 329–41.

13 Courtesy name Jihong; name changed to Zeng Zhenhan, courtesy name Shiheng, posthumous title Jingyi. Hummel, *Eminent Chinese*, 755; Jen, *Taiping Revolutionary Movement*, 404, 417, 514–15.

14 Courtesy name Chenghou. Zeng Guohuang was a *jiansheng*, holder of the lowest civil service degree, obtainable by purchase, and an expectant district magistrate. He married a woman named Wang. Hummel, *Eminent Chinese*, 755; Zeng Guofan, *Quanji*, vol. 1, *wenji*, 227.

15 Daughter of He Changling (1785–1848) of the Shanhua District of Hunan, former governor general of Yunan and Guizhou and editor of the *Huangchao jingshi wenbian* (Imperial documents on statecraft) in 1827. Madam He married Zeng Jize on April 25, 1856, when he was seventeen. She died the next year in childbirth. Li Enhan, *Zeng Jize de waijiao*, 6; Hummel, *Eminent Chinese*, 281–82.

16 Smith, *Fortune-Tellers and Philosophers*, 221–33.

17 *Ao* is rendered here as "valley." *Cihai*, 1218.

18 Original given name Peicheng, a native of the Gui District of Guangxi. Chen Yucheng was a military leader and hero of the Taipings. After internal strife resulted in a thinning of the leadership of the Taipings in 1856, Chen emerged as one of several highly effective commanders until his capture and execution by imperial forces in Henan in 1862. In 1859, in recognition of his military accomplishments, he was named Ying Wang (Brave Prince). Hummel, *Eminent Chinese*, 104–6; Cai, *Qingdai qibai mingren zhuan*, 1889–92.

19 Courtesy name Gaoxuan, younger brother of Zeng Guofan's father. Zeng Guofan, *Quanji*, vol. 5, *nianpu*, 1, 71.

20 November 10, 1812–September 5, 1885; courtesy names Jigao, Pucun; literary names Laoliang, Zhongjie, Xiansheng; posthumous title Wenxiang. A native of the Xiangyin District of Hunan, Zuo Zongtang passed the provincial-level civil service examinations for the degree of *juren* in 1832 but took and failed the

metropolitan examination for the degree of *jinshi* three times. He commanded troops of the Hunan Army against the Taipings in Jiangxi and Zhejiang; served as governor general of Fujian and Zhejiang (1863–66) and governor general of Shaanxi and Gansu (1866–80), during which time he pacified the Nian and Muslim rebellions in those provinces. While governor general of Shaanxi and Gansu, he regained control of the northwest region, which in 1884 became the province of Xinjiang. He was governor general of the Liangjiang provinces (1881–84) and imperial commissioner in charge of military affairs in Fujian (1884–85), where he directed operations against the French in the Sino-French War (1883–85). Zuo died several months after a peace was signed in Fuzhou. Gideon Chen, *Tso Tsung-t'ang*; Hummel, *Eminent Chinese*, 762–67; Dai Yi and Lin Yanjiao, *Qingdai renwu zhuangao*, 67–75; Cai, *Qingdai qibai mingren zhuan*, 1399–1412.

21 Courtesy name Mengrong, literary name Xiaxian. Liu Rong was a native of the Xiangxiang District of Hunan who served as governor of Shaanxi (1863–65). Lu Baoqian, *Liu Rong nianpu*.

22 Courtesy name Mengheng, died c. 1871. The following material on Zeng Jifen's sisters and their husbands is drawn from Shen Yunlong, *Jindaishiliao kaoshi*, 1:74, 79.

23 Courtesy name Zhongkun, died in 1881 in France.

24 Courtesy name Fengru.

25 January 19, 1808–April 12, 1856; courtesy name Zhongyue, literary name Loshan, posthumous title Zhongjie. A native of the Xiangxiang District of Hunan, Lo Zenan earned the *jinshi* in 1847. Hummel, *Eminent Chinese*, 540–41; Cai, *Qingdai qibai mingren zhuan*, 988–91.

26 Courtesy name Licheng. Known for his ability in mathematics, he was also a student of English, which he studied for the purpose of consulting English books. His granddaughter attributed his premature death (at age thirty-four in Beijing) to exhaustion from overzealous pursuit of his studies, which brought on tuberculosis, and to despair over his failure on the civil service examinations for the *jinshi* degree. Yang Yunhui, ed., *Zeng Baosun*, 1–2; Hummel, *Eminent Chinese*, 755.

27 James Legge, in *Chinese Classics*, 1:12–21, discusses the evolution of this text. Various translations are available, including Legge, 1:137–354.

28 *Cihai*, 2728; Chai Ch'u and Winberg Chai, eds., *Li Chi Book of Rites*, 1:15–17, 59–98.

29 Courtesy name Xueqin, posthumous title Gangzhi. A native of Hengyang Dis-

trict of Hunan, Peng Yulin was leader of the naval forces of the Hunan Army in the struggle against the Taipings. Hummel, *Eminent Chinese*, 617–20; Cai, *Qingdai qibai mingren zhuan*, 1233–42.

30 One of the architectural wonders of ancient China, the Yueyang Tower was originally built during the Tang dynasty (A.D. 618–907) in the year 716. Its beauty inspired poetry by Du Fu (712–770) which is carved on tablets and hung on the walls of the tower. The most celebrated literary tribute is "Yueyang lou ji" (Recalling Yueyang Tower), an essay by Fan Zhongyan (989–1052), written when the tower was rebuilt in 1045 overlooking Baling Prefecture during the Song dynasty (A.D. 960–1279). Rebuilt again in 1867, it is situated at the West Gate of the city of Yueyang where the Yangzi enters Dongting Lake. It has three stories and is 19.72 meters high, 17.24 meters wide, and 14.54 meters deep. Guojia wenwu shiye guanliju, *Zhongguo mingsheng zidian*, 784; *Cihai*, 1806. Fan's "Yueyang lou ji" may be found in Zhao Cong, ed., *Guwen guanzhi xinbian*, 912–14.

The ancient site of Huanghe Tower was at the head of the Huanghe promentory in She Mountain (also known as Huanghe Mountain), in what is today Wuhan Municipality in Hubei. According to tradition it was constructed in A.D. 223, during the Three Kingdoms (220–263). During the succeeding centuries it was destroyed and rebuilt many times. Huanghe Tower inspired poetry by Li Bo (701–762) and Cui Hao (d. 754) of the Tang dynasty (618–907) and Lu You (1125–1210) of the Song dynasty (960–1271). In the 1980s it was torn down and rebuilt at the bridge over the Yangzi at Wuhan. *Cihai*, 4710. Guojia wenwu shiye guanliju, *Zhongguo mingsheng zidian*, 727. A translation of Cui Hao's poem "Huanghe lou" (Yellow Crane Terrace) can be found in Witter Bynner, trans., *Three Hundred Poems of the T'ang Dynasty*, 142–43.

31 The Guo family originated in the Qishui District of Hubei. Guo Peilin (1809–59, courtesy name Zhongzhai, literary name Liangsan), head of the family, was awarded the *jinshi* degree in 1838, the same year as Zeng Guofan, and became a compiler of the Hanlin Academy. In 1853 he was named controller of the Lianghuai Salt District. He fell in battle against the Taipings at Dingyuan in Anhui. Li Yuning, *Jindai zhonghua funu zixu*, 61.

32 The Buddha of Immeasurable Light who presided over the Pure Land or Western Heaven. Smith, *Cultural Heritage*, 140–41.

33 Courtesy name Renshen. A native of the Huaxian District of Guangdong, Hong Xiuquan was the founder, religious leader, and king of the Taiping Revolutionary movement (1851–66). After the city wall of Nanjing was breached on

July 19, 1864, troops of the Hunan Army under the command of Zeng Guoquan poured into the city, looting and burning the residences of Taiping leaders. Estimates of those killed vary from 10,000 to more than 100,000, though the latter figure is highly improbable. The sack of Nanjing by the Hunan Army greatly enriched Zeng Guoquan and his generals but earned the revulsion of many of their comrades-in-arms.

Zeng Guofan arrived in Nanjing on July 28, 1864, and persuaded his brother to feign illness and leave the city. Zeng Guofan's subsequent report to the throne covered up the brutality and rapaciousness of Hunan Army units commanded by his brother, claiming that the Taiping leaders had stripped the city before it fell. Hummel, *Eminent Chinese*, 361–67; Jen, *Taiping Revolutionary Movement*, 13–57, 529–36.

34 February 15, 1823–November 7, 1901; courtesy names Zifu and Jianfu, literary names Shaoquan and Yisou, posthumous title Wenzhong. A native of Hefei in Anhui, Li Hongzhang was a leading provincial official during the second half of the nineteenth century. He was awarded the *jinshi* degree in 1847 and later became a compiler of the Hanlin Academy. He joined Zeng Guofan's staff in 1858, recruited the Anhui Army, and cooperated with foreigners in the defense of Shanghai (1862–64). Li served briefly as governor of Jiangsu, governor general of the Liangjiang and Lianghu provinces (Hubei and Hunan), and from 1870 to 1895 as governor general of the metropolitan province of Zhili. He later served as governor general of the Liangguang provinces (Guangdong and Guangxi, 1899–1901). Li was instrumental in crushing the Nian Rebellion in 1868. He introduced numerous military, naval, and economic reforms and was active in diplomatic negotiations on China's behalf with the major imperialist powers. Hummel, *Eminent Chinese*, 464–71; Lei Luqing, *Li Hongzhang xinzhuan*; Yuan Shu-yi, *Li Hongzhang zhuan*.

35 January 17, 1779–July 12, 1839; courtesy name Zilin, literary name Yunting, posthumous title Wenyi. Tao Zhu was a native of the Anhua District of Hunan. He earned the *jinshi* degree in 1802 and became a compiler of the Hanlin Academy in 1805. He held a series of provincial posts before being named governor of Anhui in 1823 and of Jiangsu in 1825. He was promoted to governor general of the Liangjiang provinces in 1830, a post he held until several months before his death, when illness forced him to retire. Hummel, *Eminent Chinese*, 710–11; Cai, *Qingdai qibai mingren zhuan*, 583–91; Wei Xiumei, *Tao Zhu zai jiangnan*, 3–12.

36 Literally, "thinking of clouds." The implication of this name is not clear. It may

refer to the courtesy name of a historical figure from the Qing period. Zhang Qiyun, *Zhongwen da zidian*, 4:47.

37 The word for delicate is *xi* (Giles, *Chinese-English Dictionary*, 518, entry 4163). It may have been used because it rhymes with the final syllable of the term for emperor, *di*. Mrs. Nie's characterization of the country people as ignorant probably refers to the inference that Zeng could become emperor because he had defeated the Taipings.

38 Popularly known as Seng Wang, a Mongol prince who served the Qing dynasty as a commander of the banner forces. He was successful in turning back the northern campaign of the Taipings (1853–55) but was unable to keep the combined British and French forces from entering Beijing in 1860. He commanded operations in north China against the Nian rebels until he fell in battle in 1865. Hummel, *Eminent Chinese*, 632–34; Cai, *Qingdai qibai mingren zhuan*, 980–87.

39 Courtesy name Songfen, literary name Yifang. A native of the Qishui District of Hubei, Guo Yun married Zeng Jihong, third son of Zeng Guofan, who contracted tuberculosis and died in 1881, leaving Guo Yun with four sons and a daughter. Guo Yun was educated in the classics, a poet, and the author of a well-known account of her experiences during the Taiping Revolution, *Binan shimo ji*. She had an independent spirit and advocated equal opportunities in education for women. Li Yuning, *Jindai zhonghua funu zixu*, 59–75.

40 Courtesy name Yiyong, given name Gangji, oldest son of Guo Songtao. Hummel, *Eminent Chinese*, 439.

41 April 11, 1818–July 18, 1891; courtesy names Bochen and Yunxian, literary name Yuchi Laoren. Guo Songtao was a native of the Xiangyin District in Hunan who, as a youth, became a close friend of Zeng Guofan while studying in Changsha. In 1847 he earned the *jinshi* and was inducted into the Hanlin Academy. Guo fought against the Taipings in the Hunan Army under Zeng's command in the early 1850s and in the Second Opium War (1859–60). By this time he had become an advocate of improved understanding of foreign countries' aims in China and the use of diplomacy rather than force in dealing with them. His controversial views on foreign affairs resulted in his dismissal from the governorship of Guangdong in 1866. Nevertheless, he had powerful backers, among them Li Hongzhang. The murder of British interpreter Augustus R. Margary in Yunnan Province in 1875 resulted in the signing of the Chefoo Convention in September 1876, conceding further imperialist privilege to Great Britain and binding China to an official apology mission to the British Crown. Guo was selected to head the apology mission and was concurrently named China's ambassador to the Court of St. James's; he was China's first diplomat

in the Western world. His appointment and service in Great Britain precipitated the most vicious and slanderous attacks by conservatives (in China), who viewed him as an appeaser of imperialism and a servant of the hated foreigner. Guo was allowed to return to China in 1879 and was replaced by Mrs. Nie's brother Zeng Jize. He lived in semiretirement in Hunan until his death in 1891, when Li Hongzhang succeeded in having his name entered in the Bureau of National History. Hummel, *Eminent Chinese*, 438–39; Hsu, *China's Entrance into the Family of Nations*, 180–90.

42 Meaning uncertain. *Wushi* literally is "fifty." It is rendered here as the name, probably a familiar name, of one of Zeng Guofan's nieces. To render it as "fifty" would signify that Zeng had fifty nieces and that he sent wedding presents for all at the same time. If he had done this, each niece would have received only two taels and approximately six inches of material. Eliminating this alternative, the familiar name seems the most plausible translation. Original text is in *Zeng Guofan shouxie riji*, twenty-fourth day, seventh month, ninth year of the Xianfeng reign (1859).

43 Courtesy name Changqi, posthumous title Wujing. A native of Changsha in Hunan, Huang Yisheng was orphaned at an early age and entered the military service at age thirteen. He was nominated by Zeng Guofan for naval service and subsequently distinguished himself in engagements against the Taipings. Zeng placed him in charge of the Yangzi naval force. Huang also campagined against the Nian. Cai, *Qingdai qibai mingren zhuan*, 1131–38.

44 Given name Yichen, courtesy names Weixi and Huixi. A native of Hangzhou, Shao Yichen passed the provincial-level civil service examinations for the degree of *juren* in 1831. Shao served as an imperial and provincial official and was well known as a scholar and bibliophile. Hummel, *Eminent Chinese*, 638.

Chapter 2. Zeng Guofan's Final Years

1 Mrs. Nie added these recollections about the work schedule to the *nianpu* in late September or early October 1941. The schedule itself had already been incorporated into the text under the year 1868. Nie Qijie, "Chongde laoren jiniance," 304.

2 Ibid., 304.

3 During the Ming (1368–1644) and Qing (1644–1912) dynasties, historians wrote general histories of China in the style employed by Zhu Xi (1130–1200) in his *Tongjian gangmu* (Selective mirror of history). This work selected and arranged

the events recorded in Sima Guang's (1019–86) *Zizhi tongjian* (General mirror for the aid of government) to emphasize the moral lessons of history. Examples of this genre are Yuan Huang's *Yuan Liaofan gangjian* (Yuan Liaofan's selective mirror), written during the Ming period, and Wu Chengquan's *Gangjian yizhilu* (Selective record of changing knowledge), written during the Qing period. *Cihai*, 2642.

"Official dynastic histories" refers to the twenty-four dynastic histories beginning with the *Shiji* (Annals of history) by Sima Qian (?145–90 B.C.). These histories were designated the official histories of the Chinese dynasties during the Qianlong reign (1736–96) of the Qing dynasty. *Cihai*, 3121.

4 The Nanjing Arsenal (Jinling Zhizaoju), one of China's earliest machine industries, was established outside the south gate of Nanjing in 1865 by then Liangjian governor general Li Hongzhang. Its principal mission in the late 1860s was the production of ordnance and ammunition for the Anhui Army in its struggle with the Nian rebels. The Nanjing Arsenal was under the supervision of the Liangjiang governor general, the office held by Zeng Guofan from April 10, 1867 until September 6, 1868. Kennedy, *Arms of Kiangnan*, 49–50, 66–70.

5 Traditional Chinese algebra, *tian yuan*, included solving equations by finding common denominators as in contemporary algebra. *Ciyuan*, 684. Other algebraic functions, such as linear and quadratic equations and the binomial theorem, were derived in China independently of Western mathematics. Ronan, *Shorter Science and Civilization in China*, 2:46–60.

6 Cohen, *China and Christianity*, 229–61.

7 November 3, 1821–August 23, 1870; courtesy name Gushan, literary names Yanmen and Tiefang. A native of Caozhou in Shandong Province, Ma Xinyi came from a Muslim family; he earned the *jinshi* in 1847. Ma held a variety of subprovincial and provincial posts until early 1868, when he was named governor general of Fujian and Zhejiang provinces. Later the same year, he was appointed governor general of the Liangjiang provinces. Ma's assassination was the subject of an imperial investigation; the assassin's motives were identified as revenge for personal damages suffered as a result of Ma's reform policies. Rumors persisted, however, that Ma had been in league with Muslim rebels and that high officials had conspired in his assassination. The assassination was conveniently timed to provide a high-level opening into which the court could move Zeng Guofan at a time when Zeng had incurred the wrath of antiforeign officials and gentry in north China by condemning perpetrators of the Tianjin Massacre to death and sending culpable officials into exile.

Among the antiforeign elements in north China Zeng was seen as an appeaser and a coward. Hummel, *Eminent Chinese*, 554–56. The modern view of Zeng as an appeaser of imperialism and a traitor owes much to Marxist historian Fan Wenlan's treatment of Zeng's disposition of the Tianjin Massacre case. Fan, *Zhongguo jindaishi*, 1:428–29. However, Fan's attack on Zeng may have been politically inspired; it was formulated and written at the Chinese Communist headquarters at Yanan during World War II in what appears to have been a counterattack on the near deification of Zeng that was promoted by the rival Guomindang (Nationalist) party under Chiang Kai-shek in an effort to restore public confidence in traditional Chinese values during a time of national crisis. Fan, *Zhongguo jindaishi*, 1:1; M. C. Wright, *Last Stand of Chinese Conservatism*, 305–8.

8 The career of Sir Samuel Halliday Macartney (1833–1906) epitomizes some of the problems associated with foreign technical personnel in China in the late nineteenth century. Macartney, a physician, left the British forces in China to join the staff of Li Hongzhang, whom he encouraged to establish machine production of arms and ammunition. Macartney served as director of the Nanjing Arsenal from 1865 to 1875. His tenure was marred by disputes with the Chinese staff and was terminated abruptly in 1875 when ordnance built under his supervision exploded and killed several members of a Chinese gun crew. Subsequently, Macartney served as secretary and counselor of the Chinese diplomatic mission in London. Boulger, *Life of Sir Halliday Macartney*; Kennedy, *Arms of Kiangnan*, 67–70.

9 The term used here, *gebi*, means, literally, "to cut flesh from the arm," which usually refers to an act intended to express undying love. In this context *gebi* is used for *gegu*, literally, "to cut flesh from the thigh" to be given to a sick parent to revive him or her, an act of filial piety. *Cihai*, 437.

Chapter 3. My Marriage and Life in Hunan

1 Courtesy name Zhongfang, posthumously referred to as Zhongcheng (governor), and native of Hengshan District in Hunan. After Nie's marriage to Zeng Jifen in 1875, he held minor posts in the Yunnan Likin Bureau, the Hubei Salt Distribution Bureau, and the Liangjiang Military Secretariat at Nanjing until 1883, when he was named deputy director of the Jiangnan Arsenal in Shanghai. In 1884, Governor General Zuo Zongtang of Liangjiang appointed Nie director of the Jiangnan Arsenal. Nie purchased the office of taotai on Taiwan

in 1886 through his brother-in-law Chen Zhantang, an official on the island, but Nie never actually took office in Taiwan. In 1890, on the recommendation of Zeng Jifen's uncle, Governor General Zeng Guoquan of Liangjiang, Nie was named taotai of the Suzhou-Songjiang-Taicang Circuit in eastern Jiangsu, also known as the Shanghai taotai. He was just thirty-five, the youngest official appointed to this post after the opening of Shanghai to foreign trade in 1842. Indeed, the average age of appointment to this post in the nineteenth century was approximately forty-nine. In this post Nie supervised the Imperial Maritime Customs at Shanghai. During his tenure as Shanghai taotai he acquired 54,000 taels worth of stock in the joint government-privately owned New Huaxin Cotton Mill established in 1891. In 1894 he also became an investor in the Huasheng Cotton Mill. Both of these plants enjoyed the backing of Governor General Li Hongzhang of Zhili. In 1894, on the recommendation of Taiwan governor Shao Youlian, Nie was named to a post in the Grain Tribute Bureau in Taiwan.

Nie's departure from the Shanghai taotai post was adumbrated and delayed for more than a year by a shortage of 800,000 taels in the funds for which he was responsible. Though Mrs. Nie attributes this shortage principally to the peculation of an accountant, Nie presumably used some of these funds to acquire his initial increment of stock in the New Huaxin Cotton Mill. Nie was eventually successful in balancing his books—though just how is unclear—and transferring the seals of office to his successor. Later, when the assets of the accountant were confiscated, stock in the New Huaxin Cotton Mill, greatly depreciated in value, was turned over to Nie. The matter of the shortage in the Shanghai taotai's funds and Nie's delay in leaving Shanghai was handled with the utmost discretion. It entirely escaped the notice of the ever-vigilant foreign press in Shanghai, which attributed the delay to difficulties in finding an appropriate successor and lamented Nie's departure, lauding his skill in dealing with foreigners and calling for public recognition of his achievements.

Nie left Shanghai in early 1895 to take office as provincial judge of Zhejiang, a post to which he had been named the previous year. In 1896 he became financial commissioner of Jiangsu, and, in 1899, acting governor. In 1900 he participated in negotiations with the treaty powers in Beijing to reduce tariffs. When these were interrupted by the Boxer Uprising, he returned to his post as financial commissioner of Jiangsu, serving again as acting governor. With other governors of southeastern provinces Nie acted to suppress antiforeign activities in south China and negotiated with foreign consuls in Shanghai to bar foreign troops from those provinces. Late in 1900 he was named governor of Hubei, but before he took office he was transferred to the governorship of Jiangsu. In 1901 Nie was made governor of Anhui, and in 1903 governor of Zhejiang. In 1904, acting through a new accountant, Tang Kuisheng, Nie acquired additional stock in the bankrupt New Huaxin Cotton Mill and leased it to the Futai Company, a firm that he and Tang established. Continuing to act through Tang, Nie acquired two-thirds interest in the New Huaxin Mill and placed it under the management of his son Nie Qijie. The first year's operations were a huge success thanks to the relaxation of imperialist competition in the cotton industry during the Russo-Japanese War (1904–5). The following year, 1905, Tang died and the Nie family gained sole control of the Futai Company, which continued to lease the New Huaxin Mill. Nie Qijie served as manager, and another son, Nie Qiwei, as assistant manager. Though Nie Qigui remained in the background during these dealings to avoid the appearance of engaging in business transactions while occupying high government office, it is clear that the acquisition of stock in the New Huaxin Mill and its lease to the Futai Company were done with his approval.

In 1905, pursuant to charges by imperial censors that he had mishandled government funds and engaged in cronyism while supervising the Zhejiang Provincial Mint, Nie was cashiered. In the same year he purchased more than six thousand acres of shoreline property reclaimed from the marshland along the northern shore of Dongting Lake. In 1908 the Futai Company's lease on the New Huaxin Mill expired. Since the cotton business was booming, the original stockholders of the New Huaxin Mill attempted to regain control. The Nie family then called a meeting of the board of directors and used their controlling financial interest to force a decision to sell New Huaxin's assets to compensate the original stockholders. As a result of the sale, the Nie family acquired sole ownership of the New Huaxin Cotton Mill for the price of 317,500 taels, renaming it Heng Feng. Since the Nies owned so much of the stock already, their actual outlay was only about 100,000 taels. Mrs. Nie maintains that the funds for the takeover of the New Huaxin Mill were borrowed and repaid over the next several decades. The likelihood exists, however, that they were part of the funds missing from the Shanghai taotai's accounts in 1894.

Nie succumbed in March 1911 to an illness contracted while caring for his ailing mother, who preceded him to the grave by only a few weeks. He was honored posthumously by the imperial court as a model of filial piety. Though Nie never passed a civil service examination, he had a long and distinguished official career, partly because of Zeng Jifen's powerful family connections. He moved effortlessly from the role of government official to that of private capitalist. Mrs. Nie's autobiography is the principal source of information on the life and career of Nie Qigui, further controversial aspects of which will be discussed in annotations as they appear in the following pages. See also Chen Xulu, Fang, and Wei, *Zhongguo jindaishi cidian*, 563; W. K. K. Chan, *Merchants, Mandarins and Modern Enterprise*, 55–56; Chen Zhen and Yao Luo, *Zhongguo jindai gongyeshi ziliao*, 1:397; Mesny, *Mesny's Chinese Miscellany*, 2:470; Li Xin and Sun Sibai, *Minguo renwuzhuan*, 249–50; Zhongguo kexueyuan jingji yanjiuso, *Heng Feng shachangde fasheng fazhan yu gaizao*, 3–5. *North China Herald*, Jan. 12, Feb. 16, 23, March 2, 9, 16, May 18, 25, June 1, July 15, and Sept. 14, 1894; Leung, *Shanghai Taotai*, 28–29.

2 Courtesy name Xiaoyen. A native of Nanchang in Jiangxi Province, Mei Qizhao passed the metropolitan examinations for the *jinshi* degree in 1852 and was named provincial judge of Guangdong in 1867, financial commissioner of Jiangsu in 1869, and governor of Zhejiang in 1877; he was ordered to Beijing to await assignment in 1879, named junior vice president of the Board of War in 1881, director general of conservation of the Yellow River and the Grand Canal in the same year, deprived of official rank in 1883, and died at age sixty-nine. Wei Xiumei, *Qingji zhiguan biao*, 2:20.

3 Zengzi (505–437 B.C.), courtesy name Ziyu, also known as Zengcan. A native of Wucheng in Confucius's native state of Lu in the present-day province of Shandong, Zengzi is one of the best-known disciples of Confucius. He is the putative author of parts of the *Daxue* (Great learning) and the *Xiaojing* (Classic of filial piety). To him are attributed extremes of filially pious behavior, for which he is renowned. He is said to have experienced a heart tremor when his mother bit her finger and to have divorced his wife for having served his mother some badly stewed pears. *Cihai*, 686; Giles, *Chinese Biographical Dictionary*, 2:768–69.

4 Zeng Guofan compiled or wrote at least thirty-seven works. The more important of these can be found in the so-called complete collection first published in 1876 and republished several times. The 1965 edition includes the following titles: essays, poems, letters, memorials to the throne, letters to his family, instructions to family members, diary, endorsements on correspondence, miscellaneous writings, biography, and chronological biography. Zeng Guofan, *Quanji*. Previously unpublished letters and a handwritten diary have been published separately. Zeng Guofan, *Weikan xingao*; Zeng Guofan, *Shouxie riji*; Hummel, *Eminent Chinese*, 755.

5 One of China's five sacred mountains, Mount Heng is located in the Hengshan District in eastern Hunan south of Changsha overlooking the Xiang River. It is a granite formation with seventy-two peaks, of which Zhurong (1,290 meters) is the most spectacular. It was previously known as Nanyue (south mountain) since it was the southernmost of the five sacred mountains. Each mountain was named for one of the four cardinal points of the compass, and one for the center. *Cihai*, 1859; Guojia wenwu shiye guanliju, ed., *Zhongguo mingsheng zidian*, 802.

6 The usual three-year mourning period following the death of a parent was actually interpreted as twenty-seven months. The date given here for the termination of mourning was in the twenty-eighth month following the death of Nie Erkang in the summer of 1872. Ch'u Chai and Winberg Chai, *Li Chi Book of Rites*, 1:205, 2:391.

7 The suggestion that the marriage be held one hundred days after Madam Ouyang's death was based on the rules for abbreviating mourning in the *Qing Tong Li* (General ritual practices of the Qing period), a work on rituals and ceremonies compiled during the Qianlong (1736–96) and Jiaqing (1796–1821) reigns. It was based on the ancient practice of terminating continuous wailing for the deceased after one hundred days, thereafter wailing only once in the morning and once in the evening. Taiwan Zhonghua Shuju bianjibu, *Cihai*, 469; *Ciyuan*, 416; *Cihai*, 2194.

8 West of the Xiang River (literally Xiangxi) may refer specifically to the area west of the river and south of the city of Xiangtan. This area had historically been known as Xiangxi. Playfair, *Cities and Towns of China*, 196.

9 Traditional geomancy, or the pseudoscience of *fengshui* (wind and water), has been employed in China from the earliest times to determine the locations for dwellings, cities, and burial sites. Geomancy is based on the assumption that the earth, like the human body, is an organism with channels through which the earth's natural energy (*qi*) flows in the same way that blood flows through the veins of the human body. Natural energy is maximized at places where these channels converge, and these are the most auspicious sites for dwellings, graves, and so on. Artificial or man-made channels such as roads or ditches can bring evil influences and are to be avoided. Geomancy determines the extent of the beneficial and evil forces influencing any site and its suitability for a dwelling, a grave, or a settlement. It is based on the belief that the welfare of individuals and groups is dependent on a harmonious relationship with the natural surroundings and conformity with the movements of heaven

and earth. A variety of means are employed by the practitioner of geomancy to select auspicious sites; for example, intuition, manuals explaining where natural energy occurs, and the geomancer's compass, which correlates an individual's personal data with astrological data and the conformation of the earth. Hook, *Cambridge Encyclopedia of China*, 306–7.

10 Carved wooden tablets bearing an ancestor's name, the number of his generation, his official titles, and his wives' surnames played a prominent role in the worship or veneration of ancestors as practiced by most Chinese lineages prior to 1949. Originally founded on the belief that there is a reciprocal relationship between the living and the spirits of the deceased, the propitiation of ancestral spirits became highly ritualized. Tablets bearing the names of recently deceased ancestors were placed on altars in individual homes. Large families built ancestral halls with altars on which tablets bearing the names of even distant ancestors were placed. Rituals conducted in such halls included ceremonies in which elders of the lineage assembled before the tablets to pay their respects. Hook, *Cambridge Encyclopedia of China*, 307–9.

11 *Cihai*, 996.

12 The account of this incident is adapted from Nie Qijie, "Chongde laoren jiniance," 301.

13 This was possibly a posthumous adoption, since Chunfan was older than Nie Erkang, who died in 1872, and Qichang was born in 1879. Furthermore, Qichang lived with his natural parents.

14 He Changlin, *Huangchao jingshi wenbian*. Originally compiled in 1821, this work includes essays on the theory and practice of government administration by scholars of the empirical school of Confucianism that flourished in the eighteenth century. The essays on practice are grouped under titles corresponding to the six boards of the imperial government: Civil Appointments, Finance, Rites, War, Justice, and Public Works. Eight later editions were issued between 1882 and 1902, entitled either *jingshi wen xinpian* (New documents on statecraft) or *jingshi wenxupian* (Further documents on statecraft), reflecting the significance of this collection as a handbook dealing with the practical problems of day-to-day administration. Wakeman, "Huang-ch'ao ching-shih wen-pien," 8–22.

15 I have not located this work. Gangzhou, which no longer exists as a contemporary place-name, was situated in what today is Xinhui District in coastal Guangdong. Zang, *Zhongguo gujin diming dacidian*, 458.

16 *Likin* was a mercantile tax instituted in Jiangsu Province in 1853 to support

forces battling the Taipings. Its literal meaning is "a tax of one-thousandth of the value." *Likin* was adopted by most provinces in the next several decades; it was levied on goods in transit, in inventory, and at the place of production. The rate varied from 2 to 10 percent in different localities. Collection and control of *likin* revenues were largely in the hands of provincial authorities; as such it was an important source of financial autonomy from the imperial government. *Likin* was instituted in Yunnan, in southwest China, in 1874. Lo Yudong, *Zhongguo lijin shi*, 1:1–54, 2:423–29.

17 December 16, 1818–August 14, 1887; courtesy name Zimo, literary name Yinqu, posthumous title Wushen gong. A native of Xining in Hunan. In 1849 Liu became a *bagongsheng*, or senior licentiate, through a special examination administered every twelve years to selected individuals. *Bagongsheng* were eligible for appointment to provincial office and for admission to higher examinations. Liu distinguished himself in fighting against the Taipings and in the Nian Rebellion. He served as governor of Guangxi, governor general of Guangdong and Guangxi, governor general of the metropolitan province of Zhili, and governor of Guangdong before being named governor general of Yunnan and Guizhou in 1876. He retired from that post in 1883 and died at his home in Hunan in 1887. During the Taiping Revolution, Liu Changyou served as a commander in the Hunan forces under the overall command of Mrs. Nie's father, Zeng Guofan. Hummel, *Eminent Chinese*, 515–16; Chang Chung-li, *Chinese Gentry*, 28; Michael, *Taiping Rebellion*, 1:119.

18 For a discussion of Zeng Jize's posting and the experiences of China's early envoys in Britain see Hsu, *China's Entrance into the Family of Nations*, 186–90. Early envoys observed that at the Court of St. James's, women danced in evening gowns "half naked" and men in skin-colored tight trousers. "From a distance it looks as if the lower body were bare. Most disgraceful to look at."

19 Courtesy name Dishan. Chonghou, a Manchu of the Wanyen clan, passed the provincial civil service examinations for the degree of *juren* in 1849. After filling a series of minor posts, he was assigned to the staff of the Mongol general Senggelinqin in the Second Opium War. He subsequently served as commissioner of northern ports, headed the mission of apology to France following the Tianjin Massacre, and served in China's first governmental agency dealing with foreign affairs, the Tsungli Yamen. In 1878 he was appointed ambassador to Russia to negotiate the return of the Ili territory. However, the Treaty of Livadia, which Chonghou signed in 1879, relinquished a large portion of Ili to Russia and committed China to a large indemnity (see note 20 below). After

he returned to China in 1880, Chonghou was denounced by conservatives and sentenced to death by beheading. He was saved from this fate, apparently, by the appeals of more moderate officials and the protests of European powers and the United States, including a personal appeal to spare his life by Queen Victoria to the Empress Dowager. Later that year Chonghou was released and partially rehabilitated, but he never reentered public life. Hsu, *Ili Crisis*, 47–94; Hummel, *Eminent Chinese*, 209–11.

20 The Treaty of Livadia between China and czarist Russia was signed on October 2, 1879, by Chinese envoy Chonghou. Though it nominally returned the strategic Ili territory on China's northwest border to China, it actually ceded 70 percent of the territory to Russia, awarded Russia an indemnity of five million rubles, gave Russia the right to open new consulates, established a large duty-free zone for Russian imports, and opened the Sungari River in Manchuria to Russian navigation. Hsu, *Ili Crisis*, 51–58.

21 The Shanhaiguan is at the eastern terminus of the Great Wall in Hebei Province fifteen kilometers northeast of the city of Qinghuangdao and about three hundred kilometers east-northeast of Beijing. Established in 1381, it takes its name because the pass (*guan*) is situated between the mountains (*shan*) and the sea (*hai*). It is of great strategic importance for the defense of north China from invaders. The Manchu conquest of China in 1644 came through the Shanhaiguan. Though the Treaty of Livadia between China and Russia was to go into effect upon ratification by both sides within one year from the signing, the Chinese government rejected its terms. The Chinese expected Russian pressure to secure ratification. Western consuls in China warned that Russia might invade Manchuria with twenty thousand men and land another six thousand in the Liaodong peninsula in south Manchuria. The Shanhaiguan was the most likely place for such forces to cross the Great Wall, invade north China, and threaten Beijing. The imperial government deployed its best troops under the command of generals—most of whom were Hunanese veterans of Zeng Guofan's Hunan Army—to defend the Shanhaiguan and the area northeast of Beijing. Zeng Jize's successful renegotiation of the Treaty of Livadia spared China the threatened military confrontation with Russia. Guojia wenwu shiye guanliju, ed., *Zhongguo mingsheng zidian*, 115; Hsu, *Ili Crisis*, 95–101.

22 The Treaty of St. Petersburg, signed on February 24, 1881, restored most of the Ili territory to Chinese control and reduced the number of Russian consulates to two in return for an increased indemnity of nine million rubles. Generally considered a diplomatic victory for China, the gains made at St. Petersburg

can be credited to Zeng Jize's careful preparation and well-planned strategy, which contrasted sharply with the perfunctory approach to negotiations taken by his predecessor, Chonghou, in negotiating the Treaty of Livadia. Zeng Jize's negotiations were also aided by Russia's desire to avoid conflict at a time when its economy was still feeling the effects of the Turkish War (1876–77), the government was isolated diplomatically following the Congress of Berlin (1878), and the court was fearful of a growing revolutionary movement. The Treaty of St. Petersburg encouraged the hard-liners in China's leadership (the Qingyi group) to resist Western demands even at risk of war. It also opened the way in 1884 for the incorporation of the northwest border regions into the empire as the province of Xinjiang. Li Enhan, *Zeng Jize de waijiao*, 63–163.

23 From at least the third century B.C. the imperial government had maintained an official monopoly on the production, sale, and distribution of salt. The salt monopoly (or gabelle) was based on the fact that in China, more so than in other traditional societies, there was an inelastic demand for salt as a dietary supplement. This arose from the predominance of cereals and the infrequency of meat in the Chinese diet. In addition to the universal demand for salt throughout China's huge populace, it was produced only in certain areas; if the government did not control production and distribution, private interests readily could. In the 1830s Tao Zhu, governor general of the Liangjiang provinces, introduced a system designed to break the monopoly of the handful of merchant families who under government licenses had gained complete control of the sale and distribution of salt. Under this system permits to purchase from the producer, transport, and sell salt were issued to anyone who made full payment in advance. Fairbank, Reischauer, and Craig, *East Asia: The Modern Transformation*, 113–16; M. C. Wright, *Last Stand of Chinese Conservatism*, 170–73; Wei Xiumei, *Tao Zhu zai jiangnan*, 41–49, 122–58, 283, 285, 289, 293, 297, 299.

24 This was a prefectural-level post in the office that supervised the state monopoly on salt and tea. Brunnert and Hagelstrom, *Present Day Political Organization of China*, 429.

25 The unicorn of Chinese mythology is very unlike its European cousin. It is depicted with one to three horns or a single horn covered with fur. Various descriptions give it fish scales, an ox's tail, cloven hoofs, or five-toed feet. It is one of the four supernatural creatures and symbolizes a family of many children. It also is regarded as symbolizing goodness and appears when the empire is well governed, but on occasion has been understood to mean just the opposite. Eberhard, *Dictionary of Chinese Symbols*, 303–4.

26 In traditional Chinese culture, dreams were regarded as experiences of the soul, which can leave the body during sleep to fulfill one's desires. They were interpreted as oracles of things to come by professional interpreters of dreams. Though interpreters are now rare, books that interpret dreams are in frequent use. The *Zhougong jiemeng*, attributed to the duke of Zhou (c. 1050 B.C.), is one popular work that purports to interpret dreams. Eberhard, *Dictionary of Chinese Symbols*, 86.

27 Courtesy name Yuntai, also known as Mr. C. C. Nieh; Nie Qijie was well known during his life as a cotton entrepreneur and advocate of education. Born in Changsha, he was brought to Shanghai at age two by his parents when his father became director of the Jiangnan Arsenal in that city. He was educated by private tutors and studied English with Mrs. John Fryer, wife of the well-known translator at the Jiangnan Arsenal, and with Miss M. Lawrence of Hangzhou during his father's tenure as provincial judge of Zhejiang. Though his study of English was limited to an hour or so each day over a period of no more than two years, he became known for his excellent command of the language. He pursued studies in electrical and chemical engineering informally and acquired a reputation as an efficient engineer. Nie Qijie married Ms. Xiao of Taihe in Anhui Province in 1898. In 1904–5, at age twenty-five, partially through capital and influence provided by his father, Nie became manager and partial owner of the Futai Company, which controlled the New Huaxin Cotton Mill. In 1908 the Nie family bought Futai and changed the name to Heng Feng (see note 1, above). Under the direction of Nie Qijie and assistant director Nie Qiwei (a.k.a. Guanchen, 1883–?), the Heng Feng Cotton Mill was reorganized and modernized. During World War I, with competition from foreign cotton mills greatly reduced, Heng Feng's market share grew and profits soared. The mill was expanded steadily, reaching capitalization of 1.5 million taels with thirty-five thousand spindles and more than fifteen hundred employees.

Nie Qijie established a technical school at the mill in 1909 under the direction of two Japanese engineers. Heng Feng also provided scholarships for students at the technical college at Nantongzhou as well as in France and the United States. Nie expanded his educational activities to include cooperative ties with the Department of Agriculture of Nanjing University to promote industrial development. In 1917 he founded the Chinese Vocational Education Association. Nie established a vocational school in Shanghai which gained national recognition and, in 1920, a larger one which included a cotton mill, foundry, and workshop. In 1917 he traveled in the United States as vice chairman of the

Chinese Commercial Commission. In this capacity he invited American cotton experts to visit China, which they subsequently did.

The reinvestment of profits in the modernization of production facilities at Heng Feng did not begin until after 1919. Prior to that time a large part of the mill's earnings were diverted to improvements in the Zhongfuyuan, a huge agricultural enterprise on reclaimed land along the northern shore of Dongting Lake purchased by Nie Qigui in 1904 (see chapter 7, note 8). Through 1915, the Nie family drained more than 600,000 yuan from Heng Feng to pay for the startup costs of the Zhongfuyuan. From 1916 on, the Zhongfuyuan began to show a profit from the rents that the Nies exacted from its more than three thousand tenant families. It then began to provide funds to Heng Feng.

In 1918, as a result of a dispute between members of the Nie family, the family holdings were divided into nine shares. The Heng Feng Cotton Mill was transformed into a partnership which included Mrs. Nie, Nie Qijie, and his brothers. Nie Qijie was named general manager. The position of assistant manager went to his brother, Nie Qiying (Lusheng, 1897–?). The Zhongfuyuan was not included in the division of property; it remained the property of the whole family, though Nie Qijie actually wielded the power.

After World War I, the Chinese cotton industry continued to flourish for several years. Nie Qijie invested profits from Heng Feng and rent income from the Zhongfuyuan in new production equipment. In addition, he established a second Heng Feng plant and a weaving plant. In June 1919 he began planning and raising capital for the Dazhonghua (Great China) Cotton Mill at Yunzaobang in Wusong (in the vicinity of Shanghai). Of the 900,000 taels capital required for the Great China Mill, the Nie family provided 230,000. Investors were enthusiastic, and the plant was completed and entered production in 1922. Nie Qijie was chairman of the board of directors and general manager. At this time, he also raised capital and together with other entrepreneurs established the Datong Textile Company on Chongming Island, the Huafeng Textile Company, the Zhongguo Tiegongchang (China Ironworks Company), and the Zhong Mei maoyi gongsi (China-U.S. Trading Company), serving as chairman of the board of directors, board member, or general manager in these firms. Nie also acquired interests in other cotton mills, including Dasheng (Dah Sun) at Tongzhou, the Dasheng branch on Chongming Island, and the Anglo-Chinese Cotton Mill of Shanghai. He established the Textile Trade Institute (Shabu jiaoyiso) and served as its first chairman. Members of the institute speculated through the Hengda Cotton Brokerage, which Nie also founded. In 1921 he opened the Xie Feng Grain Depot in Changsha, one of the largest in Hunan (see chapter 7, note 8). By 1920, thanks to the success of the Nie family enterprises, Nie Qijie was the acknowledged leader of Shanghai commerce. In that year he was elected director of the Shanghai General Chamber of Commerce and deputy director of the Chinese Cotton Mill Owners' Association, which he had organized in 1918.

Though Heng Feng grew to forty-one thousand spindles, more than six hundred looms, and three thousand plus workers by 1921, it did not develop as rapidly as other Chinese cotton mills. Nie family relationships may have inhibited efficient management. In 1923, a sharp increase in the influx of foreign capital caused a crisis in the Chinese cotton industry. Nie Qijie's industries all suffered serious setbacks. During 1923–24 Heng Feng had to stop production. In 1924, to maintain operations, it became necessary to borrow 600,000 taels from the Heng Long Bank. After that Heng Feng existed on long-term loans. Within three years after the Great China Cotton Mill began operations, it also sustained serious losses from foreign competition. In August 1924 the Nies were forced to sell the Great China Mill at a loss of more than 300,000 taels. The China-U.S. Trading Company lost 300,000–400,000 taels, and the Heng Feng Mill, deep in the red, was taken over by Japanese merchants. Creditors attempted to sell the China Ironwork Company, but it was destroyed by fire during the Japanese invasion of Shanghai in February 1932. The collapse of Nie Qijie's business empire forced him in 1924 to step down as leader of the family business in favor of his younger brother Nie Qiying (Lusheng). Though Qijie remained active behind the scenes, Qiying gradually assumed leadership in the family and at the Heng Feng Mill.

Nie Qijie advocated shortening the industrial workday from twelve to eight hours; his concern for workers' health was linked to a desire for greater efficiency in production. In the years 1920–26, three thousand workers were employed at Heng Feng. The majority were women, but there were many children as well. The wage scale was among the lowest in the Shanghai cotton industry, and the workers were subject to various kinds of exactions and fines. In 1923 the workers struck, protesting the arbitrary withholding of wages, and were successful in obtaining their demands. The Chinese Communist party approved an evening school for workers at Heng Feng and set up a communist organization. Thereafter, there was a successful Communist-led strike almost every year. At Heng Feng workers were active in the May 30, 1925, incident protesting imperialist domination of China's economy. Nie Qijie secured the cooperation of the Shanghai Municipal Council, the governing body of the International Concession, to dispatch police from the concessions to arrest and detain strikers; the leaders of the workers' movement were discharged. During the Northern Expedition in 1926, Nie Qijie publicly attacked the Communist-led anti-imperialist activities of the workers and peasants, appealing to the teaching of Confucius and Gandhi.

In the same year Nie became a director of the Shanghai Municipal Council. Though he retained the title of general manager at Heng Feng, he was no longer active. That year, he barely survived a serious illness. Nie's health problems persisted and he became despondent. Though he was baptized a Christian in 1915, he now embraced vegetarianism and Buddhist devotional practices, eventually becoming a devout Buddhist. In 1943 he lost a leg to tuberculosis of the bone. Thereafter, he was even less involved with business matters.

While under the direction of Nie Qiying (Lusheng) in 1929, Heng Feng borrowed 2.4 million taels from the Xingye Bank of Zhejiang to repay old debts and build a third plant. In the fall of 1935, all the Heng Feng plants were forced to shut down, and the following year, the Xingye Bank, with the Nies' approval, leased Heng Feng to the China Cotton Company, headed by T. V. Soong (Song Ziwen, 1894–1971), brother-in-law of president Chiang Kai-shek. Its name was changed to the Heng Feng zhongji fangzhi xinju (New Hengfeng Centrally Registered Textile Bureau). After war with Japan broke out in 1937, the China Cotton Company withdrew from its leasing agreement with the Xingye Bank. To protect Heng Feng's creditors from a Japanese takeover, the Xingye Bank and the Nie family registered Heng Feng as the property of British merchants. This failed to stop the Japanese military, who seized the plants in May 1938. In 1942 Heng Feng merged with the Japanese Daiko Cotton Mill and registered with the Japanese occupation government as the Heng Feng Spinning Corporation (Koho boseki kabushikikaisha), with half of its capital provided by Japan and half by China. The Nies repaid the debt owed to the Xingye Bank from the funds supplied by the Japanese.

After the Japanese defeat in 1945, Nie Qiying (Lusheng), who had worked with the occupation authorities and served as a member of the puppet government's All-China Commercial Control Commission, stepped aside. Nie Qijie, despite his physical handicap, resumed his role as leader of family affairs and spokesman. When the Nationalist government returned to Shanghai, Heng Feng was taken over by the Ministry of Economics. Nie Qijie appealed to Minister of Economics T. V. Soong, while Nie Qijie's son Nie Guangkun (a.k.a.

Liukang or Hanzhang, 1901–?) approached his second cousin, Deputy Minister of War Yu Dawei, who also lobbied T. V. Soong in the Nies' behalf. (Zeng Guangshan, daughter of Mrs. Nie's older brother Zeng Jihong, married Yu Mingyi in 1889.) Nie Qijie was also able to influence Xu Jiqu and Liu Gongyun, Nationalist officials in charge of the disposition of repossessed enemy property. The upshot was that in March 1946, Nie regained control of Heng Feng, Yu Dawei and his mother both received substantial quantities of Heng Feng stock, and Yu Dawei was named to the board of directors. Nie Qiying (Lusheng) avoided any adverse consequences for his collaboration with the Japanese.

Although Nie Qijie regained control of Heng Feng, the Nie family had been weakened financially by World War II and was no longer able to operate the plant. Consequently, they asked cotton magnates Wu Xilin and Wu Bainian to join the company, which they then converted into a joint stock company with Nie Qijie as chairman of the board, Nie Guangkun as general manager, and Wu Bainian as manager.

After the Nie and Wu families became the managers of Heng Feng, they speculated with circulating capital provided by the Wus. Taking advantage of Nationalist government economic controls and the soaring inflation, they made huge profits. Little was reinvested in production. Instead, they divided up the profits for living expenses. The foreign exchange earned from export sales was deposited in foreign banks. At the time of the Communists' victory and the establishment of the People's Republic in 1949, Heng Feng's equipment was out of date, capital was in short supply, and financial reserves were inadequate. The plant was barely able to maintain operations. Recovery began in the early 1950s thanks to assistance from and reorganization by the new government, extraordinary efforts and sacrifices by the workers, and cessation of the illegal practices of the owners. In 1953, while Heng Feng's recovery was under way, Nie Qijie died.

This picture of Nie Qijie as a calculating capitalist derives principally from the pages of the *History of the Heng Feng Cotton Mill*, compiled by the Academy of Social Sciences in Shanghai during the 1950s when the newly established government was mounting a nationwide campaign against the evils of bureaucratic capitalism. It does not tell the whole story of a man whose life and career won the admiration of many, including foreigners, who knew him. In addition to his efforts on behalf of vocational education mentioned above, Nie promoted general education. In the 1920s he served on the Shanghai Municipal Education Committee; the advisory boards of the Qiming, Mctyiere, and Qixue girls' schools; and as a director of Fudan College. In 1923 he was a member of the commission for raising educational sinking funds. After baptism in the Methodist Episcopal church in 1915, he became an active member of the YMCA, holding local and national office.

Nie Qijie was known to be an admirer of the Russian novelist Count Leo Tolstoy (1828–1910) and an advocate of the simple life that Tolstoy espoused. He took Tolstoy's Christian name at the time of his baptism. Some sources say that in emulation of Tolstoy, Nie disposed of his palatial home on Wayfare Road in 1923 and retired to a more modest abode, though it is equally likely that the downturn in his financial situation in 1923 brought on this move. Nie translated a work on wireless telegraphy in 1901 and was at work on a volume of Tolstoy's sayings in the 1920s. He was quoted as saying "the curse of modern civilization is luxury," a viewpoint that some attributed to the influence of Tolstoy, but one that also clearly bears the mark of his mother.

Nie Qijie's only child, Nie Guangkun (1901–?), married a Ms. Liu in 1924. She gave birth to three sons (see chart 5). When Nie Guangkun departed for the United States to study, Nie is reported to have sent him off with the following admonition: "I will give you a good education but do not expect a cent from my fortune." Nie's wife died in 1917 leaving a considerable fortune in jewelry, which he sold, devoting the proceeds to philanthropy. He was clearly his mother's son. W. K. K. Chan, *Merchants, Mandarins and Modern Enterprise*, 56–58; Chen Zhen and Yao Luo, *Zhongguo jindai gongyeshi ziliao*, 397–401; *Who's Who in China, 1918–1950*, 1:135–37 (1918–2?), 2:612–13 (1925–28), 3:320–21 (1931–33); Li Xin and Sun Sibai, *Minguo renwuzhuan*, 2:249–53; Zhongguo kexueyuan jingji yanjiuso, *Heng Feng shachangde fasheng fazhan yu gaizao*, 3–5, 42–45, 74–75, 96–99, 134–37; Bergere, *Chinese Bourgeoisie*, 71, 124, 138, 161–64, 175–78.

Chapter 4. Life in Nanjing and War with France

1 The long-standing practice of conferring official status in return for contributions to the imperial coffers was greatly expanded during the Qing dynasty (1644–1912), when it was frequently employed as a means of raising funds. After the outbreak of the Taiping Revolutionary movement (1851–64), provincial governments were empowered to establish agencies to solicit contributions. It became possible to obtain government offices as well as rank through fixed contributions. As the financial crisis in various provinces worsened in the

late nineteenth century, provincial governments dispatched representatives to prosperous areas to solicit contributions in return for official status. The Yunnan office for soliciting contributions in Changsha, the provincial capital of Hunan, was probably such an agency. Chen Xulu, Fang, and Wei, *Zhongguo jindaishi cidian*, 561–62; Chang Chung-li, *Chinese Gentry*, 29–30.

The General Bureau for Defense Planning in the Jiangnan area was established in 1873 by the governor general of the Liangjiang provinces, Li Zongxi (?–1884), in response to directions from the central government. Its purposes were to plan the defenses of the lower Yangzi area, to purchase military material from the West, and to construct fortifications along the river. Fang Zongcheng, "Kaixian Li shangshu zhengshu," 373–74. I am indebted to Pingfeng Chi of the Center for Chinese Research Materials, Oakton, Virginia, for bringing this source to my attention.

2 Courtesy name Xiaoquan; a native of Hefei in Anhui and older brother of Li Hongzhang. Li Hanzhang became a *bagongsheng* (senior licentiate) in 1862 through a special examination held every twelve years. He subsequently held a series of provincial posts, including governor general of Hunan and Hubei (1867, 1870–75, 1876–82) and governor general of Guangdong and Guangxi (1889–95). He retired from official life due to illness and died in 1899. Hummel, *Eminent Chinese*, 471; Wei Xiumei, *Qingji zhiguan biao*, 2:62; Cai, *Qingdai qibai mingren zhuan*, 402–5.

3 Zeng Jize was named China's ambassador to Britain and France on August 25, 1878, to replace Guo Songtao. He arrived in Paris and presented his credentials on February 10, 1879. Li Enhan, *Zeng Jize de waijiao*, 61; Hsu, *China's Entrance into the Family of Nations*, 190.

4 The Jiezi shu calls upon officials to hold to the highest standards of self-discipline, unselfishness, and compassion in personal life and in the conduct of government affairs. It may be found along with a highly laudatory sketch of Nie Jimo's life in Nie Qijie, "Chongde laoren jiniance," 283–88.

5 Probably an error for *Huangchao jingshi wenbian* (see chapter 3, note 14).

6 The military staff agency for a provincial governor or a governor general. Hucker, *Dictionary of Official Titles*, 584, no. 8028.

7 A Muslim uprising began in the northwest provinces of Shaanxi and Gansu in the early 1860s. By 1864 it had spread to Xinjiang, a region on the northwest border intermittently under Chinese rule. The uprising was complicated by a power struggle for control of Xinjiang between Britain, which saw it as a buffer against Russian expansion toward India, and czarist Russia, which took

advantage of the uprising in 1871 to occupy the rich Ili Valley. A ten-year campaign by Zuo Zongtang resulted in the pacification of the Muslims by 1878. Most of the Ili territory was recovered through the Treaty of St. Petersburg negotiated with czarist Russia by Zeng Jize in 1881. This paved the way for the incorporation of Xinjiang as a province in 1884. Hsu, *Ili Crisis*.

8 The preceding account of Nie's initial association with Zuo Zongtang is from "Zhongfanggong yishi" (Some anecdotes about Nie Qigui), in Nie Qijie, "Chongde laoren jiniance," 296–98.

9 A tributary of the Yangzi flowing north through western Nanjing.

10 Established in Shanghai in 1865 through the joint efforts of Li Hongzhang and Zeng Guofan, the Jiangnan Arsenal quickly became China's premier modern industry and the mainstay of defense production. It was supervised by the Liangjiang governor general, who was also commissioner of southern ports and responsible for maritime defense along the southern coast. With machinery purchased from Europe and the United States and a staff of British and German technicians, the arsenal produced a full range of ordnance products and ammunition, from repeating rifles to huge coastal defense artillery as well as black, brown, and smokeless powder. It also built some of the earliest steamships produced in China, though shipbuilding was virtually eliminated in the late 1870s because of the high cost. Plagued with management, personnel, and logistical problems, Jiangnan fell short of the goals its founders had set for it; yet it was the vanguard of China's industrial modernization, the recipient of enormous imperial appropriations (much of which were squandered), and regarded as crucial to the survival of the empire. It included an artillery unit, a technical school, and a bureau for the translation of Western works on science and technology. Appointment to a management post at Jiangnan, at a time when hostilities with France in Vietnam were imminent, signified the great confidence that Governor General Zuo placed in Nie. Kennedy, *Arms of Kiangnan*, 38–48, 79–112, 123–38.

11 Courtesy name Mianlin. A native of Liuyang District in Hunan, Li is listed as assistant director of Jiangnan, in 1872 and again in 1877, in *Jiangnan zhizaoju ji* (Record of the Jiangnan Arsenal). Nie is listed as assistant director in 1882–83. Although the *Jiangnan zhizaoju ji* was published by the arsenal in 1905, its personnel records are open to question. It is unclear from the listing of assistant directors whether new names represent additions to the staff or replacements. Furthermore, the listing for director, *zongban*, is the Shanghai taotai. This no doubt reflects the arsenal's dependence on funds allocated from the Shanghai

Maritime Customs, which was supervised by the Shanghai taotai, but it is inconsistent with Mrs. Nie's statements that her husband was made director in 1885. He first appears on the arsenal's list of directors in 1890, when he became Shanghai taotai, at which time she reports that he left the arsenal. In financial reports to the throne concerning Jiangnan in the years 1885–90, Nie is listed as an assistant director along with the incumbent Shanghai taotai. Presumably, in these years Nie functioned as the director at the arsenal and could be reasonably referred to as such, while the Shanghai taotai was accorded a status senior to officials at the arsenal because of his important financial role in allocating operating funds. Wei Yungong, "Jiangnan zhizaoju ji," 42–55, 170–75; Wei Xiumei, *Qingji zhiguanbiao*, 2:62.

12 The arsenal's records make no mention of Li Xingrui leaving office. Nie's cover-up of his malfeasance was probably effective, for Li went on to have a distinguished career. He was selected as a third-class tribute student by purchase (*fu gongsheng*) in 1897 and held a series of provincial posts and appointments as acting governor until he was appointed acting governor general of Fujian and Zhejiang in 1903 and governor general of the Liangjiang provinces in 1904. He died several months after this appointment and was awarded the posthumous title *chinke* (diligent and reverent).

The reasons why Nie undertook to cover up for Li and the Liangjiang governor general did not pursue the matter further are open to speculation. However, they may relate to the fact that Li Xingrui was a coprovincial from Hunan. Li Zhongjue, an official at the arsenal after the turn of the century, observed that the arsenal was controlled by a strong clique of Hunanese, among whom there was a cult of reverence for its founder, Zeng Guofan. Wei Yungong, "Jiangnan zhizaoju ji," 170–75; Wei Xiumei, *Qingji zhiguanbiao*, 2:62; Kennedy, *Arms of Kiangnan*, 124–25.

13 Presumably an alternate name for Pan Lu, who is first listed in the personnel charts of the arsenal as assistant director in 1883. Wei Yungong, "Jiangnan zhizaoju ji," 170–75.

14 Presumably an alternate name for Zhong Qixiang, first listed in the personnel charts of the arsenal as assistant director in 1884. Wei Yungong, "Jiangnan zhizaoju ji," 170–75.

15 French imperialist ambitions to control Vietnam, formulated in the mid-nineteenth century under Louis Napoleon (r. 1852–60), placed France on a collision course with China, which had held a vague claim to suzerainty over parts of Vietnam since the third century B.C. In the 1870s and 1880s, driven by the

prospect of commercial access to the mineral resources of south China, France stepped up its activities in Vietnam, eventually establishing a formidable military presence. The Vietnamese appealed for support to China, where the "war party," encouraged by China's success in dealing with Russia at St. Petersburg in 1881, advocated resistance to French moves. Others, such as Li Hongzhang, who were aware of impending Japanese and Russian moves toward Korea, were less inclined to provoke hostilities with France. In May 1884, in the Li-Fournier Convention, China and France agreed to a French protectorate over Vietnam while recognizing China's suzerainty. But the following month a stunning victory over the French garrison at Bade by Chinese irregulars, who had entered Vietnam in the early 1880s at that government's request, brought a French demand for an indemnity of 250 million francs. China rejected the idea of an indemnity as it had previously, and France determined to force the issue militarily by extending the hostilities into south China. This involved naval engagements along the south China coast and the naval blockade of Taiwan. The penetration of the French fleet into the Min River in Fujian, where on August 23, 1884, it sank eleven vessels of China's modern navy in less than an hour and laid waste to the Fuzhou Naval Dockyard (which, ironically, had been built and operated with French assistance), demonstrated not so much the superiority of French warships as it did the confusion and indecision that plagued China's naval command structure. Rawlinson, *China's Struggle for Naval Development*, 109–28; Lin Qingyuan, *Fujian chuanzhengju shigao*, 171–92; Hsu, "Late Ch'ing Foreign Relations," 96–101; Liu and Smith, "Military Challenge," 251–52.

16 The *Yangwu* was the flagship of China's Fujian squadron. The ship was under the command of Zhang Cheng, who also had tactical control of the squadron and was later beheaded for deserting his command under fire. *Yangwu* was the seventh ship completed at the Fuzhou Naval Dockyard under the direction of the French supervisor, Prosper Giquel. It was a corvette approximately 201 feet long, of 1,400 tons displacement, with a wooden hull, horizontal steam engines rated at 250 horsepower, and three masts; it carried ten three-and-one-half-ton British muzzle-loading guns and was capable of twelve knots. It was the first vessel built at Fuzhou entirely on a foreign design; it cost more than 250,000 taels. One foreign observer praised it, saying, "*Yangwu* is a fine ship. No European or States' ship of the class could be better." Rawlinson, *China's Struggle for Naval Development*, 50, 112, 127, 259; Lin Qingyuan, *Fujian chuanzhengju shigao*, 107; Leibo, *Transferring Technology to China*, 123.

17 Rawlinson states that the Chinese erroneously reported that Courbet had been killed. Courbet died in April 1885 in the Pescadores Islands, which his fleet had occupied as part of the blockade of Taiwan. Whether or not his death was due to wounds from the battle in the Min River is unclear. Rawlinson, *China's Struggle for Naval Development*, 119; Lin Qingyuan, *Fujian chuanzhengju shigao*, 189; Kuo Ting-yee, "Internal Development and Modernization of Taiwan," 216–17.

18 Presumably an alternate name for Cai Huicang, who first appears in the personnel charts of the arsenal as assistant director in 1878. Wei Yungong, "Jiangnan zhizaoju ji," 170–75.

19 About twenty miles southwest of Shanghai.

20 During October and November 1884, Commissioner of Northern Ports Li Hongzhang had contacted the French consul in Tianjin regarding French terms. Meanwhile, Sir Robert Hart, British inspector general of the Chinese Maritime Customs and a trusted adviser of the Chinese throne, entered negotiations as an intermediary with representatives of France. At about the same time Zeng Jize, China's minister to France, began a diplomatic initiative. The war was ended in June 1885 thanks largely to Hart's efforts. The success of China's ground operations in Vietnam also prodded an unstable government in Paris to abandon a costly and distant war. China, harried in the north by Russian advances and Japanese pressure on Korea, conceded French control of Vietnam in return for French withdrawal from Taiwan. China escaped without an indemnity, though the costs of the war in naval materiél and the loss of national stature were enormous. Li Enhan, *Zeng Jize de waijiao*, 224–45; Chere, *Diplomacy of the Sino-French War*, 94–97, 162–80; Hsu, "Late Ch'ing Foreign Relations," 100–101.

Chapter 5. Life in Shanghai and Financial Ruin

1 A taotai, or intendant, was an official who had administrative control over a function of provincial government (e.g., customs or police) or a circuit comprising several prefectures, independent subprefectures, or independent departments. Ch'u, *Local Government*, 5–6. For more information on the Shanghai taotai's office see Leung, *Shanghai Taotai* (which does not mention Tang Haiqiu). The German firm of J. J. Bucheister was a supplier of ordnance technology and technicians to the Jiangnan Arsenal. Kennedy, *Arms of Kiangnan*, 134.

2 The Old Chinese City of Shanghai was on the west bank of the Huangpu River just south of the French Concession.

3 The artillery training school at Jiangnan was converted to an artillery division in 1881. Wei Yungong, "Jiangnan zhizaoju ji," 73.

4 Suzhou Creek flowed eastward through the International Concession and emptied into the Huangpu.

5 Chinese dominoes, made of either ivory or bone, are used for gambling and fortune-telling. To tell fortunes, dominoes are placed facedown and mixed up, then put into rows and turned faceup. The combinations of certain numbers formed by adjacent dominoes are then interpreted through a table, and a rating from lowest to highest is obtained for each combination. This procedure is performed three times. The three sets of ratings are then used to direct the fortune-teller to certain pages in a manual where oracular verses are recorded, and the fortune-teller uses these to make his or her prognostication. Culin, *Chinese Games with Dice and Dominoes*, 517–18. Mrs. Nie's assertion that Zeng Guofan did not believe in fortune-telling is contradicted by documented examples of his interest in various forms of divination in Smith, *Fortune-Tellers and Philosophers*.

6 Chinese chess, or *weiqi* (known as *go* in Japan), is a board game in which each player has 180 pieces. The object is to gain control of territory on the board and capture the opponent's pieces. It involves both intellect and intuition. *Weiqi* has been a popular game since the Western Han dynasty (207 B.C.–A.D. 8). It should be distinguished from *xiangqi*, which resembles Western chess. Smith, *Cultural Heritage*, 230–31.

7 A gambling game that originated in its present form during the Qing dynasty (1644–1912), mahjong is played by four players with 136 pieces, or tiles. It evolved from an early card game, *madiao*, known during the Song dynasty (960–1278). During the Qing it became popular with the salt merchants of Yangzhou in Jiangsu Province. It was adapted by the Taiping armed forces (1851–65) and used for gambling. After the Taipings' defeat, mahjong became popular in the port city of Ningbo in Zhejiang Province and subsequently spread to north and south China. In the 1920s it was introduced into the United States and other foreign countries, where it was the rage for a decade or more. Mahjong enjoyed popularity in Taiwan in the 1960s and later but is often criticized by straitlaced Chinese as a waste of time and money and a sign of decadence. *Cihai*, 4717–18; Taiwan Zhonghua Shuju bianjibu, *Cihai*, 3344–45; Morehead, Frey, and Mott-Smith, *New Complete Hoyle*, 668–69.

8 There was a revival of Buddhism in late nineteenth- and early twentieth-century China sponsored chiefly by laity who hoped that Buddhism could

help reunite a Chinese society torn by class division brought on by economic change. The center of Buddhist activities (which included publishing, conferences, fund-raising, and the establishment of young men's and women's Buddhist associations (YMBA, YWBA), was in the lower Yangzi Valley. Fairs were a feature of traditional community activity. A. F. Wright, *Buddhism in Chinese History*, 114–15; Smith, *Cultural Heritage*, 236.

9 The Board of Naval Affairs, also known as the Navy Yamen, was established by imperial edict in the fall of 1885 following the disastrous defeat of China's navy in the Sino-French War. The intent was to unify the command structure and coordinate the development of a modern navy, an effort that met with limited success in the following decade. Zeng Jize did not return from England, where he was occupied with the crisis brought on by the British Indian Army's occupation of northern Burma, until the fall of 1886. When he reported to Beijing in December 1886, he was also named concurrently to the Board of Foreign Affairs, the Zongli Yamen. Rawlinson, *China's Struggle for Naval Development*, 129; Li Enhan, *Zeng Jize de waijiao*, 350–55.

10 *Cihai*, 2572; Zang, *Zhongguo gujin diming dacidian*, 446.

11 Ginseng, a plant native to Korea and Manchuria, is reputed to have a variety of curative and revitalizing powers. Its shape—a central root with two branches, a stem, and leaves—is reminiscent of the human form, hence the Chinese name *renshen* (image of a man). The roots are covered with rings which indicate the age; the older the root the more effective its medicinal powers. In earlier times ginseng was reserved for use by the imperial household and the households of high officials. In the late nineteenth century it was available at a cost of 10–14 taels per *jin* (1.33 lbs) for imported Korean ginseng, 80 taels per *jin* for domestic ginseng, and as much as 250 taels per *jin* for roots of special quality. Couling, *Encyclopedia Sinica*, 206; Giles, *Chinese-English Dictionary*, 703, item 5624.

12 Mrs. Nie occasionally refers to the wives of her male cousins of the same generation as sisters-in-law.

13 Qingjiang is situated on the banks of the Grand Canal.

14 Junior guardian of the heir apparent (*gongbao*) was a title given to officials either during their lifetime or posthumously for distinguished service to the state. Zeng Guoquan was awarded this honor for his victory over the Taipings at Nanjing in 1864, which effectively ended the Taiping Revolutionary movement. Brunnert and Hagelstrom, *Present Day Political Organization of China*, 490–91; Hummel, *Eminent Chinese*, 750.

15 John Fryer, an Englishman, was employed at the Jiangnan Arsenal as a trans-

lator of scientific books from 1868 until 1896, when he was named Agassiz professor of Oriental languages at the University of California at Berkeley, a post that he held until he retired in 1913. Bennett, *John Fryer*.

16 Though the ambitious plans for educational reform announced by imperial edict during the One Hundred Days of Reform of 1898 were aborted by the Empress Dowager in the fall of that year, they surfaced again after the turn of the century under the sponsorship of Governor General of Hubei and Hunan Zhang Zhidong. Furthermore, the reform consensus that had been growing since China's defeat in the Sino-Japanese War (1894–95) continued to develop despite the conservative coup in the fall of 1898. Ayers, *Chang Chih-tung and Educational Reform in China*, 173–244; Cohen and Schrecker, *Reform in Nineteenth-Century China*, 317–25.

17 Income exceeded expenditures at the Jiangnan Arsenal by 140,149 Shanghai taels in 1890, which, no doubt, was the basis for Mrs. Nie's observation. This figure, however, is not necessarily a reflection of Nie's expert management. The surplus was due primarily to a sharp increase in the arsenal's annual income, which was provided by a fixed percentage of the revenue collected in the Shanghai Customs House. Operating costs did not decline during Nie's tenure; on the contrary, they increased. In 1890, income shot up 50 percent above the average of the previous five years and expenditures increased 33 percent. Furthermore, Nie's directorship was the subject of sharp criticism in a series of articles that appeared in the *Zhongwai ribao* (China and foreign daily) in May and June 1904, which charged that foreign merchant houses made extensive deliveries of substandard iron to the arsenal. Jiangnan paid the price for higher-quality iron, nearly three times the correct price, but received iron that was for the most part unusable. These transactions were allegedly handled by the director's office. Personnel policies also came under attack. The paper charged Nie with mishandling trainees in the arsenal's technical training program. Curricula, length of training periods, and student support programs were reported to be lax, with no fixed periods or stipends. Accomplished students who had incurred the director's displeasure were denied access to employment in the arsenal but subsequently were hired by foreign firms. Kennedy, *Arms of Kiangnan*, 125, 163, 171; Chen Zhen and Yao Luo, *Zhongguo jindai gongye shi ziliao*, 3:73–81.

18 Original name Weiyen, courtesy name Xiaocun. A native of the Yuyao District in Shaoxing Prefecture in Zhejiang Province, Shao Youlian passed the district examinations for the degree of *juren* in 1865. In 1878 he accompanied Chong-

hou on his mission to czarist Russia to secure the return of the Ili territory. Shao remained in Russia as chargé d'affaires after Chonghou's return to China the following year. Later, Shao assisted Zeng Jize with the negotiations for the Treaty of St. Petersburg. In 1882, after his return to China, he was named Shangai taotai. Following the outbreak of the Sino-French War (1883–85), he was placed in charge of defenses on Taiwan and assisted Zeng Guoquan in talks with the French at Shanghai, in 1884, aimed at halting the hostilities. In 1894 he was named governor of Taiwan. When war broke out with Japan in 1894, he took care of the island's defenses until he was transferred to the governorship of Hunan in the fall of that year. Later in the same year, together with Zhang Yinhuan (1837–1900), former ambassador to the United States, Shao was appointed to discuss terms of peace with Japan. Their mission was rejected by the Japanese on the grounds that they had not been invested with sufficient power. Shortly thereafter, Shao retired because of health problems. Chen Xulu, Fang, and Wei, *Zhongguo jindaishi cidian*, 373; Hsu, *Ili Crisis*, 141, 164; Hummel, *Eminent Chinese*, 62.

19 The Grand Council, or Council of State (*junjichu*), was established in 1730 as the highest organ of government through which imperial policy was made and promulgated. Hucker, *Dictionary of Official Titles*, 200.

20 The poem of farewell is Wang Wei's (701–761) "Song Yuan ershi Anxi" (Farewell to Yuan the Second on his mission to Anxi), which was extended and augmented by musicians in the fifteenth century, or earlier, as a song of farewell in three parts. In each part, the original four-line verse is repeated once. It foretells Yuan the Second's journey through Yang Pass in the Dunhuang District of Gansu, on his way to Anxi in the present-day Xinjiang Uigur Autonomous Region. *Cihai*, 938; Yu, *Poetry of Wang Wei*, 176–77, 226.

21 Bao Zhao (c. 414–466), courtesy name Mingyuan, a poet and official during the Liu Song dynasty (420–79), wrote "Deng Dalei an yu mei shu" (A letter to my sister on arriving at Dalei) describing the natural beauty of Dalei, in the present-day Wangjiang District of southwestern Anhui. *Cihai*, 4621; Bao Zhao, *Bao Canjun jizhu*, 83–85.

22 The Shanghai taotai was intendant of the circuit (a subprovincial administrative unit) that included Suzhou Prefecture, Songjiang Prefecture, and Taicang Subprefecture. Brunnert and Hagelstrom, *Present Day Political Organization of China*, 424; Leung, *Shanghai Taotai*, 5.

23 Courtesy name Yangqu. A native of Hefei in Anhui province, Gong Zhaoyuan served as director of the Nanjing Arsenal in 1880, as commissary general for

Taiwan in Shanghai at the outset of the Sino-French War (1883–85), and as customs taotai at Weihaiwei in Shandong before his appointment as Shanghai taotai in July 1886. He subsequently served as provincial judge in Zhejiang in 1890 and as financial commissioner of Sichuan in 1891. In 1893 Gong was named minister to England, France, Italy, and Belgium. In the next two years he was appointed to honorary posts on the Board of Rites in the Court of Banqueting and the Court of Sacrificial Worship, both regarded as stepping-stones to higher imperial offices. In 1897 he was the subject of an investigation and reassigned. Gong Zhaoyuan was the kind of person of whom William Mesny (a self-styled expert on all things Chinese) said, "His Excellency Gong is the right kind of man to deal with; it is a great pity that China has not more of his stamp," which is a recommendation that Gong's reputation might have done better without. Wei Xiumei, *Qingji zhiguanbiao*, 91; Mesny, *Mesny's Chinese Miscellany*, 2:489; Leung, *Shanghai Taotai*, 82–83.

24 The Beginning of Spring (*lichun*) is a day marking one of the twenty-four divisions of the solar year on the traditional Chinese calendar. It usually falls a few days before or after February 4 on the Gregorian calendar and is customarily regarded as the beginning of the spring season in China. *Cihai*, 4086.

25 A volume of clinically tested traditional Chinese medicines compiled by Bao Xiangao during the Qing dynasty (1644–1912). *Cihai*, 2617.

26 The mid-autumn festival falls on the fifteenth day of the eighth month of the lunar calendar. In addition to family gatherings, ancestor worship, and feasting, it is famous for the moon cakes, or *yuebing*, that are given at this time. They have an exterior something like a piecrust, only firmer, and an interior of various flavors reminiscent of a torte. Smith, *Cultural Heritage*, 238–39.

27 In 1891 antimissionary activity directed principally against French and British missions in the Yangzi Valley spread over a thousand miles, causing the most serious losses of life and property since the Tianjin Massacre of 1870. Incited by inflammatory pamphlets, posters, and rumors, some originating with the antidynastic Gelaohui (Elder Brother Society) and some from Hunanese gentry, Chinese masses, evincing an incipient anti-imperialism, attacked British and French mission properties indiscriminately. On May 12 a Chinese woman appeared at the gate of the French Catholic mission at Wuhu demanding her missing child. This occurred in an atmosphere in which rumors of Catholic missionaries bewitching Chinese children were rampant. The incidents sparked rioting that destroyed the mission. Rioters invaded the British consulate before they were checked at the customs compound (administered by Britain).

Wehrle, *Britain, China and the Anti-Missionary Riots*, 19–44; Latourette, *History of the Christian Missions in China*, 356, 470.

28 One of China's five sacred mountains (see chapter 3, note 5).

29 The salt merchants of Yangzhou in Jiangsu Province were legendary for their affluence and luxurious life-style. Merchant families held hereditary monopolies granted by the government for the sale of salt produced in government mines, wells, or evaporation plants to distribution merchants. Ho Ping-ti, "The Salt Merchants of Yangchou: A Study of Commercial Capitalism in Eighteenth Century China."

30 Ding Xiang Wang was the Daoist god of the Chenghuang Temple in Shanhua (present-day Changsha), Hunan Province. Bian and Li, *Hunan tongzhi*, 72:1677, 1694.

31 The *North China Herald*, a British-owned weekly published in Shanghai, attributed Nie's eight-month delay in leaving office to the controversy that arose over his successor, Lu Beiyang (Lu Peh-yang). The *Herald* lamented Nie's departure, praising him as an open-minded and farsighted official well suited to work with the foreign community in Shanghai. His designated successor, Lu, was denounced by the editor of the *Herald* as one whose career had been marked by corruption, who had obtained the post through favoritism (he was an uncle of Li Hongzhang), and who was too old and lacked the qualities needed to deal with the foreign community. In late May, the imperial court withdrew Lu Beiyang's name and appointed Huang Zuluo to succeed Nie. The controversy that arose between Nie and Huang over the 800,000-tael shortage in the customs funds seems to have entirely escaped the notice of the British press. The *Herald* did report in October 1894, several months after the outbreak of the Sino-Japanese War, that Nie was in Shanghai in charge of supplies for Taiwan. He was ordered to Beijing for an imperial audience preparatory to his assumption of office in Zhejiang. *North China Herald*, Jan. 12, Jan. 19, Feb. 16, Feb. 23, March 2, March 9, March 16, March 30, April 27, May 11, May 18, May 25, June 1, June 15, July 6, and Oct. 19, 1894.

32 Mrs. Nie's account of Nie Qigui's incumbency as Shanghai taotai appears to be an effort to present those aspects that reflect well on Nie. There was more to it than appears on the pages of her autobiography, and it is likely she knew at least something of what her husband was up to. As early as 1896, William Mesny (the treaty-port gadfly and self-styled authority) charged Nie with financial gambling—using funds from the customs bank and several Chinese banks in which he held an interest in a scheme to ruin certain foreign banks. These

charges are, of course, inconsistent with the lavish praise heaped upon Nie by the editors of the British-owned *North China Herald* (see note 31). However, they do give an inkling of the nature of Nie's financial activities in Shanghai. The research of Wellington K. K. Chan discloses that Nie, like his predecessor Gong Zhaoyuan, held shares in the New Huaxin Cotton Mill, a joint government-private enterprise. Nie held 450 shares, purchased with customs funds and valued at 22,500 taels—about 5 percent of the authorized capital of Huaxin—when he took office in 1890. Albert Feuerwerker notes further that in 1893 Nie and Sheng Xuanhuai, Li Hongzhang's financial adviser, raised capital from private sources to rebuild the Huasheng Cotton Mill after it was destroyed by fire. As Chan points out, Mrs. Nie's account places the responsibility for the shortage on the accountant Xu Zijing; since Nie was an official, it would appear unseemly by Confucian standards for him to invest in private capitalist enterprise. She does not mention these shares until much later in 1908 when Nie had an opportunity to purchase the New Huaxin Cotton Mill, and then she fails to explain where the capital to purchase these shares came from in a family repeatedly portrayed as financially strapped. Mesny, *Mesny's Chinese Miscellany*, 2:470; W. K. K. Chan, *Merchants, Mandarins and Modern Enterprise*, 55, 89–90; Feuerwerker, *China's Early Industrialization*, 65, 218, 221.

Chapter 6. End of a Dynasty: Rebirth of a Family

1 There were nine grades of honorary ranks conferred upon the wives or concubines of officials, paralleling the nine honorary grades of officials. Brunnert and Hagelstrom, *Present Day Political Organization of China*, 495.

2 Literally, "Lu the Forefather." Lu Yan (A.D. 798–?), courtesy name Dongbin, literary name Chunyangzi. According to tradition, Luzu was from Jingzhao Prefecture, in which Changan, the Tang Dynasty (618–908) capital, was situated; however, he is also reputed to be from Hezhong Prefecture, the present-day Yongji District of Shanxi. In the 840s Luzu twice failed the civil service examinations for the *jinshi* degree and then wandered from place to place. During his wanderings, tradition has it that he met Zhongli Quan, an alchemist of the Han dynasty (207 B.C.–A.D. 220) who had achieved immortality; Zhongli gave Lu the elixir of life. Lu was then sixty-four years old. He lived for a while as a hermit in the Zhongnan Mountains of Shaanxi practicing self-cultivation in the Daoist tradition through communion with nature. He later traveled from place to place, decapitating a flood dragon in the Jiangsu-Anhui region, cre-

ating cranes at Yueyang on the Yangzi, and carousing at various inns. Accounts of his fabulous deeds first appeared during the Northern Song dynasty (960–1127) and subsequently became the theme for popular fiction and drama. He is one of the Eight Immortals (or saints, as they are sometimes called) who during their lifetime achieved supernatural powers and after death were elevated to the status of gods. The Eight Immortals are a special group of gods, and Luzu is regarded as one of the foremost of the eight. His symbol is the sword, and he is the patron saint of barbers. *Cihai*, 1665; Eberhard, *Dictionary of Chinese Symbols*, 170–71, 149–50, 326; Giles, *Chinese Biographical Dictionary*, 562–63; Mayers, *Chinese Readers Manual*, 147.

3 Imperial silk manufactories were under the supervision of Manchu notables, bondsmen, or eunuchs and nominally controlled by the Imperial Household Department of the imperial government. Manufactories were located at Nanjing and Suzhou in Jiangsu and Hangzhou in Zhejiang. Hucker, *Dictionary of Official Titles*, 164.

4 January 21, 1830–October 6, 1902; courtesy name Xianzhuang, posthumous name Zhongcheng. A native of Xinning in Hunan, Liu Kunyi was a *linsheng* (a holder of the lowest-level civil service degree) who by virtue of special examinations had qualified for a government stipend. He entered the Hunan Army in 1855 and served for ten years in the struggle against the Taipings. As a reward for his military service he was named governor of Jiangxi (1865–74). After this he held a series of important provincial posts, including Liangjiang governor general (1879–81 and 1890–1902). He took decisive action to suppress the 1891 antimissionary movement in the Yangzi Valley and the secret societies that supported it. In 1900 he was a leader of the league of southern governors of which Nie Qigui was a member. The governors acted independently during the Boxer Uprising to keep the Boxers out of south China and secured pledges from the foreign powers that they would not invade south China. Hummel, *Eminent Chinese*, 523–24; Chen Xulu, Fang, and Wei, *Zhongguo jindaishi cidian*, 265.

5 Subsequent to these negotiations, the French Concession and the International Concession were enlarged. Chen Xulu, Fang, and Wei, *Zhongguo jindaishi cidian*, 164; Belsky, "Bones of Contention."

6 Pujun was the son of Manchu prince Duan, a grandson of Emperor Daoguang (r. 1821–51). Prince Duan allied himself with the Empress Dowager (note 7, below) in 1898 to abort the reform movement initiated in that year by Emperor Guangxu (r. 1875–1908; see note 8, below). The Empress Dowager and Prince Duan saw the reforms as imperiling the power of the Manchu nobility. They

placed Emperor Guangxu under house arrest and conspired to depose him by February 1900 and replace him with Pujun. When the ministers of the foreign powers in Beijing heard of this plot they objected strongly, believing that Emperor Guangxu was reform-minded and that his return to active rule held out the best hope for stabilizing China's relations with the foreign powers. The Empress Dowager and Prince Duan, infuriated by this "foreign interference in domestic affairs," in 1899 set aside their plans to enthrone Pujun but gave their support to the virulently antiforeign Boxer Uprising in the hope of eliminating foreign opposition to their efforts to depose Emperor Guangxu and reaffirming Manchu control of the imperial government. Li Chien-nung, *Political History of China*, 168–70.

7 November 29, 1835–November 15, 1908; Empress Xiaoqin née Yehonala, her Manchu name, also known by the title Empress Cixi. She entered the palace as a concubine in 1851 at age seventeen. Her son was named heir apparent on August 21, 1861, one day before his father, Emperor Xianfeng (r. 1851–62), died. Through palace intrigue she gradually asserted her control over the regency council established to guide young Emperor Tongzhi (r. 1862–75). When Emperor Tongzhi died without an heir under mysterious circumstances in early 1875, she succeeded in placing a three-year-old infant on the throne in violation of the Manchu clan rules for imperial succession. She dominated young Emperor Guangxu (note 8, below), continuing to rule through intrigue and reliance on eunuch favorites until her retirement in 1889. Even after that she influenced the affairs of state—most notably by diverting large sums of government funds, earmarked for naval modernization following China's defeat in the Sino-French War (1884–85), to refurbish her retirement quarters and prepare her birthday celebration in 1894. In 1898, when Emperor Guangxu's reform program threatened the entrenched power of the Empress Dowager's Manchu cronies, she placed the emperor under house arrest and resumed direct control of the imperial government. In 1902, following the Boxer Uprising, she reluctantly set the government on the course of reform. Most reforms, however, were superficial or inadequate. The Empress Dowager died on November 15, 1908. Emperor Guangxu, whom she hated for his willingness to yield Manchu dominance and whom she was loathe to see resume power, had succumbed suddenly and mysteriously on the previous day. Hummel, *Eminent Chinese*, 295–300.

8 August 14, 1871–November 14, 1908; Manchu name Zaitian, ninth emperor of the Qing dynasty, reigned 1875–1908. Emperor Guangxu was the son of

Prince Chun (1840–91) and the younger sister of the Empress Dowager. He was adopted by the Empress Dowager and placed on the throne in 1875, in violation of Manchu clan rules governing succession. Throughout his reign, she dominated him. Though Guangxu was regarded as intelligent and progressive by foreigners, thanks to the education provided by his remarkable tutor, Weng Tonghe (1830–1904), the Empress Dowager hated him because his support for reform promised to undermine Manchu control of the imperial government. Guangxu died mysteriously on November 14, 1908, one day before the death of the Empress Dowager, who, it is believed, had him murdered. Hummel, *Eminent Chinese*, 731–33.

9 The Foreign Inspectorate of Customs had its origins in 1853 when an uprising of the Small Sword Society in Shanghai forced the closing of the Imperial Customs House. The British consul in Shanghai feared that the collection of customs dues on foreign imports would be conducted inland. Foreign scrutiny would then be impossible, and competing foreign merchants and Chinese customs officers could conspire to avoid the uniform low tariff on all foreign imports stipulated in the unequal treaties of 1842–44. Therefore, the British together with the United States and French consuls pressed the Chinese customs authorities to appoint foreign customs collectors who, with the protection of their governments' gunboats, could collect customs dues without fear of interference and turn them over to the imperial government. This system was continued, and a British inspector of customs was appointed in 1855. In 1863, Robert Hart, an Irishman who had been in China since 1854, was named inspector general of a Customs Service expanded to include eleven ports. Under Hart's leadership the Imperial Maritime Customs Service employed foreign customs officers to collect revenues for the imperial government. Though the operation of an important agency of China's government by foreign personnel was deeply resented by many Chinese, the clean-handed administration of the Customs Service under Hart's leadership provided China with an unexpected new source of income at a time when it was urgently needed. Hart's cooperative and constructive attitude in dealing with his Chinese employers won him the position of trusted adviser to high Chinese officials in times of international crises until his retirement in 1908. His biography first appeared as an obituary in the *London Times* during the summer of 1900, when it was erroneously presumed that he had perished during the Boxers' siege of the foreign legation quarters in Beijing. Spence, *To Change China*, 93–128; S. F. Wright, *Hart*

and the Chinese Customs; Bruner, Fairbank, and Smith, *Entering China's Service*; Fairbank, Bruner, and Matheson, *The I. G. in Peking*.

10 In 1899, as the time approached when China's commercial treaties with the foreign powers could be renegotiated, Sheng Xuanhuai (1844–1916), director general of the Imperial Railroad Administration, and Nie were appointed to meet with Hart and develop a strategy to revise the treaties and regain the tariff autonomy that China had surrendered in earlier treaties. Their plan was to trade immunity for foreign imports from the *likin* (the internal transit tax) for an increase in the 5 percent tariff stipulated in the treaties. Before serious consideration could be given to this proposal, the Boxer Uprising disrupted China's relations with the foreign powers. Feuerwerker, *China's Early Industrialization*, 72.

11 Courtesy name Xingwu, a native of Guyuan Independent Department in Gansu Province. Dong, a Muslim, fought alongside Zuo Zongtang in suppressing the Muslim uprising in the northwest in the 1870s. After the Sino-Japanese War (1894–95), he was made commander of all forces in the provinces of Gansu, Shaanxi, Shanxi, Henan, and Shandong. In 1898 his forces assisted the Empress Dowager in her seizure of power from Emperor Guangxu; he was quick to give his support when she turned her xenophobic rage against all foreigners and backed the Boxers. In the summer of 1900, when the Boxers entered Beijing and placed the foreign legations under siege, Dong's troops fought side by side with the Boxers, who claimed magical immunity to foreign bullets. They flourished "magic weapons such as soul-absorbing banners, sky-covering flags, thunderbolt fans, hooks and flying swords." After the Boxers were defeated by the allied expeditionary force in August 1900, Dong was condemned as an antiforeign reactionary and, as part of the Boxer settlement, was deprived of all ranks and offices. Li Chien-nung, *Political History of China*, 156, 174–79; Hummel, *Eminent Chinese*, 406–9; Mesny, *Mesny's Chinese Miscellany*, 3:243; Hsu, "Late Ch'ing Foreign Relations," 121–27.

12 The Red Gang (Hong Bang) was a secret society that originated in the 1850s among transport workers in northern Anhui Province who had been deprived of their regular employment by the disruption of grain tribute shipments (from the Yangzi Valley to the capital area) caused by the mid-nineteenth-century rebellions. In violation of imperial government regulations governing the transport and sale of salt, the Red Gang moved high-quality, low-price salt from the Changlu salt district covering parts of Henan and Anhui into the Huai District,

which included parts of the same provinces but where salt was of lower quality and higher price. Members of the Red Gang were known as Honghuzi, or Red Beards. Because of the hazards of smuggling, the Red Gang evolved into a militant organization that included adventurers, bandits, and desperados. By the late nineteenth century the Red Gang had extended its influence into the lower Yangzi Valley where it controlled transport and smuggling. Jean Chesneaux identifies the Hong Bang as the Triad Society, the principal secret society of south China, which was also known as the Hong League. The Triads had the political mission of overthrowing the ruling Qing dynasty (1644–1912) and restoring the Ming dynasty (1368–1644). The name Hong League was taken from the surname of the Ming imperial clan, Hong. This was later transformed into the homonym *hong*, meaning "red," hence the Red Gang. In the twentieth century, especially after the fall of the Qing dynasty in 1912, the Red Gang became increasingly involved in the opium trade, prostitution, gambling, and labor racketeering. Jerome Ch'en, "Rebels Between Rebellions," 807–22; Chesneaux, *Popular Movements and Secret Societies in China*, 99, 166; Chesneaux, *Secret Societies in China*, 15, 34, 49–51.

13 Liu Zi was a government student by inheritance from his father, Liu Songshan (1833–70), who distinguished himself in the struggle against the Taiping Revolutionary movement and the Nian Rebellion before losing his life in 1870 during the suppression of the Muslim uprisings in the northwest. In 1895 Liu Zi was named provincial judge, not financial commissioner, of Shanxi Province. Wei Xiumei, *Qingji zhiguanbiao*, 73; Chen Xulu, Fang, and Wei, *Zhongguo jindaishi cidian*, 265–66.

14 Provincial governments traditionally had been responsible for the issuance of coinage in China. In the late 1880s, at the urging of the imperial government, the provinces began purchasing equipment from abroad and establishing provincial mints to produce coinage through the use of machinery. King, *Money and Monetary Policy in China*, 220–28.

15 Courtesy name Zijiu, literary name Zhi'an. A native of the Shanhua District of Hunan, Qu earned the *jinshi* degree in 1871 and served as provincial director of education in Henan, Zhejiang, and Sichuan. In 1900 he accompanied the Empress Dowager in her flight from the capital during the Boxer Uprising, winning her favor. In 1901 he was appointed minister of the Board of Works, minister of the Grand Council (the highest administrative body in the imperial government), and minister of the Bureau of Government Affairs. Qu also served as president and controller of China's first Ministry of Foreign Affairs, established

in 1901, and was active in the Qing court's preparations for the establishment of constitutional government after 1902. He was removed from office in 1908 after a disagreement with the Empress Dowager. After the 1911–12 Revolution brought down the Qing dynasty, Qu lived in Shanghai. He was given the posthumous title Wenshen (cultured and prudent). Chen Xulu, Fang, and Wei, *Zhongguo jindaishi cidian*, 766; Wei Xiumei, *Qingji zhiguanbiao*, 129.

16 September 2, 1837–October 4, 1909; courtesy name Xiaoda, literary names Xiangtao, Xiangyan, Hugong, Wujingjushi, and Baoshui. A native of the Nanpi District of Zhili (present-day Hebei) Province, Zhang Zhidong earned the *jinshi* degree in 1863 and was made a compiler of the Hanlin Academy. There followed a long and distinguished career as a provincial official and reformer. He was noted for his opposition to foreign aggression on China's borders and his support of the imperial government during the Ili crisis with czarist Russia (1880–81) and the Sino-French War (1883–85). In both crises, Mrs. Nie's brother Zeng Jize represented China diplomatically. In subsequent appointments as governor general of Hunan and Hubei and governor general of Jiangsu, Jiangxi, and Anhui, Zhang pioneered railroad development, modern minting, iron and steel production, ordnance manufacture, and educational reform. In the years following China's defeat in the Sino-Japanese War (1894–95), he advocated moderate reform and supported the court, distancing himself from the radical reformers during the One Hundred Days of Reform of 1898. He remained nominally loyal though not actively supportive of the court during the Boxer Uprising (1899–1900). His philosophy of preserving Confucianism while adopting useful aspects of Western learning led him to call for an end to the civil service examination system—the stronghold of Confucian learning—and the introduction of a modern school system. The epoch-making end of the civil service examinations came in 1905 principally as a result of Zhang's advocacy. In 1907 he was named China's first minister of education. Hummel, *Eminent Chinese*, 27–31; Ayers, *Chang Chih-tung and Educational Reform in China*; Li Guoqi, *Zhang Zhidong de waijiao zhengce*.

17 After the Boxer Protocol was signed (1901), the court gave its blessing to moderate reforms. Zhang Zhidong promptly proposed the establishment of a modern school system, modification of the civil service examination system, and the dispatch of students abroad to study. Ayers, *Chang Chih-tung and Educational Reform in China*, 205–16.

18 Original given name Chunze, courtesy name Yunjie, literary name Jiongtang. A native of the Xilin District of Guangxi Province, Cen Chunxuan was the

third son of the prominent military leader and provincial official Cen Yuying (1829–89). Cen Chunxuan earned the degree of *juren* in the civil service examinations of 1885. He held office in Beijing, Guangdong, and Gansu prior to 1900 when, during the Boxer Uprising (1899–1900), he escorted the imperial court to Xi'an to avoid the foreign powers' occupation of Beijing. Cen subsequently held posts as governor of Shaanxi (1901–2), governor general of Sichuan (1902–3), and governor general of Guangdong and Guangxi (1903–6). He retired in 1907. Chen Xulu, Fang, and Wei, *Zhongguo jindaishih cidian*, 331.

19 Née Hirao Seki. Born to a samurai family in today's Gifu Prefecture in central Honshu, she served at the imperial court before her marriage to Takeo Shimoda; she was widowed in 1884. Mrs. Shimoda distinguished herself as a teacher of the Chinese and Japanese classics and as an advocate for the education of women, having established a school for that purpose in 1885. She toured the United States and Europe (1893–95) to observe women's educational institutions. In 1898 she and others founded the Teikoku fujin kyokai (Imperial Women's Association) to promote women's education; it published the magazine *Nihon fujin* (Japanese women). In 1899 she founded the Jissen Girls' School (now Jissen University) and the Joshi kogei gakko (Women's Crafts School) and in 1904 a school for Chinese women in Japan. She was founder (1901) and president (1920–31) of the Aikoku fujinkai (Patriotic Women's Society). Her publications include poetry, a diary titled *Hanafubuki* (Snow storm of flowers), and many works designed to improve women's education. *Kodansha Encyclopedia of Japan*, 7:105.

20 *Kenwuju*. Offices with this title were customarily concerned with introducing Chinese colonists to border areas or minority areas of sparse population. Brunnert and Hagelstrom, *Present Day Political Organization of China*, 365–68.

21 A censor was an official of the imperial government who maintained surveillance of officials at various levels and submitted memorials directly to the emperor on any matters the censor regarded as malfeasance in office. Such memorials frequently constituted impeachment of the named official. Censors were commonly referred to as "the ears and eyes of the Son of Heaven." Hucker, *Dictionary of Official Titles*, 592.

22 As part of the reform movement initiated by the Qing government following the signing of the Boxer Protocol in 1901, the government encouraged the dispatch of students overseas to study. The intent was to gain qualified teachers for the modern school system that was established in 1904. Most students went to Japan because of its proximity to China, its cultural affinity, and the similari-

ties in the written language. The termination of the civil service examinations in 1905 (the stronghold of traditional education) coupled with the enormous prestige that accrued to Japan following its victory in the Russo-Japanese War (1904–5) resulted in a dramatic movement of Chinese students to Japan in quest of a modern education. In 1904 there were thirteen hundred Chinese students in Japan. By 1905 this figure had increased to eight thousand. Jansen, "Japan and the Chinese Revolution of 1911," 348–53; Ichiko, "Political and Institutional Reform," 376–83.

The Commission for Army Reorganization was established in 1903 as part of the Qing government's military reforms. In 1906 it was amalgamated with the new Ministry of War. Brunnert and Hagelstrom, *Present Day Political Organization of China*, 488.

23 One of the honorary ranks conferred on the wives or concubines of officials, paralleling the nine honorary grades of officialdom. Brunnert and Hagelstrom, *Present Day Political Organization of China*, 495.

24 The Sichuan salt and tea taotai stationed in Chengde Prefecture was one of nine such provincial-level officials throughout the empire who were in charge of the revenues from provincial monopolies on salt and, in the case of Sichuan, tea. Brunnert and Hagelstrom, *Present Day Political Organization of China*, 414, 422–23.

25 A circuit, or *dao*, was a subprovincial administrative unit consisting of one or more prefectures, independent subprefectures, or independent departments under the control of an intendant, or taotai (daotai). Circuits were customarily named by combining the first characters (or syllables) of the subordinate prefectures. Playfair, *Cities and Towns of China*, ix.

26 The Lantern Festival falls on the fifteenth day of the first lunar month. It marks the end of the New Year's festivities. The spirits of ancestors who have returned to take part in the New Year's celebrations are guided back to the spirit world by the light of paper and fabric lanterns. Eberhard, *Dictionary of Chinese Symbols*, 159.

27 Guanyin, the most popular Chinese deity (in Indian Buddhist texts, Avalokitesvara) was a bodhisattva assistant to the Buddha Amitabha who presided over the Pure Land, or Western Heaven. In Buddhist belief, a bodhisattva is one who stops short of entering nirvana, or enlightenment, in order to help others toward that goal. In India, Guanyin is regarded as male; in China this helping and sympathetic figure came to be considered female and was gradually adopted into popular religions as a kindly goddess who helps the needy and

favors wives who have failed to produce male offspring. Smith, *Cultural Heritage*, 140; Thompson, *Chinese Religion*, 64.

28 *The Tale of Xiangshan* is a religious drama based on a Buddhist legend of the Song dynasty (960–1278), reiterated as a poetic drama (*chuanqi*) in the Ming dynasty (1368–1644), and absorbed into the repertoire of the popular theater in the nineteenth century. It involves Miao Shan, the daughter of King Miao Zhuang. The king, who is without a male heir, encourages Miao Shan to marry; she refuses, preferring the pious life of a Buddhist ascetic. Infuriated, her father strangles her, but she comes back to life and dwells on Xiangshan (Fragrant mountain). When King Miao Zhuang later becomes gravely ill, Miao Shan gives him her own hands and eyes, which effect a miraculous cure. The king then goes to Xiangshan, repents his crimes, and gives thanks to Buddha. Miao Shan for her self-sacrifice becomes the bodhisattva Guanyin, the goddess of mercy. Mackerras, *Rise of the Peking Opera*, 258.

29 The Hong Kong and Shanghai Banking Corporation (Huifeng Yinhang), established in 1865 by British merchants, was one of the oldest foreign financial institutions operating in China. Its initial capital of $5 million (Spanish) was paid up in two years and increased, by 1891, to $10 million as a result of the bank's leading role in financing foreign trade, currency exchange, industrial investments, and underwriting government loans. Of the 45 million taels that the Chinese government borrowed prior to 1895, 17 million were underwritten by the Hong Kong and Shanghai Banking Corporation. King, *Money and Monetary Policy in China*, 99–101.

The Kaiping Mines were established by Li Hongzhang, governor general of Zhili Province, in 1877 at a site about halfway between Tianjin and the Shanhaiguan (the pass where the Great Wall approaches the sea). They were a government-supervised merchant undertaking managed by Tang Tingshu (Tong King-sing, 1832–92), a former employee of Western firms in China and an English-language interpreter. The Kaiping Mines initially employed Western mining engineers and machinery to produce coal competitive in quality and price with imported coal, in an effort to recapture the market from foreign competitors in north China and Shanghai. Specifically, Kaiping coal fueled the vessels of the China Merchant's Steam Navigation Company, China's first domestic carrier, which carried Kaiping coal southward to the markets of Shanghai. By 1883 the Kaiping Mines had established a machine-building plant and introduced a railroad and telegraph to service the mines. Production reached 250,000 tons of coal per year, most of which was consumed in north

China. After Tong's death in 1892, the mines came under the management of a Manchu official; resources were severely depleted, and the mines gradually became dependent on foreign loans. In 1900 Kaiping was taken over by a British firm represented by an American mining engineer who later became president of the United States, Herbert Hoover. In 1912 the Kaiping Mines became part of the Sino-British Kailan Mining Administration. Carlson, *Kaiping Mines*, 1–142; Wang Xi, *Zhong Ying Kaiping guangquan jiaoshe*.

30 Modern national defense industries were first established in China in the 1860s and 1870s under government auspices with capital and operating funds provided from customs revenues and other public sources. Examples of such industries include the Jiangnan Arsenal in Shanghai and the Fuzhou Naval Dockyard. In the 1870s and 1880s the industrialization movement was broadened to include enterprises of a commercial nature designed to compete with the growing imperialist domination of China's domestic economy. Examples of such industries include the China Merchant's Steam Navigation Company (1872), the Kaiping Mines (1877), the Moho Gold Mines (1887), and the Shanghai Cotton Cloth Mill (1878). These were government-supervised merchant enterprises (that is, capitalized principally with private funds but managed by government officials). Although they employed private capital, they frequently enjoyed monopolistic privileges in the marketplace and were marked by bureaucratic corruption and inefficiency. The New Huaxin Cotton Mill (Huaxin fangzhi xinju, also translated as New Huaxin Spinning and Weaving Mill) represented still another organizational structure for modern business in China, collaboration between private and official investors to capitalize an industry that was without government supervision. It was essentially private in nature, though some of the official investors' funds appear to have been siphoned off from Shanghai customs revenues.

The New Huaxin Cotton Mill was originally advertised in the late 1880s as a government-private joint enterprise (*guanshang heban*). The initial promoter, Shanghai taotai Gong Zhaoyuan, secured authority to establish the mill in Shanghai despite the ten-year monopoly that Li Hongzhang's Shanghai Cotton Cloth Mill held on milling cotton in that city, suggesting that Li was also a silent partner or at least a backer of New Huaxin. Initial shareholders included Gong, other officials, and at least one merchant. The New Huaxin Cotton Mill was a moderate-sized enterprise for 1890, with twelve thousand spindles, eighty looms, and eight gins. The authorized capital was 450,000 taels in 4,500 shares, of which probably half, or 225,000 taels, was paid up. Nie received 450 shares worth 22,500 taels in 1890 when he replaced Gong as Shanghai taotai. This was probably arranged by Yan Xinhou, a stockholder and manager of the New Huaxin Cotton Mill who was also in charge of the Huitong Customs Bank, which the Shanghai taotai supervised and employed as a depository for customs revenues. Mrs. Nie either did not know, or if she knew did not disclose, that public funds may have been transferred from the Customs Bank to purchase stocks for her husband. This transfer may explain part of the shortages in the customs funds discovered when Nie surrendered the seals of office in 1894. Mrs. Nie implies that the acquisition of the New Huaxin stock was the accountant Xu Zijing's doing, not Nie's. Yet, in 1904, she considers the stock Nie's property. Her view seems to be that because Nie borrowed and later replaced the 800,000 taels in 1894, the stocks were therefore his. He had in effect purchased them. W. K. K. Chan, *Merchants, Mandarins and Modern Enterprise*, 89–90; Hsu, *Rise of Modern China*, 284–85.

31 By 1893 the New Huaxin Mill had added three thousand spindles and 150 more looms. In 1894 it became a subsidiary of the Huasheng Spinning and Weaving Mill, a government-supervised industry—successor to Li Hongzhang's Shanghai Cotton Cloth Mill. The New Huaxin Cotton Mill seems to have declined after it was taken over by Huasheng, probably due to stiffer competition from foreign-owned mills and bureaucratic mismanagement. W. K. K. Chan, *Merchants, Mandarins and Modern Enterprises*, 91; Li Xin and Sun Sibai, *Minguo renwuzhuan*, 249.

32 Mrs. Nie characterizes her husband as loathe to become involved in business dealings while holding office. Nie himself does not seem to have suffered such qualms. If he owned the stocks, as Mrs. Nie infers, then he was one of the lessors who contracted with Mr. Tang. This passage seems to be deliberately vague with respect to how Nie came to own these stocks and how he became involved with the mill, probably because it offended Mrs. Nie's sense of propriety that her husband, an imperial official, should be so involved with pecuniary concerns. She may have sought to protect his reputation, or she may not have known the details because she didn't want to know them. W. K. K. Chan, *Merchants, Mandarins and Modern Enterprise*, 89–90.

33 Where the purchase price of 325,000 taels came from is unclear. Mrs. Nie refers to loans, but one could also assume that the 60 percent of profits realized during the four-year lease period (1904–8) while the plant was managed by Qijie and operated as a commercial enterprise, Futai, may have supplied part of the purchase price. W. K. K. Chan, *Merchants, Mandarins and Modern Enterprise*, 92.

34 Hengfeng fangzhi xinju (New Heng Feng Spinning and Weaving Mill). By 1921 Heng Feng had expanded to forty thousand spindles and 354 looms. Annual production reached 128,000 bales of four-, ten-, and sixteen-count cotton yarn and 300,000 bolts of cloth. After 1924 Heng Feng suffered losses and in 1936 was leased to its major creditor, the Zhejiang Development Bank (Zhejiang xingye yinhang), and operated by the China Cotton Company (Zhongmian gongsi) under the name New Heng Feng Centrally Registered Spinning and Weaving Mill (Hengfeng zhongji fangzhi xinju). Chen Zhen and Yao Luo, *Zhongguo jindai gongyeshi ziliao*, 397–98; Zhongguo kexueyuan jingji yanjiuso, *Heng Feng shachangde, fasheng, fazhan, yu gaizao*, 44 (see chapter 3, note 27).

35 Da zhonghua shachang or Da zhonghua fangzhi chang. The Great China Cotton Mill was founded in June 1919 in the aftermath of the May Fourth movement of 1919, which protested the decision of the World War I Allies at the Paris Peace Conference to award the former German economic rights in China's Shandong Province to Japan. This action by the Allies touched off a nationwide boycott of Japanese goods in China and created a demand for cotton that Chinese mills could not meet. The Great China Cotton Mill formally opened in November of that year in the Baoshan District north of Shanghai on the north bank of Yunzao Creek, several hundred yards east of the mouth of the Huangpu River and the Wusong-Shanghai railroad station. By the summer of 1922 it had twenty-five thousand spindles operational and twenty thousand more awaiting installation. Under the general management of Nie Qijie, it sought to increase its capital and expand operations. However, by 1924, the Great China Mill had suffered severe financial setbacks resulting from heightened foreign competition. As a result, the Nies were obliged to sell at a loss of more than 300,000 taels. Chen Zhen and Yao Luo, *Zhongguo jindai gongyeshi ziliao*, 1:398–99 (see chapter 3, note 27).

36 May 7, 1877–June 30, 1927; courtesy name Ziwu, literary name Wujing jushi. Zhang Qihuang came from a distinguished south China gentry family. He was a precocious youth educated at the prestigious Kuangya Academy established by Zhang Zhidong in Guangzhou. He passed the civil service examinations for the *jinshi* in 1904, the year before the examination system was eliminated. He then served as magistrate at Zhijiang in western Hunan until 1910. During this time, his first wife died and he married Nie Qide. After the revolution of 1911, Zhang served as commissioner of military affairs for Hunan under Governor Tan Yenkai. In 1918 he joined the staff of warlord Wu Peifu and served as an adviser to Wu in the Zhili-Anhui War of 1920 and the Zhili-Fengtian War

of 1922. When the latter conflict ended, Zhang was named provincial governor of Guangxi, a post he held until 1924, when he again joined Wu Peifu's staff for the Second Zhili-Fengtian War. In 1927, as Wu was moving his army toward Sichuan, Zhang was killed by sniper fire at Fancheng in the Henan-Hubei border area. Zhang was an artist, a writer, a man of letters, and devotee of fortune-telling. Boorman and Howard, *Biographical Dictionary of Republican China*, 1:22–24.

37 Societies for the encouragement of industry were part of the government reform program in the early twentieth century. They were to be established in each province by 1912–13. Brunnert and Hagelstrom, *Present Day Political Organization of China*, 360.

38 The State Historiographer's Office (also translated Historiography Institute) was attached to the Hanlin Academy and was responsible for preparation of the chronicles of each reign. Hucker, *Dictionary of Official Titles*, 299, no. 3537. The basic annals of Emperor Xuantong (r. 1908–12) state that in March 1911 the name of former Zhejiang governor Nie Qigui, who had died of grief following the demise of family members, was promulgated and transmitted to the state historiographer because of his filial behavior. Qingshi bianxuan weiyuanhui, *Qingshi*, 1:378.

Chapter 7. Widowhood

1 The exact location of Tangping is unclear. The text states it is in the Hexi District; however, there is no Hexi District (literally, the District West of the River) in Hunan. Therefore, I have assumed that Tangping is in the Changsha District in an area known generally as *hexi* (i.e., west of the river).

2 Revolutionary party is used here to translate the term *min dang* (literally, People's party) to distinguish this group from the Constitutional party. The Revolutionary party in Hunan included poor people, drifters, laborers, and peasants—those who had suffered from the collapse of the rural economy brought on by imperialist penetration. These groups were organized and led by secret societies, principally the Gelaohui (Elder Brothers). The Gelaohui joined forces with the revolutionary Hunan gentry, who had earlier advocated constitutional government rather than revolution, to topple the old regime in Changsha on October 22, 1911. However, by the end of October, Constitutionalists had seized power in Changsha and installed Tan Yankai (note 6, below)

as military governor of Hunan. Eto and Schiffrin, *1911 Revolution in China*, 193–208.

3 Established in 1872 by Li Hongzhang to compete with the foreign firms that already dominated China's domestic shipping, the China Merchant's Steam Navigation Company was the first government-supervised merchant enterprise in China. It underwent several changes in management but always enjoyed close links with the government, resulting in preferential treatment and, frequently, inefficient business practices. Feuerwerker, *China's Early Industrialization*, 96–188; Xia Dongyuan, *Zheng Guanying zhuan*, 35–60, 93–135, 214–38, 256–59.

4 The Constitutionalists comprised gentry, merchants, and intellectuals who in the first decade of the twentieth century advocated peaceful transition to constitutional government rather than revolution. After the election of provincial assemblies in 1909 as part of the imperial government's reform measures, these advocates of constitutional government frequently took leadership roles in the assemblies. In Hunan, Constitutionalist leader Tan Yankai (note 6, below), chairman of the provincial assembly, persuaded his colleagues to declare independence shortly after the uprising at Wuchang on October 10, 1911, a move that amounted to joining forces with the popular movement, the Revolutionaries. By the end of October, however, the Constitutionalists had gained power and installed Tan as military governor. Mary C. Wright, *China in Revolution*, 143–45, 176–77.

5 The rearguard of the Hunan provincial forces comprised thirteen battalions trained by Zhang Qihuang. These were experienced troops recruited in Zhang's home province of Guangxi. Five thousand were selected from the rearguard to be the Nanwu Army under the command of Ren Dingyuan and Nie Qixian. The Nanwu Army was organized as a defense battalion and equipped with recent-model German ordnance. The name Nanwu, meaning "military power of the south," was given to the force by an official on the staff of Tan Yankai, military governor of Hunan, following the revolutionary uprising in that province. Zhongguo Shixuehui, *Xinhai geming*, 6:163–64.

6 Courtesy name Zu'an, literary names Weisan and Wuwei. Born in Hangzhou, Zhejiang Province, Tan Yankai's native place was Chaling in Hunan. Tan held the *jinshi* degree and was a member of the Hanlin Academy. He was president of the Hunan Provincial Assembly established in 1909 and a leader of the gentry-based Constitutionalist party in that province. When the revolt broke out at Wuchang in neighboring Hubei Province on October 10, 1911, imperial

troops were moved from Hunan to reinforce the garrison at Wuchang. Revolutionaries then seized power in Changsha, the capital of Hunan, and, in an effort to allay public anxiety, the Revolutionary party leaders appointed the moderate Tan Yankai director of military affairs. Within days, Revolutionary military forces were dispatched from Hunan to support the uprising at Wuchang. Constitutional party leaders took advantage of the power vacuum thus created to assassinate the Revolutionary military governors and install Tan Yankai as military governor, a post he held until he broke with President Yuan Shikai in 1913. Tan subsequently served twice as governor of Hunan until he was ousted in a factional struggle in 1920. From 1924 to 1928, he held high positions in the Guomindang government at Guangzhou and during the Northern Expedition. Tan served as president of the Executive Yuan (cabinet) of the Guomindang government in Nanjing from 1928 until his death. Boorman and Howard, *Biographical Dictionary of Republican China*, 3:220–23; Chen Xulu, Fang, and Wei, *Zhongguo jindaishi cidian*, 740.

7 Established in 1854, the Shanghai Municipal Council administered the International Concession on the west bank of the Huangpu River north of the Old Chinese City of Shanghai. The International Concession was originally the British Concession, which was administered under an agreement with the Chinese government by diplomats and merchants who resided there under the protection of the extraterritoriality provisions of the unequal treaties of 1842 and 1860. Gradually, it expanded to include the United States Concession and extended the right of residency to other foreigners and to Chinese. The council was originally constituted of British landowners and rate payers but came to include nationals of other powers residing in the concession. In 1931, it included five British, two American, two Japanese, and five Chinese members. The concession, and the council that governed it until the Japanese takeover in 1941, remained a constant reminder to Chinese of imperialist power on Chinese soil. Murphey, *Shanghai: Key to Modern China*, 15–28, 80; *Cihai*, 1154; Fairbank, "Creation of the Treaty System," 237–43.

8 In the 1920s these lands became a highly organized agricultural enterprise, the profits from which were an important source of funds for the development of the Heng Feng Cotton Mill. At the beginning of World War I, the Nies used 600,000 yuan from the huge profits that the Heng Feng Cotton Mill made at this time to purchase additional land adjacent to the original acreage and to make improvements. The whole tract was known as the Zhongfuyuan. It bordered Datung Lake, an arm of Dongting Lake, on the east, extending about

eight kilometers east and west and five kilometers north and south. The total area comprised approximately 7,500 hundred acres. The dykes to keep out the waters of the lake were seven to eight meters in height and sixty-five to seventy meters wide at the base.

After 1920, formal management was established, with a director, a deputy director, a chairman of the dykes, a police force, and agencies for external relations, overall supervision, auditing, and so on. The authorities could arrest, try, and take the tenants into custody. All matters related to tenancy were handled in the form of official instructions as though the Zhongfuyuan was a government agency. The chairman of the dykes was nominally appointed by the district magistrate; however, the deputy director of the Zhongfuyuan always held the post and was the de facto boss of the Zhongfuyuan. There were twenty to thirty men in the police force under his command, including officers of various ranks. The external relations people developed personal ties with officials and other external agencies. The general supervisor had jurisdiction over the tenants. The auditor had responsibility for supervising and inspecting income and expenditures as well as rent collection. Altogether there were about thirty clerks, forty laborers, and thirty security personnel, with a monthly payroll of about fifteen hundred yuan.

The land of the Zhongfuyuan was divided into four zones: north, south, east, and west. These were further subdivided: the east zone into ten plots, the west into ten, the south into five, and the north into nine. Each plot varied in size from about 150 to 335 acres. The plot headman for each plot collected rents. There were approximately three thousand tenant families: two thousand who paid rent directly to the owners and one thousand who sublet land. The total population was more than twenty thousand. Before a tenant rented land, he first had to give a rent deposit. The landlord then gave him a property receipt which had on the face the amount of the rent and the deposit given. On the back there were six conditions listed. This constituted the tenant's rental contract. The conditions for rental were very rigid: for example, the land could not be sublet; if it were, the landlord could reclaim it and rent it to someone else; if the tenants didn't pay the full rent in kind, then the landlord could deduct the amount due from the rent deposit. The rent deposit was three to six yuan for each *mou* (one-sixth of an acre). It averaged about four yuan; initially it was as low as two yuan but it gradually increased. It was also stipulated that 3 percent of the area rented could be used for a domicile and rent would not be collected on that.

The principal income of the Zhongfuyuan came from land rents. The vast majority were from rice paddies; a smaller amount came from cotton. In general, rents equaled half the annual harvest. Of all the land rented in the Zhongfuyuan, cotton fields made up about 8 percent. The annual rents from these totaled about 7,500 kilograms of cotton. The rest of the land was rice paddies. The annual rent from these was fifty to sixty thousand piculs. In addition to the land rent, there were various other levies. The conditions for rental also stipulated that rent or additional levies owed by the tenants were charged interest. The rate went as high as 30 percent. Tenant indebtedness mounted with the passage of time, and some tenants were reduced to virtual serfdom.

In 1921 the Zhongfuyuan established the Xiefeng Wholesale Grain Depot in Changsha to store the enormous harvests from the Zhongfuyuan and to corner the grain market. It was one of the largest grain depots in Hunan, with a storage capacity of more than 180,000 bushels of grain and machinery for milling. Although sales, storage, and milling of grain were its primary business, the Xiefeng Grain Depot also served as an economic link between the Heng Feng Cotton Mill and the Zhongfuyuan. Xiefeng was the channel for funds between the Zhongfuyuan and Heng Feng, promoting the sales of Heng Feng products in Hunan and accepting loans from the Zhongfuyuan for Heng Feng. This triangular relationship also carried commercial remittances between the Zhongfuyuan and Changsha and between Changsha and Shanghai. Not only were large profits gained from making the remittances, but it was also possible to use large amounts of the remittance fund interest free for the Heng Feng Cotton Mill and the establishment of the Heng Feng Mill Number 2. Hunan shengzhi bianzuan weiyuanhui, *Hunan shengzhi*, 1: "Hunan jinbainian dashi jishu"; Bergere, *Chinese Bourgeoisie*, 161.

9 Chen Zhen and Yao Luo, *Zhongguo jindai gongyeshi ziliao*, 1:397.

10 The Chinese Cotton Mill Owners' Association had been organized in 1917 to lobby for the retention of an export tax on raw cotton that Japanese interests sought to have removed. Bergere, *Chinese Bourgeoisie*, 133–34.

11 The information in this paragraph concerning Nie Qijie's leadership in the world of commerce prior to 1920 is incorporated from collateral sources to explain his rise to the presidency of the Shanghai General Chamber of Commerce, which Mrs. Nie recorded in 1920. Bergere, *Chinese Bourgeoisie*, 136; Bergere, "Chinese Bourgeoisie, 1911–1937," 757.

12 See chapter 4, note 2.

13 West Lake, so called since the Tang dynasty (618–907), lies to the west of the city of Hangzhou, capital of Zhejiang and southern terminus of the Grand

Canal. Its shoreline is 15 kilometers, and the surface area is 5.2 square kilometers. The lake is flanked by high mountains and divided into several sections by embankments. Numerous temples and recreation areas are situated along its shoreline, including the temple of the well-known patriot and martyr of the Southern Song dynasty (1133–1279) Yue Fei (1103–41). It is among the most renowned scenic spots in China. *Cihai*, 4196–97; Guojia wenwu shiye guanliju, *Zhongguo mingsheng cidian*, 360–61 and photograph in front matter.

14 Another interpretation of the division of assets at this time is that it was brought on by family squabbling and that the Heng Feng Cotton Mill became in effect a general partnership of Nie's sons, grandsons, and widow. The sources also differ over who received shares and half shares. In 1924, after a series of setbacks, Nie Qijie was obliged to yield the directorship of Heng Feng to his brother and partner, Nie Qiying (Lusheng), who during World War II collaborated with the Japanese puppet government in Shanghai. In 1943 Nie Lusheng became a member of the mixed Sino-Japanese Executive Committee for the administration of the Heng Feng Cotton Mills. After the Nationalist government regained control of Shanghai in 1945, Nie Qijie, who had not collaborated with the puppet government, resumed the presidency of the Associated Heng Feng Cotton Mills. Following Qijie's death in 1953, his son Nie Guangkun (Liukang, Hanzhang) was named manager of the Heng Feng Cotton Mills, by then a joint state-private enterprise in socialist transition. Bergere, *Chinese Bourgeoisie*, 161–62; Zhongguo kexueyuan jingji yanjiuso, *Heng Feng shachangde fasheng, fazhan, yu gaizao*, 45, 74, 96–98; Li Xin and Sun Sibai, *Minguo renwuzhuan*, 251–55.

15 Established in 1897 in Shanghai by Sheng Xuanhuai, industrialist and financial adviser to Li Hongzhang, the Nanyang School was originally supported by two of Sheng's commercial enterprises: the Imperial Telegraph Administration and the China Merchant's Steam Navigation Company. It underwent several name changes and reorganizations before the 1911 revolution, after which it was taken over by the Ministry of Communications and renamed the Shanghai Industrial School. In 1921 the Shanghai Industrial School merged with several other technical schools and adopted the name Jiaotong (Communications) University. The following year, 1922, it reverted to the name Nanyang until 1927, when it became the First Jiaotong University. In 1928 the name was shortened to Jiaotong University. Since then the university has undergone displacements, reorganization, and expansion. At this writing, it is a comprehensive university with faculties of philosophy, science, and engineering called Shanghai Jiaotong University. *Cihai*, 305, 797.

16 See note 15, above.

17 Courtesy name Zhongliang, posthumous title Wenzhuang. A native of the Lujiang District in Anhui Province, Liu Bingzhang earned the *jinshi* degree in 1860 and was inducted into the Hanlin Academy. He served as a commander in Li Hongzhang's Huai (Anhui) Army during the Taiping Revolutionary movement and the Nian Rebellion. After several provincial appointments in the 1860s, Liu was named governor of Jiangxi (1875–78), governor of Zhejiang (1882–86), and governor general of Sichuan (1886–94). Though he owed his appointments to high office to the influence of Li Hongzhang, Liu Bingzhang was known for his opposition to the introduction of Western technology and learning favored by Li. Liu spent his final years in Beijing awaiting assignment. Cai, *Qingdai qibai mingren zhuan*, 1181–84; Wei Xiumei, *Qingji zhiguanbiao*, 75.

18 Literary name Xiaoxia. A native of Lianping District in Guangdong Province, Yan Zhongji passed the civil service examinations, attaining the *jinshi* degree in 1863. In the first decade of the twentieth century, he served as provincial judge in Hunan and Zhejiang as well as financial commissioner in Shaanxi and Zhejiang. Wei Xiumei, *Qingji zhiguanbiao*, 2:232.

19 A native of He District of Guangxi, Lin Zhaoyuan was a *lingsheng*, or government stipendiary, a status achieved through success on special provincial examinations. Before serving as governor of Guizhou (1881–83), he held the posts of judge and financial commissioner in that province. Wei Xiumei, *Qingji zhiguanbiao*, 2:65.

20 Courtesy name Cihuang. A native of He District of Guangxi, Lin Shitao held the *jinshi* degree and was a compiler in the Hanlin Academy. After the establishment of the Republic in 1912, he served as a compiler in the State Office of Historiography and in 1917 was a member of the provisional parliament. Tahara Tennan, *Shinsue minsho chugoku kanshin jinmeiroku*, 37.

21 April 2, 1874–December 4, 1939; courtesy name Ziyu. A native of Penglai in Dengzhou Prefecture, Shandong, Wu Peifu passed the district-level civil service examinations in 1896 but followed a military rather than a civil service career. After graduating in 1902 from the Baoding Military Academy in Zhili, Wu rose through the commissioned ranks of the Beiyang Army commanded and controlled by Yuan Shikai, later first president of the Republic (1912–16). Following Yuan's death in 1916, the Beiyang military clique, which he headed, split into two factions in 1918. Wu became identified with the Zhili faction. By 1921 Wu had gained control of the Zhili faction and the following year emerged as the dominant figure in the warlord melee of north China. He controlled the government in Beijing until 1924, when he was dislodged by a rival war-

lord faction. Wu continued, however, to dominate the provinces of Henan, Hubei, and Hunan until 1926, when his forces were defeated by the Northern Expeditionary Forces of the Guomindang. Wu devoted the rest of his days to scholarship and study, declining several offers from Japan to head puppet governments in north China during the 1930s. Boorman and Howard, *Biographical Dictionary of Republican China*, 3:444–50; Chen Xulu, Fang, and Wei, *Zhongguo jindaishi cidian*, 338.

22 The National Revolutionary Army of the Guomindang party, including elements from the Chinese Communist forces incorporated under the United Front agreement of 1923, launched the Northern Expedition from the south China province of Guangdong in 1926. Commanded by General Chiang Kai-shek (1887–1975), the Northern Expedition aimed at ridding China of warlord cliques and imperialist controls and establishing unity under Guomindang rule. The uneasy coalition of the Guomindang and Communists came apart in the summer of 1927 after the National Revolutionary Army had occupied the Yangzi Valley and begun a drive toward Beijing. Communist military units driven from the National Revolutionary Army withdrew to a remote base on the Jiangxi-Hunan border in south-central China. Chiang Kai-shek led the remaining Guomindang troops of the National Revolutionary Army northward, capturing Beijing and declaring China unified under Guomindang rule in June 1928. In the course of the Northern Expedition, Chiang entered alliances with major warlords and assured the principal imperialist powers of his intention to respect legitimate treaty rights, thereby compromising the original goals of the expedition and making the Guomindang's "unification of China" nominal at best. Because of this, Chiang shifted his capital from Beijing to Nanjing in the lower Yangzi Valley, where his actual control was strongest. Wilbur, "The Nationalist Revolution," 575–720.

23 See chapter 6, note 36.

24 After the breakup of the United Front of Communists and Guomindang in the summer of 1927, the Communists dispersed and went underground. Communist military units withdrew to a remote area on the Jiangxi-Hunan border, where they enlarged the Red Army through recruitment of peasants. After the failure of several Communist-led urban uprisings, the Moscow-based Communist International urged the Chinese party led by Li Li-san (b. 1898) to employ the rurally recruited Red Army to capture urban industrial centers. Accordingly, in late July 1930 the Red Army took and held Changsha for ten days before Guomindang units forced it to withdraw. Though the Communist forces

threatened to take the city again in September, they were ultimately unsuccessful. The Changsha debacle indicated that the strategy of initiating Communist revolution in the cities favored by Moscow could not succeed; without well-organized urban support the Red Army was unable to fend off the systematic attacks of better trained and equipped Guomindang forces. After Changsha, the Red Army remained in rural areas of Jiangxi where it came under the leadership of Mao. The urban activities of the Chinese Communist party came under the direction of the Moscow-recognized leaders known as the "Twenty-eight Bolsheviks" or "Returned Students" (because of their previous study in the Soviet Union). Ch'en, "The Communist Movement," 198–204.

25 *Fangjian* literally means "street checks." The meaning is unclear.

26 Originally, *qipao* referred to the dress worn by women in the households of the Manchu Banners, the hereditary Manchu military units stationed throughout China (1644–1911). The literal meaning is "banner gown." After the revolution of 1911 ended Manchu rule in China, Chinese women adopted this dress. It has undergone numerous improvements in style. In general, the *qipao* has a high collar, overlaps and opens on the right side in the front, is snug around the waist, extends below the knee, and is slit on both sides of the skirt. The sleeves vary in length. *Cihai*, 3553; E. Wu, "The Enduring Legacy of the Chi Pao."

27 In 1909 the districts of Hunan Province bordering on Dongting Lake experienced floods and poor harvests. Governor of Hunan Cen Chunming (1868–1923), other officials, landlords, unscrupulous gentry, and foreign firms had bought up grain, hoarded it, and driven up the price. They also shipped large quantities to neighboring provinces, seeking to maximize profits. This aggravated the situation throughout the whole province. Starving crowds converged on Changsha. The price of rice doubled and then tripled in one day. On April 12 a crowd of more than one hundred people destroyed the rice-hulling firms that had forced up prices, demanding a fair price. Governor Cen issued orders to suppress the protesters, but on April 23 several thousand people stormed the governor's offices, beating up the police taotai, Lai Chengyu. That night rice shops were ransacked. The next day all businesses in the city ceased operation. Governor Cen then gave the order to open the grain storage facilities. More than twenty people lost their lives. The infuriated mob burnt the governor's office, the Tax Bureau, several banks, the residences of the foreign consuls, foreign business firms, churches, the post office, wharves, and godowns. In April, Great Britain, the United States, France, Japan, and Germany dispatched gunboats to support the imperial troops suppressing the angry crowds. Hundreds

of protesters were arrested, and an untold number were injured and killed. A nationwide outcry followed, and the imperial government was obliged to remove Governor Cen from office. The provincial government began importing rice and banned rice exports, resulting in lower prices; the disturbances then began to subside. Chen Xulu, Fang, and Wei, *Zhongguo jindaishi cidian*, 126. The interpretation of the Changsha rice riots as a spontaneous uprising of the starving masses against the greed and exploitation of government officials and gentry has been called into question by Arthur Rosenbaum, who shows that the progressive gentry of Hunan (the Constitutionalists), alienated by the government's inept efforts at reform, sided with the hungry peasants and exploited the rioters to drive the reactionary governor Cen Chunming from office. Rosenbaum, "Gentry Power and the Changsha Rice Riot of 1910," 689–715.

28 The Middle Way, or Mean, is a central notion in Confucian thought—"impartial and unbiased, without excess and without shortcoming." *Cihai*, 3225.

Epilogue

1. The easy correspondence between Mrs. Nie's Christian faith and the Confucian teachings of Zeng Guofan are clear from the following poem, in which Zeng proclaims his faith in the power of goodness, condemns malevolence, and disdains the desire for worldly riches.

Hate Not and Seek Nothing
(A Poetic Summary)
Zeng Guofan

The greatest virtue is mercy; the greatest vice is envy.
The deeds of one with a jealous heart are like the bickering of wives and concubines—petty, neither straightforward nor upright.
Without talent, such a person disdains the ability of others.
Encountering ill fortune, he envies the advances of others.
Without accomplishments, he begrudges others the chance for success.
Without support, he covets the help that others receive.
With position and influence the same as others, he only fears they will draw near or surpass him; therefore, he hates them.
Without fame, he looks with jealousy upon the admiration that others enjoy for their literary distinction.

Having no distinguished descendants, he hates those that have prosperous progeny.
Scurrying about night and day striving for fame, hurrying frantically hither and yon to grasp possessions,
Ever hoping one day to enjoy great prestige, caring not if others suffer his evil influences,
Hearing of a disaster and feeling joyful, if asked why, not knowing,
Not only the gods come to your help, even demons nurture your great abilities.
Universal and eternal logic warns of retribution.
If you are such a person who jealously hates others, you will bring only misfortune on yourself.
In extreme cases you will suffer physical harm.
In lesser cases your life will be shortened.
Therefore, the younger generation must be constantly aware to yield to others.
If you do, you will lose nothing.
Always pray for and wish others well.
If you do, you will suffer no loss.
If you can eliminate jealous hate, then all people will experience blessings like those we hope will descend on the entire world.
I will fear nothing and hate not.

If one can be content with things, such a person will feel that heaven and earth are vast and rational.
If one constantly is grasping, then even the vastness of space will seem narrow and confined.
If his desires are too many, it surely is harmful.
While living a frugal life, he will wish for more wealth.
When living is difficult, he will wish for greater ease.
After he has gained wealth, he will want a thousand carriages.
If he does not get them, he will seek frantically.
When he has them, he will want them to last forever, to be fragrant as orchids and as durable as stone.
Thus, seeking splendor and wealth and knowing no limit to desire causes avarice to be great and conceit to grow.
However, just as the cold clear light of the moon is sometimes hidden by clouds,
When we enjoy good fortune, everything is smooth; but when good fortune deserts us, then calamities follow.
Not only can we not expect good luck, all kinds of disasters actually befall us.
If we say anything, we are blamed.

We can do nothing, melancholy and depression set in, and the spirit gradually weakens.
Lift up your head and look about you, discover how great are heaven and earth.
Peace and prosperity do not come to us in a single stroke,
Nor do troubles come upon us from a single fault.
Nine out of ten people have no means of subsistence.
Many are worse off than I.
I can endure a life of poverty, not to mention times like these when all is going smoothly.
Ah, no matter what happens, I am ready.
If one asks a little less of this world, one can live happily.
Until death, I will seek nothing from life, then I will have no regrets.

The values expressed in this poem together with family solidarity, diligence, frugality, honesty, and respect for learning, all of which Zeng impressed upon Mrs. Nie in her youth, constituted the core of her moral code. Mrs. Nie seems to have assimilated the Christian notions of faith, hope, and charity effortlessly into this code.

Judging from a memorial essay written by Mrs. Nie's sons shortly after her death, she continued practices associated with Buddhist beliefs into her old age. They attributed her longevity to her moral qualities: respect for living things, frugality, simplicity, charity, good works, selflessness, and concern for others. Respect for life led her to engage in the traditional Buddhist practice of "releasing living creatures" (*fang sheng*), such as fish and frogs, back into the wild on her birthday and on the Buddha's birthday. Buddhists believe that this practice will bring benefit in the afterlife. Mrs. Nie presumably continued to release living things after her conversion to Christianity in 1915 since her sons credited this practice as one of the factors that brought her longevity. Her moral eclecticism seems to have gone beyond the obvious correspondence of Christian and Confucian values to include at least this aspect of Buddhist belief. Nie Qijie, "Chongde laoren jiniance," 299–303.

Translator's Afterword

1 Rowe, *Hankow Conflict and Community in a Chinese City*, 345–46.
2 Cohen, "Self-strengthening in China-centered Perspective," 33–34.
3 Chen Jiang, "Recent Chinese Historiography on the Western Affairs Movement," 117.

4 Shen Chuanjing, "Zhongguo jindaishide jiben xiansuo he xinwenhua yundong," 1–14.

5 Rowe, *Hankow Conflict and Community in a Chinese City*, 345–52.

6 Bergere, *Chinese Bourgeoisie*, 13–98.

7 Ibid., 160–63, 175–77.

8 Ibid., 272–97.

9 For a brief but comprehensive review of the literature see K. T. Wei, *Women in China*, which includes sections on biographies, autobiographies, and memoirs as well as works of historical perspective. An earlier, more specialized, work is Reynolds, *Preliminary Bibliography*. M. Young, *Women in China: Studies in Social Change and Feminism*, 243–48, contains a brief but well-annotated bibliography on "Women in Traditional China."

10 Wu Pei-yi, *Confucian's Progress*, especially x–xii, includes an enlightening discussion of the tension between the standards for verisimilitude and the urge for self-revelation in traditional autobiographical writing.

11 A woman well known for her advocacy of change was Qiu Jin, the heroine of revolutionary nationalism at the turn of the century, a contemporary of Mrs. Nie whose life stands in sharp contrast to hers; see Wolf and Witke, *Women in Chinese Society*. Snow, *Women in Modern China*, and Smedley, *Portraits of Chinese Women in Revolution*, contain many biographies and autobiographies—in a similar vein—from the early twentieth century. The victimization of women is dealth with in a stirring and realistic autobiography, *A Daughter of Han: The Autobiography of a Chinese Working Woman*, trans. Ida Pruitt. See also Rowbotham, *Women, Resistance, and Revolution*, 170–75; Wolf and Witke, *Women in Chinese Society*, 111–41; Guisso and Johannesen, *Women in China*, 163–77.

12 Wu Pei-yi, *Confucian's Progress*, 32–41.

13 Li Yuning, "Historical Roots of Changes in Women's Status in Modern China," in Li, *Chinese Women Through Chinese Eyes*, 102–22; Li, "Hsu Tsung-han," 91–110; Guisso and Johannesen, *Women in China*, 179–238.

14 Li Yuning, *Chinese Women Through Chinese Eyes*, 117–18.

15 Chang Chung-li, *Chinese Gentry*, 51–70. As Rowe points out, this assumption of gentry functions by the emerging bourgeoisie was already under way in nineteenth-century Hankow. Rowe, *Hankow Commerce and Society in a Chinese City*, 345.

WORKS CITED

Ayers, William. *Chang Chih-tung and Educational Reform in China*. Cambridge: Harvard University Press, 1971.

Bao, Zhao. *Bao Canjun jishu* [The collected and annotated works of Adjudant Bao Zhao]. Shanghai: Quji chubanshe, 1980.

Belsky, R. D. "Bones of Contention: The Siming Gongsuo Riots of 1874 and 1898." *Papers on Chinese History* (Harvard University) 1.1 (Spring 1992): 56–73.

Bennett, Adrian Arthur. *John Fryer: The Introduction of Western Science and Technology into Nineteenth-Century China*. Cambridge: Harvard University Press, 1967.

Bergere, Marie-Claire. "The Chinese Bourgeoisie, 1911–1937." In John K. Fairbank, ed., *The Cambridge History of China*. Vol. 12: *Republican China, 1911–1949*, 721–825. New York: Cambridge University Press, 1983.

———. *The Golden Age of the Chinese Bourgeoisie, 1911–1937*. Translated by Janet Lloyd. New York: Cambridge University Press, English edition, 1989.

Bian, Baodi, and Li Hanzhang, comps. *Hunan tongzhi* [Comprehensive gazetteer of Hunan]. Edited by Zeng Guoquan and Guo Songtao. Reprint. Shanghai: Quji chubanshe, 1990.

Biggerstaff, Knight. *The Earliest Modern Government Schools in China*. Ithaca, N.Y.: Cornell University Press, 1961.

Boorman, Howard L., and Richard C. Howard, eds. *Biographical Dictionary of Republican China*. New York: Columbia University Press, 1967–71.

Borton, Hugh. *Japan's Modern Century from Perry to 1970*. 2d ed. New York: Ronald Press, 1970.

Boulger, Demetrius. *The Life of Sir Halliday Macartney*. London: John Lane, 1908.

Bruner, Katherine F., John K. Fairbank, and Richard J. Smith. *Entering China's Service: Robert Hart's Journals, 1854–1863*. Cambridge: Harvard University Press, 1986.

Brunnert, H. S., and V. V. Hagelstrom. *Present Day Political Organization of China*. Taipei: Wenxing shudian, 1963.

Bynner, Witter, trans. *Three Hundred Poems of the T'ang Dynasty, 618–906*. Reprint.

Taipei: Book World Company, n.d.

Cai, Guanlo, ed. *Qingdai qibai mingren zhuan* [Biographies of seven hundred famous people of the Qing period]. 3 vols. Beijing: Zhongguo shuju, 1984.

Carlson, Ellsworth C. *The Kaiping Mines (1877–1912).* 2d ed. Cambridge: Harvard University, East Asian Research Center, 1971.

Chai, Ch'u, and Winberg Chai, eds. *Li Chi Book of Rites.* 2 vols. Translated by James Legge. New Hyde Park, N.Y.: University Books, 1967.

Chan, Anthony B. *Arming the Chinese: The Western Armaments Trade in Warlord China, 1920–1928.* Vancouver: University of British Columbia Press, 1982.

Chan, Wellington K. K. "Government, merchants and industry to 1911." In John K. Fairbank and Kwang-Ching Liu, eds., *The Cambridge History of China.* Vol. 11: *Late Ch'ing, 1800–1911,* part 2, 416–62. New York: Cambridge University Press, 1980.

———. *Merchants, Mandarins and Modern Enterprise in Late Ch'ing China.* Cambridge: Harvard University Press, 1977.

Chang, Chung-li. *The Chinese Gentry: Studies on Their Role in Nineteenth-Century Chinese Society.* Seattle: University of Washington Press, 1955.

Chang, Hao. "Intellectual Change and the Reform Movement, 1890–98." In John K. Fairbank and Kwang-Ching Liu, eds., *The Cambridge History of China.* Vol. 11: *Late Ch'ing, 1800–1911,* pt. 2. New York: Cambridge University Press, 1980.

———. *Liang Ch'i-ch'ao and Intellectual Transition in China, 1890–1907.* Cambridge: Harvard University Press, 1971.

———. "On the Ching-shih Ideal in Neo Confucianism." *Ch'ing-shih wen-t'i.* 3.1 (November 1974): 36–61.

Chang, Hsin-pao. *Commissioner Lin and the Opium War.* Cambridge: Harvard University Press, 1964.

Chen, Gideon. *Tso Tsung-t'ang: Pioneer Promoter of the Modern Woolen Mill in China.* Peiping: Yenching University Press, 1938.

Ch'en, Jerome. "The Chinese Communist Movement to 1927." In John K. Fairbank, ed., *The Cambridge History of China.* Vol. 12: *Republican China, 1912–1949* pt. 1, 505–26. New York: Cambridge University Press, 1983.

———. "The Communist Movement 1927–1937." In John K. Fairbank and Albert Feuerwerker, eds., *The Cambridge History of China.* Vol. 13: *Republican China, 1912–1949,* pt. 2, 168–229. New York: Cambridge University Press, 1986.

———. "Rebels Between Rebellions—Secret Societies in the Novel *Péng Kung An.*" *Journal of Asian Studies* 29.4 (August 1970): 807–22.

Chen, Jiang. "Recent Chinese Historiography on the Western Affairs Movement: Yangwu Yundong, 1860–1895." *Late Imperial China* 7.1 (June 1986): 112–27.

Chen, Xulu, Fang Shiming, and Wei Jianyou, eds. *Zhongguo jindaishi cidian* [Dictionary of modern Chinese history]. Shanghai: Cishu chubanshe, 1982.

Chen, Zhen, and Yao Luo, eds. *Zhongguo jindai gongyeshi ziliao* [Materials on the industrial history of modern China]. 3 vols. Beijing: Sanlian shuju, 1957.

Chere, Lewis M. *The Diplomacy of the Sino-French War (1883–1885): Global Complications of an Undeclared War*. Notre Dame, Ind.: Cross Cultural Publications, 1989.

Chesneaux, Jean, ed. *Popular Movements and Secret Societies in China, 1840–1950*. Stanford, Calif.: Stanford University Press, 1972.

———. *Secret Societies in China in the Nineteenth and Twentieth Centuries*. Translated by Gillian Nettle. Ann Arbor: University of Michigan Press, 1971.

Chiang, Siang-tseh. *The Nien Rebellion*. Seattle: University of Washington Press, 1954.

Chow, Tse-tsung. *The May Fourth Movement: Intellectual Revolution in Modern China*. Reprint. Stanford, Calif.: Stanford University Press, 1967.

Chu, Samuel C. *Reformer in Modern China: Chang Chien, 1853–1926*. New York: Columbia University Press, 1965.

Ch'u, Tung-tsu. *Local Government in China under the Ch'ing*. Cambridge: Harvard University Press, 1988.

Cihai bianji weiyuanhui, ed. *Cihai* [Encyclopaedic dictionary of Chinese]. 3 vols. Shanghai: Cishu chubanshe, 1979.

Ciyuan, xiudingzu [Ciyuan revision group], with Shangwu yinshuguan bianjibu [Commercial Press editorial department], eds. *Ciyuan Xiudingben* [Etymological dictionary, rev. ed.]. 4 vols. Beijing: Shangwu yinshuguan, 1984.

Cohen, Paul A. *China and Christianity: The Missionary Movement and the Growth of Antiforeignism, 1860–1870*. Cambridge: Harvard University Press, 1963.

———. "Christian Missions and Their Impact to 1900." In John K. Fairbank, ed., *The Cambridge History of China*. Vol. 10: *Late Ch'ing, 1800–1911*, pt. 1, 543–90. New York: Cambridge University Press, 1978.

———. *Discovering History in China: American Historical Writing on the Recent Chinese Past*. New York: Columbia University Press, 1984.

———. "Self-strengthening in China-centered Perspective: The Evolution of American Historiography." *Qingji ziqiang yundong yantaohui lunwenji* [Proceedings of the Conference on the Self-strengthening Movement in Late Ch'ing China, 1860–1894]. 2 vols. Taipei: Zhongyang yanjiuyuan jindaishi yanjiusuo, 1988.

Cohen, Paul A., and John E. Schrecker, eds. *Reform in Nineteenth-Century China*. Cambridge: Harvard University Press, 1976.

Couling, Samuel. *The Encyclopedia Sinica*. London: Oxford University Press, 1917.

Culin, Stewart. *Chinese Games with Dice and Dominoes*. Extract from the Smithsonian Institute Report of 1893. Seattle: Shorey Book Store, facsimile reproduction, 1972.

Dai, Yi, and Lin Yanjiao, eds. *Qingdai renwu zhuangao* [Draft biographies of famous persons of the Qing period]. Vol. 1, pt. 2. Shenyang: Liaoning renmin chubanshe, 1984.

de Bary, William Theodore. *East Asian Civilizations: A Dialogue in Five Stages*. Cambridge: Harvard University Press, 1988.

de Bary, William Theodore, and the Conference on Seventeenth-Century Chinese Thought. *The Unfolding of Neo-Confucianism*. New York: Columbia University Press, 1975.

Eastman, Lloyd E. "Nationalist China during the Nanking Decade, 1927–1937." In John K. Fairbank and Albert Feuerwerker, eds. *The Cambridge History of China*. Vol. 13: *Republican China, 1912–1949*, pt. 2, 116–67. New York: Cambridge University Press, 1986.

Eberhard, Wolfram. *A Dictionary of Chinese Symbols*. London: Routledge and Kegan Paul, n.d.

Ebrey, Patricia Buckley, ed. *Chinese Civilization and Society: A Source Book*. New York: Free Press, 1981.

Esherick, Joseph W. *The Origins of the Boxer Uprising*. Berkeley: University of California Press, 1987.

Eto, Shinkichi. "China's International Relations, 1911–1931." In John K. Fairbank and Albert Feuerwerker, eds., *The Cambridge History of China*. Vol. 13: *Republican China, 1912–1949*, pt. 2, 74–115. New York: Cambridge University Press, 1986.

Eto, Shinkichi, and Harold Z. Schriffrin, eds. *The 1911 Revolution in China*. Tokyo: University of Tokyo Press, 1984.

Fairbank, John K., "The Creation of the Treaty System." In John K. Fairbank, ed., *The Cambridge History of China*. Vol. 10: *Late Ch'ing, 1800–1911*, pt. 1, 213–63. New York: Cambridge University Press, 1978.

———. *The Great Chinese Revolution 1800–1985*. New York: Harper and Row, 1987.

Fairbank, John K., Edwin O. Reischauer, and Albert Craig. *East Asia: The Modern Transformation*. Boston: Houghton Mifflin, 1965.

———. *East Asia: Tradition and Transformation*. Boston: Houghton Mifflin, 1978.

Fairbank, John King, Katherine Frost Bruner, and Elizabeth MacLeod Matheson. *The I. G. in Peking Letters of Robert Hart: Chinese Maritime Customs, 1868–1907*. 2 vols. Cambridge: Harvard University Press, 1975.

Fan, Wenlan. *Zhongguo jindaishi* [Modern Chinese history]. 9th ed. 2 vols. Beijing: Renmin chubanshe, 1955.

Fang, Zongcheng, ed. "Kaixian Li shangshu (Zongxi) zhenshu" [The official papers of Li Zongxi]. In Shen Yunlong, ed. *Jindai Zhongguo shiliao congkan* [Collected historical materials on modern China]. Series 47, no. 2. Taipei: Wenhai chubanshe, 1966.

Feuerwerker, Albert. *China's Early Industrialization: Sheng Hsuan-huai (1844–1916) and Mandarin Enterprise*. New York: Atheneum, 1970.

Fung, Yulan. *A History of Chinese Philosophy*. 2 vols. Translated by Derk Bodde. Princeton: Princeton University Press, 1952, 1953.

Giles, Herbert A. *A Chinese Biographical Dictionary*. 2 vols. Reprint. Taipei: Literature House, 1962.

———. *A Chinese-English Dictionary*. 1912. Reprint. Taipei: Literature House, 1964.

Giquel, Prosper. *A Journal of the Chinese Civil War, 1864*. Edited by Steven Leibo. Honolulu: University of Hawaii Press, 1985.

Guisso, Richard W., and Stanley Johannesen, eds. *Women in China: Current Directions in Historical Scholarship*. Youngstown, N.Y.: Philo Press, 1981.

Guojia wenwu shiye guanliju, ed. *Zhongguo mingsheng zidian* [Dictionary of famous places in China]. Shanghai: Cishu chubanshe, 1981.

He, Changling, ed. *Huangchao jingshi wenbian* [Collected writings on statecraft of the reigning dynasty]. Reprint. Taipei: Shijie shuju, 1963.

He, Yikun. *Zeng Guofan pingzhuan* [Critical biography of Zeng Guofan]. Reprint. Taipei: Zhongzheng shuju, 1979.

Ho, Ping-ti. *The Ladder of Success in Imperial China: Aspects of Social Mobility, 1368–1911*. New York: Columbia University Press, 1962.

———. "Salient Aspects of China's Heritage." In Ho Ping-ti and Tsou Tang, eds., *China in Crisis*. 2 vols. Chicago: University of Chicago Press, 1968, 1:1–92.

———. "The Salt Merchants of Yangchou: A Study of Commercial Capitalism in Eighteenth-Century China." *Harvard Journal of Asiatic Studies* 17 (1954): 130–68.

———. "The Significance of the Ch'ing Period in Chinese History." *Journal of Asian Studies* 26.2 (February 1967): 189–95.

———. *Studies on the Population of China, 1368–1953*. Cambridge: Harvard University Press, 1959.

Hook, Brian, ed. *The Cambridge Encyclopedia of China*. New York: Cambridge University Press, 1982.

Hsiao, Kung-chuan. *A Modern China and a New World: K'ang Yu-wei, Reformer and Utopian, 1858–1927*. Seattle: University of Washington Press, 1975.

Hsu, Immanuel C. Y. *China's Entrance into the Family of Nations: The Diplomatic Phase, 1858–1880*. Cambridge: Harvard University Press, 1960.

———. *The Ili Crisis: A Study of Sino-Russian Diplomacy, 1871–1881*. London: Oxford University Press, 1965.

———. "Late Ch'ing Foreign Relations, 1866–1905." In John K. Fairbank and Kwang-Ching Liu, eds., *The Cambridge History of China*. Vol. 11: *Late Ch'ing, 1800–1911*, pt. 2. New York: Cambridge University Press, 1980.

———. *The Rise of Modern China*. 4th ed. New York: Oxford University Press, 1990.

Hu, Sheng. *Imperialism and Chinese Politics*. Beijing: Foreign Language Press, 1978.

Huang, Philip. *Liang Ch'i-ch'ao and Modern Chinese Liberalism*. Seattle: University of Washington Press, 1972.

Huard, Pierre, and Wong, Ming. *Chinese Medicine*. New York: McGraw-Hill, 1972.

Hucker, Charles O. *A Dictionary of Official Titles in Imperial China*. Stanford: Stanford University Press, 1985.

Hummel, Arthur W., ed. *Eminent Chinese of the Ch'ing Period*. Reprint. Taipei: Literature House, 1964.

Hunan shengzhi bianzuan weiyuanhui. "Hunan jinbainian dashi jishu" [Record of major events in Hunan over the past hundred years]. In *Hunan shengzhi* [History of Hunan Province]. Vol. 1. Changsha: Hunan renmin chubanshe, 1959.

Ichiko, Chuzo. "Political and Institutional Reform, 1901–1911." In John K. Fairbank and Kwang-Ching Liu, eds., *The Cambridge History of China*. Vol. 11: *Late Ch'ing, 1800–1911*, pt. 2, 375–415. New York: Cambridge University Press, 1980.

Iriye, Akira, "Japanese Aggression and China's International Position, 1931–1949." In John K. Fairbank and Albert Feuerwerker, eds., *The Cambridge History of China*. Vol. 13: *Republican China, 1912–1949*, pt. 1, 492–546. New York: Cambridge University Press, 1986.

Jansen, Marius. "Japan and the Chinese Revolution of 1911." In John K. Fairbank and Kwang-Ching Liu, eds., *The Cambridge History of China*. Vol. 11: *Late Ch'ing, 1800–1911*, pt. 2, 339–74. New York: Cambridge University Press, 1980.

Jen, Yu-wen [Jian Yuwen]. *The Taiping Revolutionary Movement*. New Haven: Yale University Press, 1973.

Jian, Yuwen. *Taiping Tianguo quanshi* [The complete history of the Taiping heavenly kingdom]. 3 vols. Hong Kong: Jianshi mengjin shuwu, 1962.

Kann, Eduard. *The Currencies of China*. Shanghai: Kelly and Walsh, 1927.

Kennedy, Thomas L. *The Arms of Kiangnan: Modernization in the Chinese Ordinance Industry, 1860–1895*. Boulder Colo.: Westview Press, 1978.

———. "Self-strengthening: An Analysis Based on Some Recent Writing." *Ch'ing-shih wen-t'i* 3.1 (November 1974): 3–35.

Kessler, Lawrence D. "Ethnic Composition of Provincial Leadership during the Ch'ing Dynasty." *Journal of Asian Studies* 28.3 (May 1969): 489–511.

King, Frank H. H. *Money and Monetary Policy in China, 1845–1895*. Cambridge: Harvard University Press, 1965.

Kodansha Encyclopedia of Japan. 9 vols. Tokyo: Kodansha, 1983.

Kuhn, Philip A. "The Taiping Rebellion." In John K. Fairbank, ed., *The Cambridge History of China*. Vol. 10: *Late Ch'ing, 1800–1911*, pt. 1, 264–317. New York: Cambridge University Press, 1978.

Kuo, Ting-yee. "Internal Development and Modernization of Taiwan, 1683–1891." In Paul K. T. Sih, ed., *Taiwan in Modern Times*. New York: St. John's University Press, 1973.

Latourette, Kenneth Scott. *A History of the Christian Missions in China*. London: The Society for Promoting Christian Knowledge, 1929.

Legge, James, trans. *The Chinese Classics*. 2d reprint ed. 5 vols. Taipei: Wenxing shudian, 1966.

Lei, Luqing. *Li Hongzhang xinzhuan* [A new biography of Li Hongzhang]. Taipei: Wenhai chubanshe, 1983.

Leibo, Steven A. *Transferring Technology to China: Prosper Giquel and the Self-strengthening Movement*. Berkeley, Calif.: Institute of East Asian Studies, 1985.

Leung, Yuen-sang. *The Shanghai Taotai: Linkage Man in a Changing Society, 1843–90*. Honolulu: University of Hawaii Press, 1990.

Levy, Howard. *Chinese Footbinding: The History of a Curious Erotic Custom*. New York: Walton Rawls, 1966.

Li, Chien-nung. *The Political History of China, 1840–1928*. Edited and translated by Teng Ssu-yu and Jeremy Ingalls. Princeton, N.J.: Van Nostrand Company, 1956.

Li, Enhan. *Zeng Jize de waijiao* [The diplomacy of Zeng Jize]. Taipei: Jindaishi yanjiusuo, 1966.

Li, Guoqi. *Zhang Zhidong de waijiao zhengce* [Zhang Zhidong's foreign policy]. Taipei: Jindaishi yanjiusuo, 1970.

Li, Xin, and Sun Sibai, eds. *Minguo renwuzhuan* [Biographies of figures of the republican period]. Beijing: Zhonghua chubanshe, 1978.

Li, Yuning [Bernadette Li], ed. *Chinese Women Through Chinese Eyes*. Armonk, N.Y.: M. E. Sharpe, 1992.

———. "Hsu Tsung-han (c. 1877–1944): Tradition and Revolution." *Chinese Studies in History* 20.2 (Winter 1986–87): 91–110.

———. *Jindai zhonghua funu zixu shiwenxuan* [Selected autobiographical poetry and literature by modern Chinese women]. First collection. Taipei: Lianjing chuban shiye gongsi, 1980.

Li, Zongxi. "Kaixian Li shangshu zhengshu" [Memorials of Li Zongxi]. In Shen Yunlong, ed., *Jindai zhongguo shiliao congkan* [Collected historical materials on modern China], no. 462. Taipei: Wenhai chubanshe, 1966.

Lin, Qingyuan. *Fujian chuanzhengju shigao* [Draft history of the Fujian naval dockyard]. Fuzhou: Fujian renmin chubanshe, 1986.

Lin, Yutang. *The Importance of Living*. New York: Capricorn Books, 1974.

Liu, Kwang-Ching. "The Ch'ing Restoration." In John K. Fairbank, ed. *The Cambridge History of China*. Vol. 10: *Late Ch'ing, 1800–1911*, pt. 1, 407–90. New York: Cambridge University Press, 1978.

———. ed. *Orthodoxy in Late Imperial China*. Berkeley: University of California Press, 1990.

———. "Cong Zeng Guofan jiashu shuoqi" [A preliminary discussion of Zeng Guofan's letters to family members]. In *Jinshi jiaxu yu zhengzhi bijiao lishi guoji xuexu yantaohui* [International Conference on Comparative Family and Political History], 1–22. Taipei: Academia Sinica, Institute of Modern History, 1992.

Liu, Kwang-Ching, and Richard J. Smith, "The Military Challenge: The Northwest and the Coast." In John K. Fairbank and Kwang-Ching Liu, eds., *The Cambridge History of China*. Vol. 11: *Late Ch'ing, 1800–1911*, pt. 2, 202–73. New York: Cambridge University Press, 1978.

Lo, Yudong. *Zhongguo lijin shi* [The history of the Chinese *likin*]. 2 vols. Shanghai: Shangwu yinshuguan, 1936.

Long Shengyun. *Xiangjun shigao* [Draft history of the Xiang Army]. Chengdu: Sichuan renmin chubanshe, 1990.

Lu, Baoqian. *Liu Rong nianpu* [Chronological biography of Liu Rong]. Taipei: Jindaishi yanjiusuo, 1979.

Mackerras, Colin P. *The Rise of the Peking Opera, 1770–1870: Social Aspects of the Theatre in Manchu China*. Oxford: Clarendon Press, 1972.

Mayers, William Frederick. *The Chinese Reader's Manual*. Reprint. Taipei: Ch'eng Wen Publishing Company, 1971.

Mesny, William. *Mesny's Chinese Miscellany*. 4 vols. Shanghai, 1896, 1897, 1899, 1905.

Metzger, Thomas A. *Escape from Predicament: Neo-Confucianism and China's Evolving Political Culture*. New York: Columbia University Press, 1977.

Michael, Franz. *The Taiping Rebellion*. 3 vols. Seattle: University of Washington Press, 1966.

Morehead, Albert H., Richard L. Frey, and Geoffrey Mott-Smith. *The New Complete Hoyle*. Rev. ed. New York: Doubleday, 1956.

Morse, Hosea Ballou. *The Trade and Administration of the Chinese Empire*. Taipei: Ch'eng-wen Publishing Company, n.d.

Murphey, Rhoads. *Shanghai: Key to Modern China*. Cambridge: Harvard University Press, 1953.

Nie, Qijie, ed. "Chongde laoren jiniance" [Memorial volume for a parent of great virtue]. In Shen Yunlong, ed., *Jindai Zhongguo shiliao congkan* [Collected historical materials on modern China]. Series 3, no. 22. 281–345. Taipei: Wenhai chubanshe, 1966.

Nie, Zeng Jifen. *Chongde laoren bashi ziding nianpu* [Chronological biography of a parent of great virtue edited by herself at age eighty]. Shanghai: 1931, 1933.

———. *Chongde laoren bashi ziding nianpu* [Chronological biography of a parent of great virtue edited by herself at age eighty]. Rev. ed. Shanghai: 1935.

———. "Chongde laoren ziding nianpu" [Chronological biography of a parent of great virtue edited by herself]. Including a synopsis of years 1931–42 by Qu Duizhi. In Nie Qijie, ed., "Chongde laoren jiniance" [Memorial volume for a prent of great virtue]. In Shen Yunlong, ed., *Jindai Zhongguo shiliao congkan* [Collected historical materials on modern China]. Series 3, no. 22. 307–45. Taipei: Wenhai chubanshe, 1966.

———. "Chongde laoren ziding nianpu" [Chronological biography of a parent of great virtue edited by herself]. In Yang Yunhui, ed., *Zeng Baosun huiyilu* [The memoirs of Zeng Baosun]. Changsha: Yuelu shushe, 1986.

North China Herald and Supreme Court and Consular Gazette. Weekly newspaper published in Shanghai, 1850–1941.

Playfair, G. M. H. *The Cities and Towns of China*. Reprint. Taipei: Ch'eng Wen Publishing Company, 1971.

Porter, Johnathan. *Tseng Kuo-fan's Private Bureaucracy*. Berkeley Calif.: University of California, Center for Chinese Studies, 1972.

Pruitt, Ida. *A Daughter of Han: The Autobiography of a Chinese Working Woman*. Stanford, Calif.: Stanford University Press, 1967.

———. *Old Madam Yin: A Memoir of Peking Life, 1926–1938*. Stanford, Calif.: Stanford University Press, 1979.

Qingshi bianxuan weiyuanhui, ed. *Qingshi* [History of the Qing dynasty]. 8 vols. Taipei: Guofang yanjiuyuan, 1961.

Rawlinson, John L. *China's Struggle for Naval Development, 1839–1895*. Cambridge: Harvard University Press, 1967.

Reischauer, Edwin O., and John K. Fairbank. *East Asia: The Great Tradition*. Boston: Houghton Mifflin, 1958.

Reynolds, Douglas C. *Preliminary Bibliography of Chinese Autobiographies in English*. New York: Columbia University, East Asia Institute, 1969.

Ronan, Colin A. *The Shorter Science and Civilization in China*. Vol. 2: *An Abridgement of Joseph Needham's Original Text*. New York: Cambridge University Press, 1981.

Rosenbaum, Arthur L. "Gentry Power and the Changsha Rice Riot of 1910." *Journal of Asian Studies* 34.3 (May 1975): 689–715.

Rowbotham, Sheila. *Women, Resistance and Revolution: A History of Women and Revolution in the Modern World*. New York: Vintage Books, 1974.

Rowe, William T. *Hankow Commerce and Society in a Chinese City, 1796–1889*. Stanford, Calif.: Stanford University Press, 1984.

———. *Hankow Conflict and Community in a Chinese City, 1796–1895*. Stanford, Calif.: Stanford University Press, 1989.

Schwartz, Benjamin I. "Themes in Intellectual History: May Fourth and After." In John K. Fairbank, ed., *The Cambridge History of China*. Vol. 12: *Republican China, 1912–1949*, pt. 1, 406–51. New York: Cambridge University Press, 1983.

Shen, Chuanjing. *Fuzhou chuanzhengju* [The Fuzhou naval dockyard]. Chengdu: Sichuan renmin chubanshe, 1987.

———. "Zhongguo jindaishide jiben xiansuo he xinwenhua yundong" [The basic continuity in modern Chinese history and the New Culture movement]. Zhongguo jindaishi tixi taolunhui lunwen [Paper presented at the Conference on the Organization of Modern Chinese History]. Chengdu, Sichuan University, Department of History, 1987.

Shen, Yunlong, ed. *Jindaishiliao kaoshi* [Evidence and exegesis on historical materials on the modern period]. First collection. Taipei: Chuanji wenxue, 1969.

Sheridan, James E. "The Warlord Era: Politics and Militarism under the Peking Government, 1916–1928." In John K. Fairbank, ed. *The Cambridge History of China*. Vol. 12: *Republican China, 1912–1949*, pt. 1, 284–321. New York: Cambridge University Press, 1983.

Smedley, Agnes. *Portraits of Chinese Women in Revolution*. Old Westbury, N.Y.: Feminist Press, 1976.

Smith, Richard J. *China's Cultural Heritage: The Ch'ing Dynasty, 1644–1912*. Boulder, Colo.: Westview Press, 1983.

———. *Fortune-Tellers and Philosophers: Divination in Traditional Chinese Society*. Boulder, Colo.: Westview Press, 1991.

———. *Mercenaries and Mandarins: The Ever-Victorious Army in Nineteenth Century China*. Millwood N.Y.: K.T.O. Press, 1978.

Snow, Helen Foster. *Women in Modern China*. Paris: Mouton and Company, 1967.

Spence, Jonathan. *To Change China: Western Advisers in China, 1620–1960*. New York: Penguin Books, 1980.

Tahara, Tennan. *Shinsue minsho chugoku kanshin jinmeiroku* [A directory of Chinese officials and gentry from the late Qing dynasty and early Republic]. Tokyo: Chugoku kenkyukai.

Taiwan Zhonghua Shuju bianjibu. *Cihai* [Encyclopaedic dictionary of Chinese]. 8th ed. Taipei: Zhonghua shuju, 1955.

Tan, Chester. *The Boxer Catastrophe*. New York: Columbia University Press, 1955.

Teng, Ssu-yu, and John K. Fairbank. *China's Response to the West: A Documentary Survey, 1839–1923*. New York: Atheneum, 1963.

Thompson, Laurence G. *Chinese Religion: An Introduction*. 4th ed. Belmont, Calif.: Wadsworth Publishing, 1979.

Unschuld, Paul V. *Medicine in China: A History of Ideas*. Berkeley: University of California Press, 1985.

———. *Medicine in China: A History of Pharmaceutics*. Berkeley: University of California Press, 1986.

Van Slyke, Lyman. "The Chinese Communist Movement during the Sino-Japanese War, 1937–1945." In John K. Fairbank and Albert Feuerwerker, eds., *The Cambridge History of China*. Vol. 13: *Republican China, 1912–1949*, pt. 2, 609–722. New York: Cambridge University Press, 1986.

Wakeman, Frederic. "The Canton Trade and the Opium War." In John K. Fairbank, ed., *The Cambridge History of China*. Vol. 10: *Late Ch'ing, 1800–1911*, pt. 1, 163–212. New York: Cambridge University Press, 1978.

———. "Huang-ch'ao ching-shih wen-pien." *Ch'ing-shih wen-t'i* 1.10 (February 1969): 8–22.

Wales, Nym. *Red Dust: Autobiographies of Chinese Communists*. Stanford, Calif.: Stanford University Press, 1952.

Wang, Ermin. *Qingji junshishi lunji* [Collected essays on late Qing military history]. Taipei: Lianjing chuban shiye gongzi, 1980.

Wang, Xi. *Zhong Ying Kaiping guangquan jiaoshe* [Sino-British negotiations on the Kaiping mining rights]. Taipei: Zhongyang yanjiuyuan jindaishi yanjiusuo chuban, 1962.

Wang, Yi-chu. *Chinese Intellectuals and the West, 1872–1949*. Chapel Hill: University of North Carolina Press, 1966.

Wehrle, Edmund S. *Britain, China and the Anti-Missionary Riots, 1891–1900*. Minneapolis: University of Minnesota Press, 1966.

Wei, Karen T. *Women in China: A Selected and Annotated Bibliography*. Westport, Conn.: Greenwood Press, 1984.

Wei, Xiumei, ed. *Qingji zhiguanbiao* [Offices and personnel in the late Ch'ing period]. 2 vols. Taipei: Zhongyang yanjiuyuan jindai lishisuo, 1977.

———. *Tao Zhu zia jiangnan* [Tao Zhu in Jiangnan]. Taipei: Jindaishi yanjiusuo, 1985.

Wei, Yungong. "Jiangnan zhizaoju ji" [Records of the Jiangnan Arsenal]. 10 vols. Excerpted in Yang Jialuo, ed., *Yangwu yundong wenxian huibian* [Collected documents on the foreign matters movement]. 8 vols., 4:1–175. Taipei: Shijie shuju, 1963.

Wilbur, C. Martin. "The Nationalist Revolution: From Canton to Nanking, 1923–28." In John K. Fairbank, ed., *The Cambridge History of China*. Vol. 12: *Republican China, 1912–1949*, 527–721. New York: Cambridge University Press, 1983.

———. *Sun Yat-sen, Frustrated Patriot*. New York: Columbia University Press, 1976.

Wolf, Margery, and Roxane Witke, eds. *Women in Chinese Society*. Stanford, Calif.: Stanford University Press, 1975.

Wright, Arthur F. *Buddhism in Chinese History*. New York: Atheneum, 1965.

Wright, Mary C., ed. *China in Revolution: The First Phase, 1900–1913*. New Haven: Yale University Press, 1968.

———. *The Last Stand of Chinese Conservatism: The T'ung-Chih Restoration, 1862–1874*. New York: Atheneum, 1966.

Wright, Stanley F. *Hart and the Chinese Customs*. Belfast: William Mullen and Son, 1950.

Wu, Emma. "The Enduring Legacy of the Chi Pao." *Free China Review* 41.6 (June 1991): 33–38.

Wu, Hsiang-hsiang. "The Construction of the Summer Palace and Naval Funds in the Late Ch'ing Dynasty." Translated by Thomas L. Kennedy. *Chinese Studies in History* 12.1 (Fall 1978): 3–36.

Wu, Pei-yi. *The Confucian's Progress. Autobiographical Writing in Traditional China*. Princeton, N.J.: Princeton University Press, 1990.

Xia, Dongyuan. *Zheng Guanying zhuan* [The biography of Zheng Guanying]. Shanghai: Huadong shifan daxue chubanshe, 1981.

Yang, Yunhui, ed. *Zeng Baosun huiyilu fu chongde laoren ziding nianpu* [The memoirs of Zeng Baosun with chronological autobiography of a virtuous parent]. Changsha: Yuelu shushe, 1986.

Young, Ernest P. *The Presidency of Yuan Shih-k'ai: Liberalism and Dictatorship in Early Republican China*. Ann Arbor: University of Michigan Press, 1977.

Young, Marilyn. *Women in China: Studies in Social Change and Feminism.* Ann Arbor: University of Michigan, Center for Chinese Studies, 1973.

Yu, Pauline. *The Poetry of Wang Wei.* Bloomington: Indiana University Press, 1980.

Yuan, Shuyi. *Li Hongzhang zhuan* [Biography of Li Hongzhang]. Beijing: Renmin chubanshe, 1991.

Zang, Lihe. *Zhongguo gujin diming dacidian* [Dictionary of Chinese ancient and modern place-names]. Taipei: Shangwu yinshuguan, 1966.

Zeng, Guofan. *Zeng Guofan shouxie riji* [Zeng Guofan, handwritten diary]. Held at Academia Sinica, Institute of Modern History, Taipei.

———. *Zeng Guofan weikan xingao* [Previously unpublished letters of Zeng Guofan]. Beijing: Zhonghua shuju, 1959.

———. *Zeng Wenzhenggong quanji* [Complete works of Zeng Guofan]. 5 vols.; *nianpu* [chronological biography]; *wenji* [collected writings]; *riji* [diary]. Taipei: Shijie shuju, 1965.

Zhang, Qiyun [Chang Ch'i-yun], ed. *Zhongwen da zidian* [The encyclopaedic dictionary of the Chinese language]. 10 vols. Taipei: Huagang chuban youxian gongsi, 1962.

Zhao, Cong, ed. *Guwen guanzhi xinbian* [Selections from classical literature, newly edited]. 2 vols. Hong Kong: Youlian chubanshe, 1960.

Zhongguo kexueyuan jingji yanjiusuo. *Heng Feng shachangde fasheng, fazhan, yu gaizao* [The establishment, development, and reform of the Heng Feng Cotton Mill]. Shanghai: Renmin chubanshe, 1958.

Zhongguo Shixuehui, ed. *Xinhai geming* [The 1911 Revolution]. 8 vols. Shanghai: Renmin chubanshe, 1957.

Zhu, Dongan. *Zeng Guofan zhuan* [Biography of Zeng Guofan]. Chengdu: Sichuan renmin chubanshe, 1985.

GLOSSARY

Ao	坳
Bagongsheng	拔贡生
Buzhi Buqiu Shi	不恃不求诗
Cai Eryuan	蔡二源
Cao Mingxian	曹铭先
Chang'er	长儿
Changzhao	常昭
Chao Chongshan	巢崇山
Chen Naihan	陈乃翰
Chen Songsheng	陈松生
Chen Yuandui	陈源兑
Chen Zhantang	陈展堂
Chenghuang	城隍
Chongde Laoren bashi ziding nianpu	崇德老人八十自订年谱
Chongde Laoren jiniance	崇德老人纪念册
Chongming	崇明
Chongqian	崇谦
Chunfan	春帆
Dao	道
Daxue	大学
Deng	邓
Deng dalei an yu mei shu	登大雷岸与妹书
Deng Yinjie	邓寅皆
Ding	丁
Ding Xiang Wang	定湘王
Duogui	多桂
Fangjian	坊检
Feijing	飞鲸
Fu Hou	富厚
Fu Qingyu	傅青余
Fugongsheng	附贡生
Fulong	伏龙
Futai	复泰
Gan	甘
Gangzhou gongdu	冈州公犊
Gebi	割臂
Gegu	割股
Gong Zhaoyuan	龚照瑗
Goulin Guan	构林关
Guanchen	管臣
Guanshang heban	官商合办
Guanxi	关系
Guanyin	观音
Guangchi	光坻
Guangchi	光墀
Guangdi	光地
Guangjian	光坚
Guangjun	广钧
Guangjun	光钧
Guangkun	光坤
Guangluan	广銮
Guangming	广铭
Guangqi	光圻
Guangquan	广铨
Guangshan	广珊
Guangtan	光坦

Guangxiao 光孝
Guangxuan 广璇
Guangyang 广锡
Guangyao 光曜
Guangyong 光墉
Guangzhao 光昭
Guangzhi 光址
Guangzhong 广钟
Gujia 贾家
Guo 郭
Guo Yiyong 郭依永
Guo Yun 郭筠

Hanlin 翰林
Hao 郝
He 贺
Heng Feng 恒丰
Heng Feng fangzhi xinju 恒丰纺织新局
Hexi 河西
Hongkou 虹口
Hongjiajing 洪家井
Hou 侯
Huang 黄
Huang Aitang 黄蔼堂
Huang Chengxuan 黄承暄
Huangchao jingshi wenbian 皇朝经世文编
Huangqing jingshi wenbian 皇清经世文编
Huang Zuluo 黄祖络
Huangniduan 黄泥塅

Jiang 江
Jiangnan (Kiangnan) 江南
Jiangnan zhizao ju ji 江南制造局记
Jiansheng 监生
Jiao 角
Jiaotong 交通
Jiazhengxue 家政学
Jichen 纪琛
Jichun 纪纯
Jiezi shu 诫子书
Jijing 纪静
Jin 斤
Jingansi 静安寺
Jingshi wenbian 经世文编
Jinpenling 金盆岭
Jinshi 进士
Jiqu 纪渠
Jirong 季融
Jiyao 纪耀
Jubolaisi 巨波来斯
Juren 举人

Kenwuju 垦务局
Kunshan 昆山

Lai Chengyu 赖承裕
Lexintian 乐心田
Liji (*Li Chi*) 礼记
Li Xiao'an 李晓庵
Li Xingrui 李兴锐
Li Youxian 李幼仙
Li Yuning 李又宁
Likin 厘金
Lin Boying 林佰颖
Lin Shitao 林世焘
Lin Zhaoyuan 林肇元
Liu Gengxin 刘更新
Liu Jie 刘杰
Liu Kangsi 刘康俟
Liu Shoulin 刘寿林
Liu Songshan 刘松山
Liu Tiqian 刘体乾
Liu Zi 刘鼒
Liuyangmen 浏阳门
Lujiang 庐江
Lunyu 论语
Luzu 吕祖

Ma Peizhi 马培之
Madao 马道

Mahjong	马将	Qianjili	谦吉里
Mei Qizhao	梅启照	Qianyi	乾益
Meng He	孟河	Qibi	其璧
		Qibin	其宾
Nan	南	Qichang	其昌
Nanwu	南武	Qichun	其纯
Nian Pu	年谱	Qide	其德
Nie Boyuan	聂伯元	Qiganshan	七干山
Nie Erkang	聂尔康	Qijun	其焌
Nie Gaomin	聂镐敏	Qikun	其焜
(Jingpu)	(京圃)	Qilin	麒麟
Nie Hanzhang	聂含章	Qipao	旗袍
Nie Jimo	聂继模	Qipu	其璞
Nie Jingmin (Xinru)	聂镜敏 (心如)	Qishui	祈水
		Qiu	邱
Nie Jixuan	聂季萱	Qiu Liying	邱丽英
Nie Liukang	聂留康	Qixian	其贤
Nie Lusheng	聂潞生	Qixun	其勳
Nie Qigui	聂缉椝	Qiying	其煐
Nie Qijie	聂其杰	Qu	瞿
Nie Qiwei	聂其炜	Qu Duizhi	瞿兑之
Nie Samin	聂钑敏	Quhongji	瞿鸿禨
Nie Tao	聂铸	Quan'er	全儿
Nie Xianmin (Rong Feng)	聂铣敏 (蓉峰)	Riqing	日清
Nie Yingchan	聂应禅		
Nie Zeng Jifen	聂曾纪芬	Sanhe	三河
Nie Zhaokui	聂肇奎	Shen Chuanjing	沈传经
Nie Zhenmin	聂镇敏	Shen-shang	绅商
		Shen-shi	绅士
Ouyang	欧阳	Shou	寿
Ouyang Cangming	欧阳沧溟	Siming	四明
Ouyang Futian	欧阳福田	Siyun	思云
Ouyang Muyun	欧阳牡云	Sun Yi	孙怡
		Sungari	松花
Pan Jingru	潘镜如		
Pan Wenzhi	潘文质	Taiji Chang	台吉厂
Peikai'er	培开而	Tang Haiqiu	汤海秋
Ping'er	平儿	Tang heting	唐河厅
Pingsantao	平三套	Tang Kuisheng	汤癸生
Pingtang	平塘	Tang Zhixian	汤蛰仙

Tangping	塘坪	Yongni	咏霓
Taotai	道台	*Youxue*	幼学
Tianrantai	天然台	Yu	俞
Tianxia	天下	Yu Shoucheng	俞寿丞
Tongjian gangmu	通鉴纲目	Yuan Fangying	袁芳瑛
		Yuan Yusheng	袁榆生
Weilingmi	威灵密	Yuanjiang	沅江
Weisai	威赛	Yuzhen	玉振
Weng Bingnan	翁炳南		
Wenzheng	文正	Zeng Jiyun	曾骥云
Wushi	五十	Zengzi	曾子
Xia Yingtang	夏应堂	Zhang Pengyuan (Chang Peng-yuan)	张朋圆
Xiang Jiuxiao	想九霄	Zhang Shaotang	张绍棠
Xiang'er	祥儿	Zhang Shuren	章淑人
Xiangshan	香山	Zhao Zhongfu (Chao Chung-fu)	赵中孚
Xieqiao	斜桥		
Xihuade	西华德	Zhen'an	镇安
Xingsheng	杏生	Zhong Yungu	钟云谷
Xu Zijing	徐子静	*Zhongfang gong yishi*	仲芳公轶事
Yamen	衙门	Zhongfuyuan	种福垸
Yan Zhongji	颜钟骥	Zhou	周
Yanfang xinbian	验方新编	Zhou Zijing	周子竟
Yang Dating	杨达亭	Zhoujiakou	周家口
Yang Jinlong	杨金龙	Zhu	朱
Yang Tianhong	杨天洪	Zhu Guixin	朱桂辛
Yangwu	扬武	Zhu Ruren	朱孺人
Yao Shu	姚舒	Zhu Youhong	朱幼鸿
Ye Guangliang	叶光亮	Zhu Yutian	朱宇田
Yi sui	一岁	Zhuo Junwei	卓君卫
Yijing	易经	Zhuo Zhinan	卓芝南
Yin Hebai	尹和白	Ziding nianpu	自订年谱
Yin Sunfang	尹孙舫	Zitian	梓田
Yingu	银姑	Zixu nianpu	自叙年谱

INDEX

Adoption, xxxi, 10, 20, 28, 38, 39, 41, 46, 81
Algebra, 26
Anti-Christian activity, xl, xliii, 27, 65, 74, 152 (n. 4). *See also* Boxer Uprising; Tianjin Massacre
Autobiography, 107–8, 111 (n. 2)

Book of changes, xxxii
Book of rites, xxix, xxx, 13
Bourgeoisie, xxi, xxiii, xliv–xlvii, 105–10
Boxer Protocol, xliii, 158 (n. 22)
Boxer Uprising, xliii, 73, 74, 152 (n. 4), 153 (n. 6), 154–55 (nn. 9, 10, 11)
British imperialism, xxxvii–xxxix, xlii, 11, 122 (n. 41)
Buddhism, xxix, 15, 58, 159 (n. 27), 160 (n. 28), 175

Capitalism, 104–5. *See also* Bourgeoisie
Cen Chunxuan, 75
Changsha rice riots, 98–99
Chen Songsheng. *See* Zeng Jiyao
Chen Yucheng, 10, 14, 15
Chen Zhantang, 48, 49–50, 57
Chiang Kai-shek, xlviii–l, 171 (n. 22)
China Merchant's Steam Navigation Company, xl, 87, 160 (n. 29)
Chonghou, 45
Christian missions, xxxviii. *See also* Anti-Christian activity
Civil service examinations, xxiv–xxvii, xliv, 6, 41, 42, 51, 52, 66, 75, 157 (n. 16). *See also* Education, Hanlin Academy
Clothing, 15–16, 19, 23, 24, 65, 96, 98
Communists, xlvii–l, 125 (n. 7), 136–37 (n. 27), 171 (nn. 22, 24)
Concubinage, xxxi, 19, 47, 50, 51–52, 68, 70, 153 (n. 7)
Confucianism, xxiv, xxxv, xxxix, xlii, xlvi, xlvii, 3–4, 34, 42, 52, 85–86, 99, 108–10, 114 (n. 36), 128 (n. 3), 173 (n. 1)
Constitutionalists, xlv, 87, 164 (n. 2), 165 (n. 6), 173 (n. 27)
Continuity of Chinese society, xxxv, 104–5
Culture. *See* Society and culture

Daoism, xxxii, 151 (n. 2)
Division of property, 40, 71, 90–91
Documents on statecraft, 42, 52
Dong Fuxiang, 73
Dreams, 48, 71–72

Education, xxiv–xxvii, xliv, 13, 23, 24, 61, 75, 77, 109, 134 (n. 27), 157 (nn.

Education (*continued*)
16, 17), 158 (n. 19). *See also* Civil service examinations
Empress Dowager, xli–xliii, 73, 74, 155 (n. 11)

Family, xxviii–xxxii, 23–24, 33–35, 109. *See also* Nie Zeng Jifen
Festivals, xxxii, 24, 58, 63, 65, 77, 99
Food, 24, 26, 53, 98–99, 149 (n. 26)
Foot-binding, xxviii–xxix
Foreign aggression, xxxvii–li, 11, 45, 54, 73, 106, 137 (n. 27), 140 (n. 7), 172 (n. 27). *See also* International Concession
Foreign concessions. *See* International Concession
French imperialism, xxxviii, xl–xli, 11, 54, 56, 73. *See also* Sino-French War
Fryer, John, Mr. and Mrs., 61

Gentry, xxii–xxvii, xliv, 106
Geomancy, xxix, 39, 94
German imperialism, xlii
Gong Zhaoyuan, 63, 161 (n. 30)
Government, xxiv–xxvii, 54
Guangxu, Emperor, xlii, 73
Guanyin, 78
Guomindang, xlvi–l, 94, 107, 125 (n. 7), 137–38, 165 (n. 6), 169 (n. 14), 171 (nn. 22, 24)
Guo Songtao, 19, 48, 52
Guo Yun, 18. *See also* Zeng Jihong

Hairstyles, 15, 95–97 (illustration)
Hanlin Academy, xxv, 18, 41, 42, 164 (n. 38)
Hart, Robert, 73, 144 (n. 20)
Heng Feng Cotton Mill, 79, 106, 134–38, 166 (n. 8), 169 (n. 14). *See also* New Huaxin Cotton Mill
Historiography, current, xxxiii–xxxv
Hong Xiuquan, xxxv, 15. *See also* Taiping Revolutionary movement
Hoover, Herbert, 161 (n. 29)
Houses, 14, 16–17, 38, 60

Imperialism. *See* Foreign aggression
Imperial Maritime Customs Service, 73, 126
Inheritance. *See* Division of property
International Concession, xxxviii, 56, 57, 152 (n. 5), 166 (n. 7)

Japanese imperialism, xli–xlii, xlvi–xlvii, xlix–li, 137 (n. 27)
Jiangnan Arsenal, xxxix–xl, 53–54, 55, 62, 161 (n. 30)
Jiaotong University, 91, 169 (n. 15)

Kaiping Coal Mines, xl, 78
Kang Youwei, xlii

Liang Qichao, xliv
Li Hanzhang, 49–50, 89
Li Hongzhang, xxvii, xxxvi, xl, 16, 24, 28, 44, 89, 122 (n. 41), 125 (n. 8), 141 (n. 10), 144 (n. 20), 160 (n. 29), 165 (n. 3)
Lin Shitao, 93
Lin Zhaoyuan, 93
Liu Bingzhang, 93
Liu Kunyi, 73
Liu Rong, 12
Liu Zi, 75
Long March, xlix
Lo Zenan, 12. *See also* Zeng Jichen
Luzu, 71

Macartney, Samuel Halliday, 28
Manchus (and Qing dynasty), xxiii,

xxxv–xlv passim, xlix, 132 (n. 21), 139 (n. 1), 156 (n. 12), 158 (n. 22), 172 (n. 26). *See also* Empress Dowager
Mao Zedong, xlviii–xlix, 172 (n. 24)
Marriage. *See* Nie Zeng Jifen; Women
Ma Xinyi, 28
May Fourth movement, xlvii, 109, 163 (n. 35)
Medicine and health, xxxii–xxxiii, 26, 27, 28, 29, 47, 59–60, 63, 64, 65, 72, 74, 102
Mesny, William, 149 (n. 23), 150 (n. 32)
Muslim uprisings, xli, 53, 140 (n. 7), 155 (n. 11)

Nanjing Arsenal, 26, 125 (n. 8)
Nationalists. *See* Guomindang
Natural Foot movement, xxix
Neo-Confucianism. *See* Confucianism
New Culture movement, xxxix, 105
New Huaxin Cotton Mill (Futai), xl, 78, 105, 126–27, 134, 151 (n. 32). *See also* Heng Feng Cotton Mill
Nian Rebellion, xxxvi–xxxvii, 17
Nie Erkang, 36, 40–42, 43 (chart), 71
Nie Guangkun, 80, 89, 91, 92 (chart), 137–39
Nie Lusheng. *See* Nie Qiying
Nie Qibin, 44, 47, 66, 67 (chart), 74, 91
Nie Qichang, 48, 61, 66, 67 (chart), 70, 74, 76, 91, 92 (chart)
Nie Qigui, xxi, xl, xliii, 34 (photo), 36; as official, xxvii, xliii, 33, 44, 52–54, 68; parents and ancestors of, 36–44 (chart, 43); and concubines, 47, 70, 73, 77, 79, 80, 89, 91; in Shanghai, 53–69, 126–27; in Zhejiang, 66, 70, 72–73, 75–77; descendants of, 67 (chart), 92 (chart); financial problems of, 69, 79, 126; in Jiangsu, 72, 74; in Anhui, 75; as landowner, 76, 88–89, 135; as cotton entrepreneur, 78–79, 126–27, 151 (n. 32); death and burial of, 79, 81, 87
Nie Qijie, xxi, 48, 61, 66, 67 (chart), 70, 76, 80, 86 (photo), 90, 91, 92 (chart); as cotton entrepreneur, 78–79, 89, 106, 134–38, 169 (n. 14); as education advocate, 134–39
Nie Qiwei, xxi, 55, 67 (chart), 74, 75, 79, 80, 92 (chart)
Nie Qixian, 63, 67 (chart), 77, 87–88, 91, 92 (chart)
Nie Qiying (Lusheng), 67 (chart), 73, 89, 92 (chart), 135–38, 169 (n. 14)
Nie Zeng Jifen, x (photo); marriage of, xxx–xxxi, 36–41; as daughter, 3–4; parents and grandparents of, 5–8 (chart, 7); and servants, 6, 14, 16, 47, 48, 51; and siblings, 11–13, 14, 16, 18–19, 25 (chart), 46–47; education and training of, 13, 22–26; and hairstyles, 14–15; and clothing, 15–16, 23, 65, 96; and death of parents, 29, 39; as wife, 33–35; and mother-in-law (Madam Zhang), 33–49 passim (chart, 43), 57, 64–65, 70–72, 75, 76, 77, 79–81; births and deaths of children of, 44, 47, 48, 53, 55, 57, 63, 65, 66, 67 (chart), 70, 88; in Nanjing, 49–53; in Shanghai, 55–69, 88–100; illnesses of, 60, 63, 65, 72, 74, 103; marriages of children of, 66, 70, 72, 75, 77, 79–80, 92 (chart); as widow, 85–86; and conversion to Christianity, 90, 175; and division of property, 90–91; and last decade of life, 101–3
1911 Revolution, xliv–xlv, 79, 87–88, 105, 164 (n. 2), 165 (nn. 4, 5, 6)
Northern Expedition, xlviii, 94

One Hundred Days of Reform, xlii, xliv, 147 (n. 16)
Opium (and Opium Wars), xxxvii–xxxviii, 88

Peng Yulin, 13, 46
People's Republic of China, 107, 138
Population growth, xxxv
Pujun, Prince, 73

Qing dynasty. *See* Empress Dowager; Manchus
Qu Hongji, 75, 89

Recreation, xxxii, 21, 58, 77–78. *See also* Festivals
Red Army, 171 (n. 24)
Red Gang (Triad Society), 74
Reform, xxxix–xliv, 75, 105, 147 (n. 16), 152–54 (nn. 6, 7, 8), 158 (n. 22), 164 (n. 37)
Republic of China, xlv, 88
Ritual, xxvii–xxxii, 10, 15, 29, 33, 39–40, 129 (nn. 6, 7), 130 (n. 10)
Russian imperialism, xli, xlii, 45, 140 (n. 7)
Russo-Japanese War, xlii, xliv

Salt, 46, 77, 155 (n. 12)
Sayings of Confucius, The, 13
Selective mirror of history, 26
Self-strengthening movement, xxxix, 104, 105
Senggelinqin, Prince, xxxvi, 17
Shanghai Banking Corporation, 78
Shanghai Municipal Council, 88, 91, 137
Shao Weixi, 20
Shao Youlian, 62, 66, 68
Sino-French War, xli, 54, 56, 146 (n. 9)
Sino-Japanese War, xli, xliv, xlix–li
Society and culture, xxi–xxxiii. *See also* Adoption; Buddhism; Clothing; Concubinage; Confucianism; Daoism; Division of property; Dreams; Education; Family; Food; Gentry; Geomancy; Government; Hairstyles; Houses; Medicine and health; Recreation; Ritual; Transportation; Women
Soong, T. V., 137
Summary of the rules of ceremony, 13
Sun Yatsen, xliv–xlv, xlvi, xlviii

Taiping Revolutionary movement, xxv, xxxv–xxxvi, xxxviii–xxxix, 5, 6, 8, 9 (map), 10–11, 15, 105, 130 (n. 16), 146 (n. 14)
Tale of Xiangshan, 78
Tan Yankai, 88, 165 (nn. 4, 5, 6)
Tianjin Massacre, xl, xli, 27–28
Tolstoy, Leo, 139
Transportation, 99–100
Treaty of Livadia, 45
Treaty of St. Petersburg, 45
Treaty of Shimonoseki, xli
Treaty of Versailles, xlvii
Treaty port system. *See* Unequal treaties
Twenty-one Demands, xlvi

Unequal treaties, xxxvii–xxxviii, 154 (nn. 9, 10), 166 (n. 7)
United Front, xlviii, 171 (nn. 22, 24)

Warlords, xlvi, xlviii, 170 (n. 21), 171 (n. 22)
Women, xvii, xxi–xxii, xxviii–xxxi, 12, 14, 15, 23–26, 33–34, 39–41, 51–52, 58–59, 75–76, 95, 107–8, 122 (n. 39),

158 (n. 19). *See also* Nie Zeng Jifen
Wu Peifu, xlvi, 94, 163 (n. 36)

Yuan Shikai, xlii, xlv–xlvi, 170 (n. 21)

Zeng Guobao, 7 (chart), 10, 13, 19, 39
Zeng Guofan, xxi, xxvii, 3, 4 (photo), 7 (chart), 25 (chart), 101; as head of household, xxix, 12, 14, 15–16, 19–20, 22–24, 37, 58; as military commander, xxxvi, xxxix, 8, 10, 11, 18, 20, 121 (n. 33); as official, xl, 5, 6, 17, 27–28, 124 (n. 7); as governor of Liangjiang provinces, 11, 22, 28, 124 (n. 4), 141 (n. 10); as governor of Zhili, 17, 26; death and burial of, 29, 37, 39; as author, 37, 101
Zeng Guohuang, 7 (chart), 10, 17, 22
Zeng Guoquan, 3, 7 (chart), 10, 16, 17, 18, 19, 36, 39, 55, 57, 60–61, 62, 63; as military commander, xxxvi, 8, 11, 45, 121 (n. 33)
Zeng Jichen, 12, 14, 18, 25 (chart), 45, 48, 51–52
Zeng Jichun, 18–19, 25 (chart), 51
Zeng Jihong, 13, 14, 18, 22, 25 (chart), 26, 28, 38, 47, 51, 57
Zeng Jiyao, 12, 16, 25 (chart), 28, 40, 45–47, 51
Zeng Jize, 8, 10, 11–12, 19, 24, 25 (chart), 27, 28, 29, 37, 38, 59–60, 62–64, 73; as ambassador, xli, 45, 52, 123 (n. 41), 144 (n. 20)
Zhang Qihuang, 79, 88–89, 94
Zhang Zhidong, xliv, 75, 163 (n. 36)
Zhongfuyuan, 76, 88–89, 135 (n. 27)
Zuo Zongtang, xxxvi, xxxix, 11, 50, 52–53, 54, 55–56

www.ingramcontent.com/pod-product-compliance
Lightning Source LLC
LaVergne TN
LVHW050619100826
845148LV00011B/1652